Karel J Rob

A Gentle Introduction
to the Art of
Object-Oriented
Programming in Java

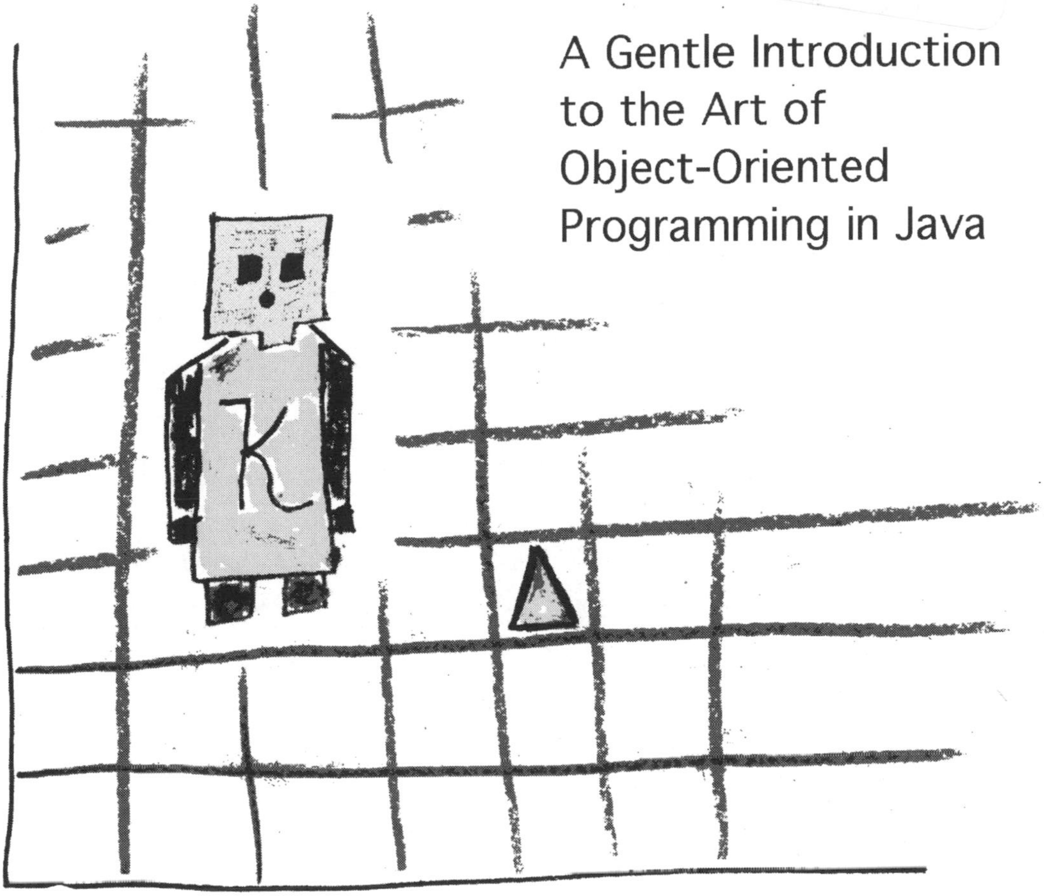

Joseph Bergin

Mark Stehlik

Jim Roberts

Richard Pattis

Published by Dream Songs Press, February 2005

April 24, 2005
January 2, 2008 Update and corrections

ISBN 0-9705795-1-9

Karel J Robot

A Gentle Introduction to the Art of Object-Oriented Programming in Java

Joseph Bergin, Mark Stehlik, Jim Roberts, Richard Pattis

Preface

The programming landscape has changed significantly since the initial publication of Karel the Robot in 1981. Today there are new programming languages, new programming paradigms, and new and more powerful computers. Pascal no longer enjoys the popularity it did in the 1980s. However, the concepts of Karel are still as vibrant and valid an introduction to the programming and problem-solving processes as they were when first introduced. However, the object-oriented programming paradigm has begun to dominate the world of commercial software production.

Karel J. Robot updates Karel the Robot and even Karel ++ to provide a means of introducing novice programmers to object-oriented programming (OOP). This book maintains the simplicity of the original and yet provides instruction that is thoroughly object-oriented from the beginning. Where the original used a syntax and methodology derived from Pascal, the present text is 100% Java. In object-oriented programming, a computation is carried out by a set of interacting objects. Here, the objects are robots that exist in a simple world. There can be one or several robots assigned to a task. The programming task is divided into two parts. The first part is defining the capabilities of the robots that are needed. The second is providing a description of the task for the robots to perform. The programmer uses his or her problem solving skills on both parts of this task. This version goes beyond the earlier Karel++ to put more emphasis on polymorphism, the primary distinction between procedural programming and object-oriented programming. There is also an introduction to simple but important design patterns, such as those that have recently revolutionized software practice.

Like its predecessors, Karel J. Robot is a Turing complete language that can be mastered in a few weeks. While not convenient for many tasks, it is theoretically possible to solve any computer programming problem in this simple language. This gives it educational power. Instead of using many many language features to solve problems, students must apply a few simple tools in combination to solve some hard problems. This puts the focus clearly on problem solving rather than language syntax. At the same time they are learning the core of an important modern programming language and the core concepts of the object-oriented programming paradigm.

We believe that most people will not actually have to program a computer as part of their everyday lives, either now or in the future. However, many people will need to be able to use a computer and will occasionally need to do something with the machine beyond the "ordinary." Simply put, they will have to solve some type of computer problem. We solve various kinds of problems every day; problem solving is part of our lives. This book will introduce you to problem-solving approaches that can be used with computers. Unfortunately, some people believe programming requires a "different" way of thinking. We don't agree with this statement. Instead of changing the way you think, this book will change how you apply your problem-solving skills to different kinds of problems.

The original Karel the Robot used procedures as the fundamental problem solving medium, as is appropriate in procedural programming. Here we apply our problem solving skills, instead, to the design of classes that describe objects (robots), since classes are the primary means of breaking a complex problem into manageable parts in object-oriented programming. The skills of procedural programming and object-oriented programming are very similar, though we look at problems from a slightly different perspective when using OOP.

For the experienced student programmer, this edition should provide insights into the problem-solving and program design processes that will make the student an even better programmer. It will also improve understanding of computer science concepts such as polymorphism, loop invariants and recursion. For individuals who want to begin a thorough sequence of training and education in programming, computer science, or both, Karel J. Robot provides a solid foundation on which to begin your work.

For novice programmers, this book will give some insight into the programming process from two distinctly different points of view: the planner's and the implementer's. All the problems can be thought about, discussed, and planned in English. Once you have developed your plan, the actual syntax of the robot programming language has very few rules to get in your way as you become the implementer or programmer.

For individuals who do not want to program but need to have a feel for the process, Karel J. Robot is an excellent tool for providing that insight.

Supplements

An Instructor's Manual will be available for the text, and contains numerous pedagogical suggestions for teaching the material based on many years of using Karel the Robot, Karel ++, and Object-Orientation in introductory programming courses at the college level. It should contain solutions to most of the in-text exercises.

Software to simulate Karel J. Robot is available on the Web. http://www.cafepress.com/kareljrobot

Joseph Bergin, Pace University
Mark Stehlik, Carnegie-Mellon University
Jim Roberts, Carnegie-Mellon University
Richard Pattis, Carnegie-Mellon University

March, 2004

Dedication. The authors would like to dedicate this work to the memory of Kristen Nygaard, who, along with his friend and colleague Ole-Johan Dahl, invented object-oriented programming in the 1960s and who worked since then to refine and extend it. Kristen was an interesting and lively person who worked his entire life to make things better for others, both in technology and otherwise. We, who came to know him, miss him and his continuing inspiration greatly. He died suddenly in August 2002 at the age of 75.

CONTENTS

Preface iii

Dedication v

Chapter 1 The Robot World 1
1.1 The Robot World 1
1.2 Robot Capabilities 3
1.3 Tasks and Situations 4
1.4 Robots and Objects 4
1.5 Important Ideas From This Chapter 5
1.6 Problem Set 5

Chapter 2 Primitive Instructions and Simple Programs 7
2.1 Changing Position 7
2.2 Turning in Place 8
2.3 Finishing a Task 9
2.4 Handling Beepers 9
2.5 Robot Descriptions 9
2.6 A Complete Program 11
2.6.1 Executing a Program 12
2.6.2 The Form of Robot Programs 14
2.7 Error Shutoffs 15
2.8 Programming Errors 16
2.8.1 Bugs and Debugging 19
2.9 A Task for Two Robots 19
2.10 An infinity of Beepers 20
2.11 Some Terminology 20
2.12 Important Ideas From This Chapter 21
2.13 Problem Set 21

Chapter 3 Extending the Robot Programming Language 30
3.1 Creating a More Natural Programming Language 30
3.2 A Mechanism that Defines New Classes of Robots 31
3.3 Defining the New Methods 32
3.4 The Meaning and Correctness of New Methods 35
3.5 Defining New Methods in a Program 36
3.6 Modifying Inherited Methods 39
3.7 An Ungrammatical Program 41
3.8 Tools for Designing and Writing Robot Programs 42
3.8.1 Stepwise Refinement-a Technique for Planning, Implementing, and Analyzing Robot Programs 42
3.8.2 The Second Step-Planning harvestTwoRowsand positionForNextHarvest 46
3.8.3 The Third Step-Planning harvestOneRow and goToNextRow 48
3.8.4 The Final Step-Verifying That the Complete Program is Correct 50
3.9 Advantages of Using New Instructions 52

3.9.1 Avoiding Errors 53
3.9.2 Future Modifications 54
3.9.3 A Program Without New instructions 56
3.10 Writing Understandable Programs 58
3.11 Important Ideas From This Chapter 59
3.12 Problem Set 59

Chapter 4 Polymorphism 65
4.1 Robot Teams 65
4.2 Similar Tasks 67
4.3 Choreographers 71
4.4 Object Oriented Design -- Clients and Servers 73
4.5 Using Polymorphism 79
4.6 Still More on Polymorphism -- Strategy and Delegation 83
4.7 Java Enumerations and More on Strategies 89
4.8 Decorators 93
4.9 Observers 95
4.10 Final Words on Polymorphism 98
4.11 Important Ideas From This Chapter 99
4.12 Problem Set 99

Chapter 5 Conditionally Executing Instructions 103
5.1 The IF Instruction 103
5.2 The Conditions That Robots Can Test 104
5.2.1 Writing New Predicates 106
5.3 Simple Examples of the IF Instruction 108
5.3.1 The harvestOneRowMethod 108
5.3.2 The faceNorthIfFacingSouth Method 109
5.3.3 The faceNorthMethod 110
5.3.4 Determining the correctness of the IF Instruction 113
5.4 The IF/ELSE Instruction 113
5.5 Nested IF Instructions 115
5.6 More Complex Tests 119
5.7 When to Use an IF Instruction 121
5.8 Transformations for Simplifying IF Instructions 123
5.9 Polymorphism Revisited 127
5.10 Important Ideas From This Chapter 130
5.11 Problem Set 130

Chapter 6 Instructions That Repeat 136
6.1 The FOR-LOOP Instruction 136
6.2 The WHILE Instruction 139
6.2.1 Why WHILE is Needed 139
6.2.2 The Form of the WHILE Instruction 140
6.2.3 Building a WHILE Loop - the Four Step Process 141
6.2.4 A More Interesting Problem 142
6.3 Errors to Avoid with WHILE Loops 144
6.3.1 The Fence Post Problem 145
6.3.2 Infinite Execution 147
6.3.3 When the test of a WHILE is Checked 147

6.4 Nested WHILE Loops 148
6.4.1 A Good Example of Nesting 148
6.4.2 A Bad Example of Nesting 151
6.5 WHILE and IF Instructions 157
6.6 Reasoning about Loops 158
6.7 A Large Program Written by Stepwise Refinement 161
6.8 Enumerations and the While Statement 166
6.9 When to Use a Repeating Instruction 167
6.10 Important Ideas From This Chapter 169
6.11 Problem Set 169

Chapter 7 Advanced Techniques for Robots 184
7.1 Introduction to Recursion 184
7.2 More on Recursion 186
7.3 Tail Recursion and Looping 190
7.4 Going Formal 191
7.5 Searching 191
7.6 Doing Arithmetic 196
7.7 Polymorphism--Why Write Many Programs When One Will Do? 201
7.8 Conclusion 203
7.9 Important Ideas From This Chapter 204
7.10 Problem Set 204

Chapter 8 Concurrent Robot Programs 209
8.1 Simple Concurrent Programs 209
8.2 Robot Runs In Its Own Thread 210
8.3 Cooperation 211
8.4 Race Conditions 212
8.5 Deadlock 213
8.6 Important Ideas From This Chapter 215
8.7 Problem Set 216

Appendix 217
1 Java main 217
2 KarelRunner 218
3 Compiling and Executing Robot Code 219
4 Constructors in Java 220
5 Controllers and Inner Classes 221
6 Java Cloning 225

Index of Terms 227

1 The Robot World

This chapter introduces a class of robots and sketches the world they inhabit. In later chapters, where a greater depth of understanding is necessary, we will amplify this preliminary discussion.

1.1 The Robot World

Robots live in a world that is unexciting by today's standards (there are no volcanoes, Chinese restaurants, or symphony orchestras), but it does include enough variety to allow robots to perform simply stated, yet interesting tasks. Informally, the world is a grid of streets that robots can traverse. It also contains special things that a robot can sense and manipulate.

Figure 1-1 is a map illustrating the structure of the robot world, whose shape is a great flat plane with the standard north, south, east, and west compass points. The world is bounded on its west side by an infinitely long vertical wall extending northward. To the south, the world is bounded by an infinitely long horizontal wall extending eastward. These boundary walls are made of solid neutronium, an impenetrable metal that restrains robots from falling over the edges of the world.

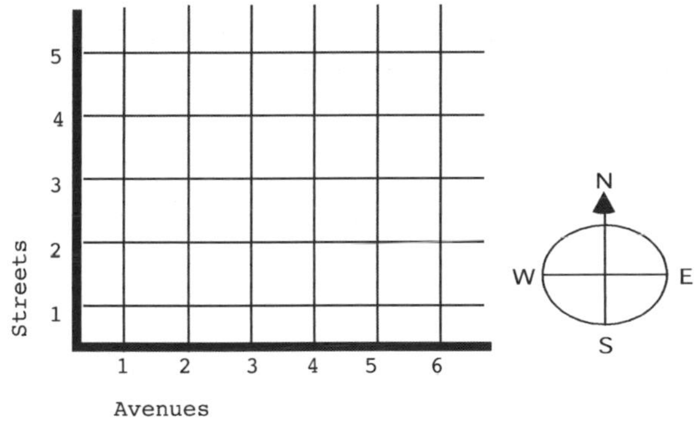

Figure1-1 The Robot World

Crisscrossing the world are horizontal streets (running east-west) and vertical avenues (running north-south) at regular, one-block intervals. To help you distinguish between streets and avenues, remember that the A in "Avenue" points north and the V points south. A corner, sometimes called a street corner or intersection, is located wherever a street and an avenue intersect.

One or more robots can occupy any corner, facing any of the four major compass directions. Any number of robots may occupy the same corner, because the streets and avenues are quite wide. We will usually work with only one robot at a time, however. Robots have names so that we can send them messages individually. When we work with a single robot we will often call it Karel,[1] though you are free to name the robots that you create with any names you like.

Both streets and avenues have numbers; consequently, each corner is identified uniquely by its street and avenue numbers. The corner where 1st Street and 1st Avenue intersect is named the origin. The positions of robots and other things in this world can be described using both absolute and relative locations. The absolute location of the origin, for example, is the intersection of 1st Street and 1st Avenue. An example of a relative location would be to say that a robot is two blocks east and three blocks north of some thing in the world. The origin also has a relative location; it is the most southwesterly corner in the robot world. Sometimes we will describe a robot task using language that gives a different interpretation to the robot world, with north as up, south down, and west and east being left and right, respectively. This is how we (in the Northern Hemisphere) normally look at maps, of course.

Besides robots, two other kinds of things can occupy this world. The first of these kinds of things is a wall section. Wall sections are also fabricated from the impenetrable metal neutronium, and they can be manufactured in any desired length and pattern. They are positioned half way between adjacent street corners, effectively blocking a robot's direct path from one corner to the next. Wall sections are used to represent obstacles, such as hurdles and mountains, around which robots must navigate. Enclosed rooms, mazes, and other barriers can also be constructed from wall sections. Figure 1-2 shows some typical wall arrangements a robot might find in the world.

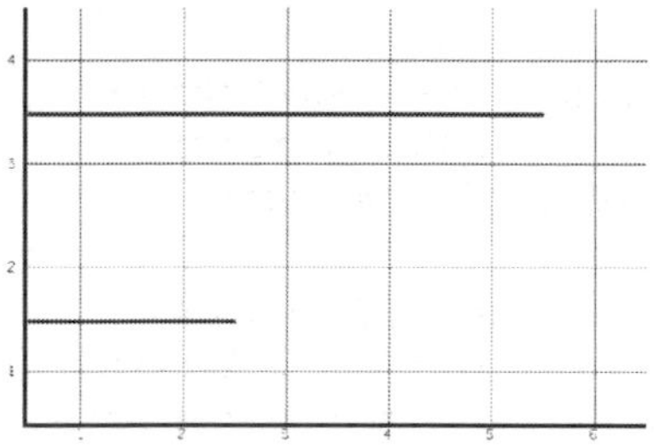

Fig 1-2a North South wall segments

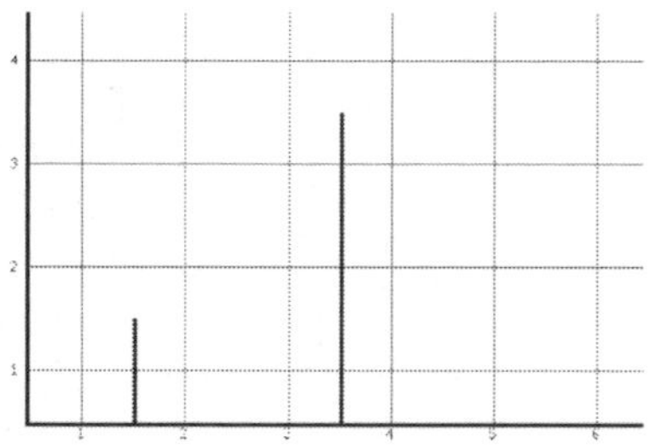

Fig 1-2b Vertical (East-West) wall segments

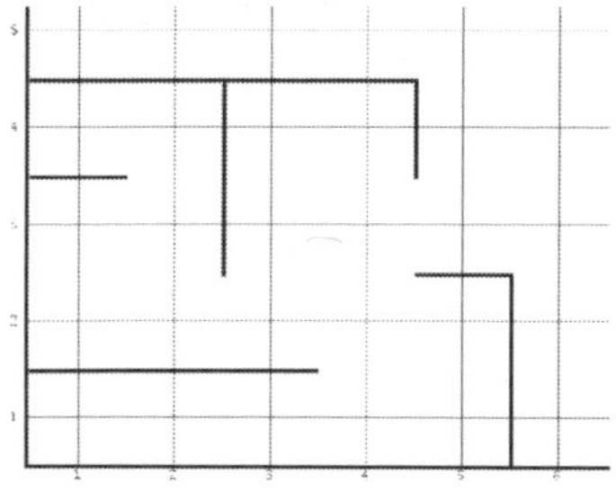

Fig 1-2c A maze of wall segments

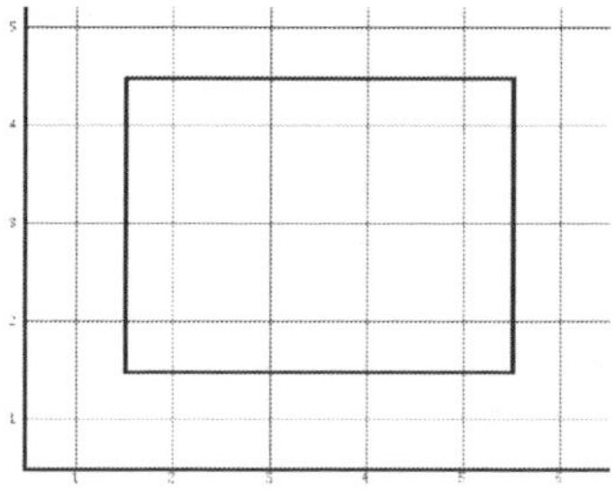

Fig 1-2d A room with no doors or windows

Figure 1-2 Different Wall Segment Arrangements in the Robot World

---

[1] The name Karel is used in recognition of the Czech dramatist Karel Capek, who popularized the word robot in his play R.U.R. (Rossum's Universal Robots). The word robot comes from the Czech word robota, meaning "forced labor."

The second kind of thing in the world is a beeper. Beepers are small plastic cones that emit a quiet beeping noise. They are situated on street corners and can be picked up, carried, and put down by robots. Some tasks require one or more robots to pick up or put down patterns made from beepers or to find and transport beepers. Figure 1-3 shows one possible pattern of beepers. Beepers are small so there can be several on a corner, and they don't interfere with robot movement. There can even be an infinite number on a corner.

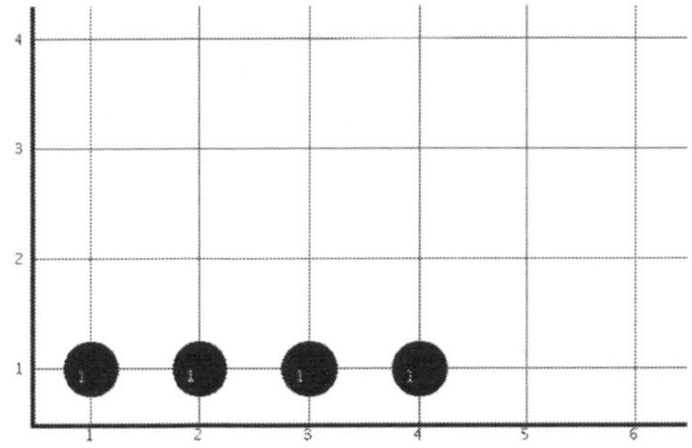

Figure 1-3 One Pattern of Beepers in the Robot World

1.2 Robot Capabilities

Let's now shift our attention away from the robot world and concentrate on the robots themselves. Robots are mobile; a robot can move forward (in the direction it is facing), and it can turn in place. Robots can also perceive their immediate surroundings using rudimentary senses of sight, sound, direction, and touch.

A robot sees by using its TV camera, which points straight ahead. This camera is focused to detect a wall exactly one-half block away from the robot. A robot also has the ability to hear a beeper, but only if the robot and the beeper are on the same corner; the beepers beep very quietly. By consulting its internal compass, a robot can determine which direction it is facing. Finally, each robot is equipped with a mechanical arm that it can use to pick up and put down beepers. To carry these beepers, each robot wears a soundproof beeper-bag around its waist. A robot can also determine whether it is carrying any beepers in this bag by probing the bag with its arm. A robot can also use its arm to determine whether there are other robots on the same corner that it occupies. Finally, a robot can turn itself off when its task is complete.

As you might expect, robots are made in factories. All robots come from the main factory, Karel-Werke, which can actually supply several different models of robots. When we need a robot for a task, we can use the standard model, or we can write a specification for a new model. Karel-Werke is able to build specialized robots that are modifications or extensions of the existing models.

Whenever we want a collection of robots to accomplish a task in the robot world, we must supply a detailed set of instructions that describe any special features of the robots that are needed and also explain how to perform the task. For most tasks one robot is all that is needed. When a robot is ordered from the factory, it is delivered to the robot world by helicopter. The helicopter pilot sets up the robots according to our specifications and sends each new robot a sequence of messages to detail its task, which it is then able to carry out.

What language do we use to program (here we use "program" to mean "write instructions for") robots? Instead of programming these robots in English, a natural language for us, we program them in a special programming language. This language was specially designed to be useful for writing robot programs. The robot programming language-like any natural language-has a vocabulary, punctuation marks, and rules of grammar, but this language, unlike English, for example, is simple enough for robots to understand. However, it is a powerful and concise language that allows us to write brief and unambiguous programs for them. This language is built from and based on the Java Programming Language.

1.3 Tasks and Situations

A task is something that we want a robot to do. The following examples are tasks for robots:

- Move to the corner of 15th St. & 10th Ave.
- Run a hurdle race (with wall sections representing hurdles).
- Escape from an enclosed room that has a door.
- Find a beeper and deposit it on the origin.
- Escape from a maze.

A situation is an exact description of what the world looks like. Besides the basic structure of the world, which is always present, wall sections and beepers can be added. To specify a situation completely, we must provide answers for the following questions.

- What is each robot's current position? We must specify both the robot's location (which corner it is on) and what direction it is facing.
- What is the location and length of each wall section in the world?
- What is the location of each beeper in the world? This information includes specifying the number of beepers in each robot's beeper-bag.

Situations are specified in this book by a small map or brief written description. If we know the number of beepers that each robot has in its beeper-bag, then the maps in Figure 1-4 completely specify different situations. The initial situation for any task is defined to be the situation in which all of the robots are placed at the start of the task. The final situation is the situation that each robot is in when it turns itself off. Figure 1-4 shows six initial situations that are typical for tasks that a single robot will accomplish in the coming chapters.

1.4 Robots and Objects

Robots are examples of things called Objects. An object is an electronic thing, though it is useful to think of objects as if they were real, just as robots can be real. Objects can **do** things and they can **remember** things. We can ask robots (and objects in general) to do the things they know how to do, and we can ask them about the things they remember. We will explore this idea throughout this book. Java is a computer language in which it is easy to create objects, and in particular, robots. The robot programming language was created using ideas like the ones presented in this book. In Chapter 4 we shall see other, somewhat more abstract, kinds of objects. Objects can be used to represent things like robots or ideas like a game strategy.

1.5 Important Ideas From This Chapter

robot
task
situation
program
object

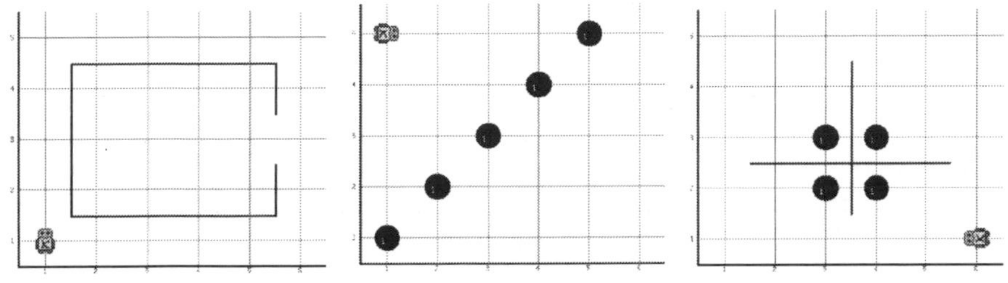

(A) A room has one door. A robot is at the origin and facing North. Robot must enter the room.

(B) A diagonal line of beepers. Robot is facing East and must pick all of the beepers

(C) A '+' wall arrangement with beepers. From a starting position robot must pick all beepers

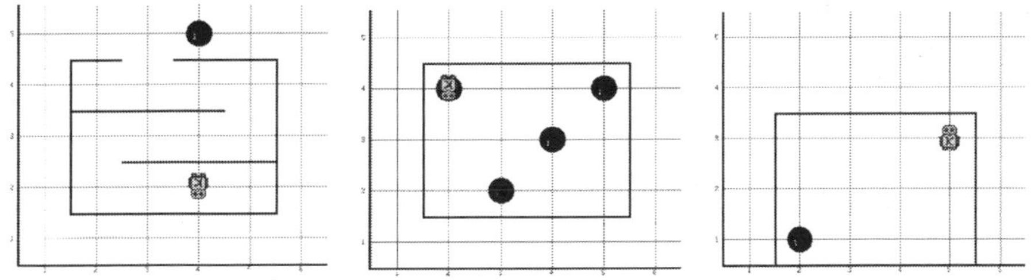

(D) Robot must escape the maze.

(E) Beepers are scattered in a box. Robot is facing South in the North West corner and must pick all the beepers in the box.

(F) Box with a beeper. Robot is facing North in the North East Corner. Robot must find the beeper.

Figure 1-4 Six Sample Tasks for a Robot to Perform

1.6 Problem Set

The purpose of this problem set is to make sure that you have a good understanding of the robot world and the capabilities of robots before moving on to robot programming.

1. Which of the following directions can a robot face?

- northeast
- east

- south-southwest
- north
- 164 degrees
- vertical
- down

2. What things other than robots can be found in the robot world?

3. Which of the things listed in Problem 2 can a robot manipulate or change?

4. What reference points can be used in the robot world to describe a robot's exact location?

5. How many robots can we have in a given robot world?

6. Give the absolute location of each robot in each of the worlds shown in Figure 1-5. Give a relative location of each robot in the worlds.

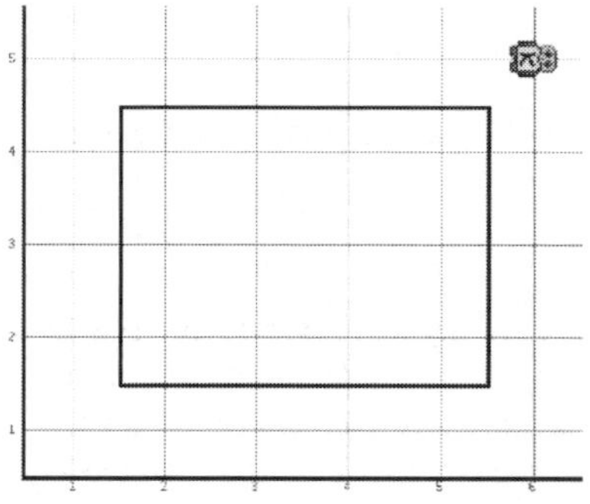

Fig A

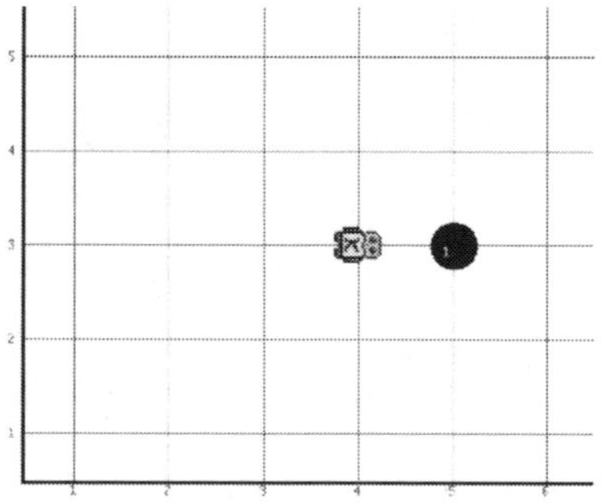

Fig B

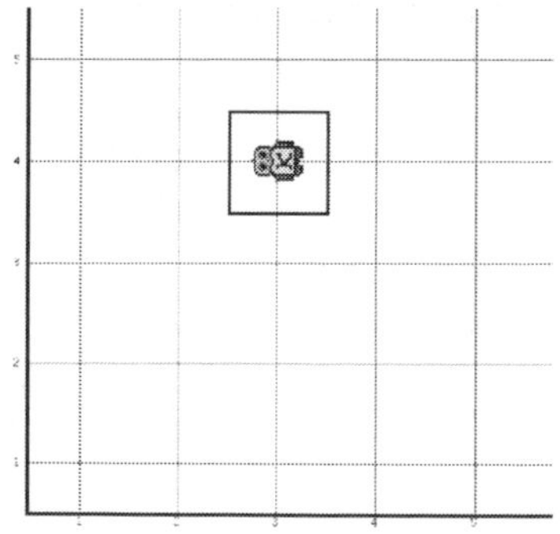

Fig C

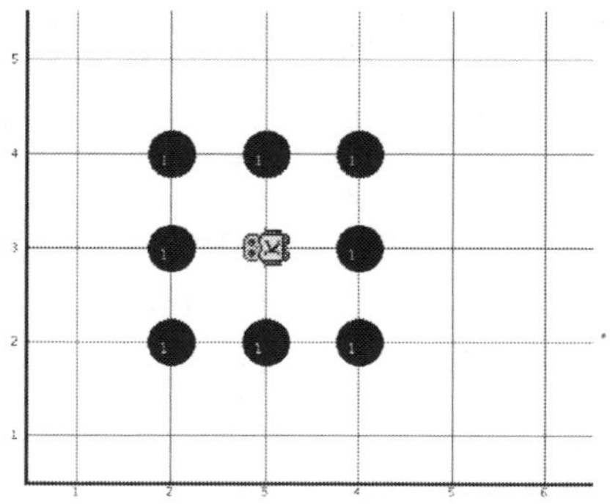

Fig D

Figure 1-5 Different Robot Situations

2 Primitive Instructions and Simple Programs

This chapter begins our study of the robot programming language. We will start with a detailed explanation of the primitive instructions that are built into every robot's vocabulary. Using these instructions, we can instruct any robot to move through the world and handle beepers. Section 2.6 shows a complete robot program and discusses the elementary punctuation and grammar rules of the robot programming language. By the end of this chapter we will be able to write programs that instruct robots to perform simple obstacle avoidance and beeper transportation tasks.

Before explaining the primitive instructions of the robot programming language, we must first define the technical term *execute*: A robot executes an instruction by performing the instruction's associated action or actions. The robot executes a program by executing a sequence of instructions that are given to it by the helicopter pilot. Each instruction in such a sequence is delivered to the robot in a message, which directs one robot to perform one instruction in the program.

2.1 Changing Position

Every robot understands two primitive instructions that change its position. The first of these instructions is **move** , which changes a robot's location.

move

When a robot is sent a **move** message it executes a **move** instruction and moves forward one block; it continues to face the same direction. To avoid damage, a robot will not move forward if it sees a wall section or boundary wall between its current location and the corner to which it would move. Instead, it turns itself off. This action, called an error shutoff, will be explained further in Section 2.7.

From this definition we see that a robot executes a **move** instruction by moving forward to the next corner. However, the robot performs an error shutoff when its front is blocked. Both situations are illustrated in

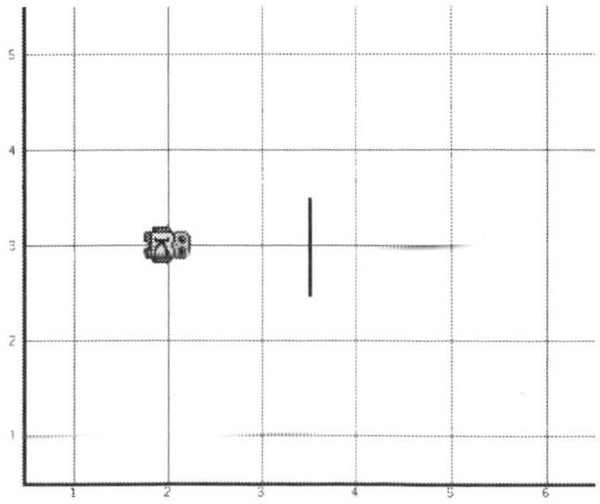

Figure 2-1 A: A Robot in the Initial Situation before a move Instruction

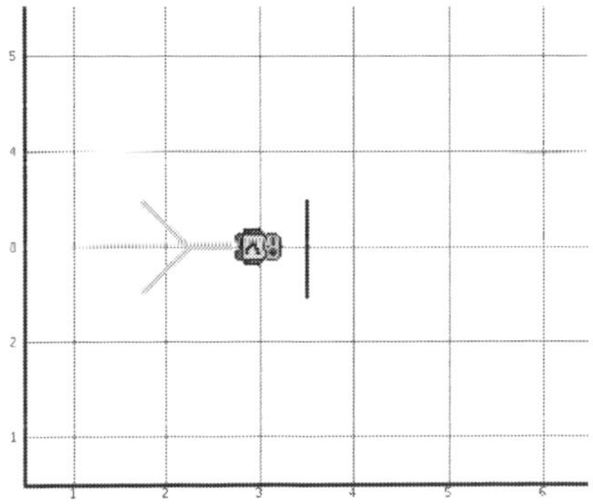

Figure 2-1 B: A Robot in the Final Situation after Executing a move Instruction

Figure 2-1. Figure 2-1 shows the successful execution of a **move** instruction. The wall section is more than one half-block away and cannot block this robot's move.

In contrast, Figure 2-2 shows an incorrect attempt to move. When this robot tries to execute a **move** instruction in this situation, it sees a wall section. Relying on its self-preservation instinct, it performs an error shutoff.

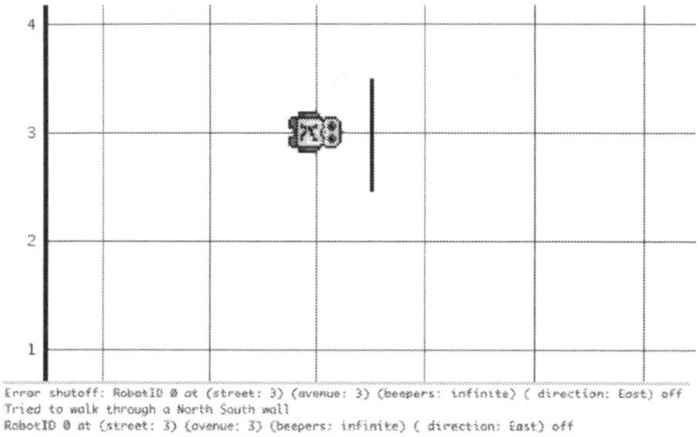
4
3
2
1
Error shutoff: RobotID 0 at (street: 3) (avenue: 3) (beepers: infinite) (direction: East) off
Tried to walk through a North South wall
RobotID 0 at (street: 3) (avenue: 3) (beepers: infinite) (direction: East) off

Figure 2-2 The Result of a robot Attempting to move When Its Front Is Blocked Is an Error Shutoff.

2.2 Turning in Place

The second primitive instruction that changes a robot's position is **turnLeft** . This instruction changes the direction in which the robot is facing but does not alter its location.

turnLeft

> When a robot is sent a **turnLeft** message it executes a **turnLeft** instruction by pivoting 90 degrees to the left. The robot remains on the same street corner while executing a **turnLeft** instruction. Because it is impossible for a wall section to block a robot's turn, **turnLeft** cannot cause an error shutoff.

A robot always starts a task on some corner, facing either north, south, east, or west. A robot cannot travel fractions of a block or turn at other than 90 degree angles. Although **move** and **turnLeft** change the robot's position, after executing either of these instructions, the robot still is on some corner and still is facing one of the four compass directions.

Karel-Werke's designer purposely did not provide a built-in **turnRight** instruction. Would adding a **turnRight** to the primitive instructions allow the robot to perform any task it cannot accomplish without one? A moment's thought-and the right flash of insight-shows that the **turnRight** instruction is unnecessary; it does not permit robots to accomplish any new tasks. The key observation for verifying this conclusion is that a robot can manage the equivalent of a **turnRight** instruction by executing three **turnLeft** instructions.

2.3 Finishing a Task

We need a way to tell a robot that its task is finished. The **turnOff** instruction fulfills this requirement.

turnOff

When a robot is sent a **turnOff** message, it executes a **turnOff** instruction. It turns off and is incapable of executing any more instructions until restarted on another task. The last instruction executed by every robot in a program is usually a **turnOff** instruction. This is not strictly necessary, however. The robot will ignore all messages after it executes **turnOff**.

2.4 Handling Beepers

Every robot understands two instructions that permit it to handle beepers. These two instructions perform opposite actions.

pickBeeper

When a robot is sent a **pickBeeper** message, it executes a **pickBeeper** instruction. It picks up a beeper from the corner on which it is standing and then deposits the beeper in its beeper-bag. If a **pickBeeper** instruction is attempted on a beeperless corner, the robot performs an error shutoff. On a corner with more than one beeper the robot picks up one, and only one, of the beepers and then places it in the beeper-bag.

putBeeper

When a robot is sent a **putBeeper** message, it executes a **putBeeper** instruction by extracting a beeper from its beeper-bag and placing the beeper on the current street corner. If a robot tries to execute a **putBeeper** instruction with an empty beeper-bag, the robot performs an error shutoff. If the robot has more than one beeper in its beeper-bag, it extracts one, and only one, beeper and places it on the current corner.

Beepers are so small that robots can move right by them; only wall sections and boundary walls can block a robot's movement. Robots are also very adept at avoiding each other if two or more show up on the same corner simultaneously.

2.5 Robot Descriptions

All robots produced by Karel-Werke have at least the capabilities just described. As we will see, such robots are very primitive, and we might like robots with additional abilities. Therefore, we must have some way to describe those extra abilities so that the factory can build a robot to our specifications. Karel-Werke employs a simple robot programming language to describe both robot abilities and the lists of robot instructions, called programs. The formal name for the description of a robot instruction is **method**. The simple model of robot described above is called the **UrRobot** class[2]. A class is a description of robots of the same kind. A class is like a production line in the factory that makes robots. The specification, or interface, of the **UrRobot** class in the robot programming language follows.

---

[2] Ur is a German prefix meaning "original" or "primitive." The pronunciation of ur is similar to the sound of "oor" in "poor."

```
public class UrRobot
{
        public void move(){...}
        public void turnOff(){...}
        public void turnLeft(){...}
        public void pickBeeper(){...}
        public void putBeeper(){...}
        ...
}
```

Following the model class name is a list of instructions (methods) for this kind of robot. The list is always written in braces { and }. The use of elipsis in the above {...} indicates that there are some things that belong here that are not being shown. These are the descriptions of how an UrRobot would carry out each of these instructions. Public simply means the names are visible everywhere in a robot program.

The five methods, **move** through **putBeeper**, name actions that **UrRobots** can perform. We defined each of these actions in the foregoing sections, and we will see many examples of their use throughout this book. The word **void** prefixes each of these methods to indicate that they return no feedback when executed. Later we will see additional methods that do produce feedback when executed, rather than changing the state of the robot as these instructions all do. Said differently, **void** means that these instructions do something as opposed to telling us something that the robot remembers: robots **do** things and they **remember** things. The matching parentheses that follow the method names mark them as the names of actions that a robot will be able to carry out. We will begin to study the kinds of things that can replace the elipises in the above starting in Chapter 3.

Note that a class is not a robot. It is just a description (blueprint, specification) of robots of the same kind. The class *of* a robot tells us its capabilities (methods). If we know the class of a robot we know what the robot can do and what it can remember. We haven't created any robots yet, but are about to do so.

A sample task for an **UrRobot** might be to start at the origin, facing east, and then walk three blocks east to a corner known to have a beeper, pick up the beeper, and **turnOff** on that corner. A complete program to accomplish this task is shown next. In this program we name the robot **karel** , but we could use any convenient name. Note that we don't capitalize the names of robots. They aren't people, after all. In Java, the name used to refer to an object (including a robot) is called a "reference variable" and the convention is not to capitalize these in our Java programs. The names of classes like UrRobot, on the other hand, are usually capitalized.

```
public static void main(String [] args)
{
      UrRobot karel = new UrRobot(1, 1, East, 0);
            // Deliver the robot to the origin (1,1),
            // facing East, with no beepers.
      karel.move();
      karel.move();
      karel.move();
      karel.pickBeeper();
      karel.turnOff();
}
```

2.6 A Complete Program

In this section we describe a task for a robot named karel and a complete program that instructs it to perform the task. The task, illustrated in Figure 2-3, is to transport the beeper from 1st Street and 4th Avenue to 3rd Street and 5th Avenue. After karel has put down the beeper, it must move one block farther north before turning off.

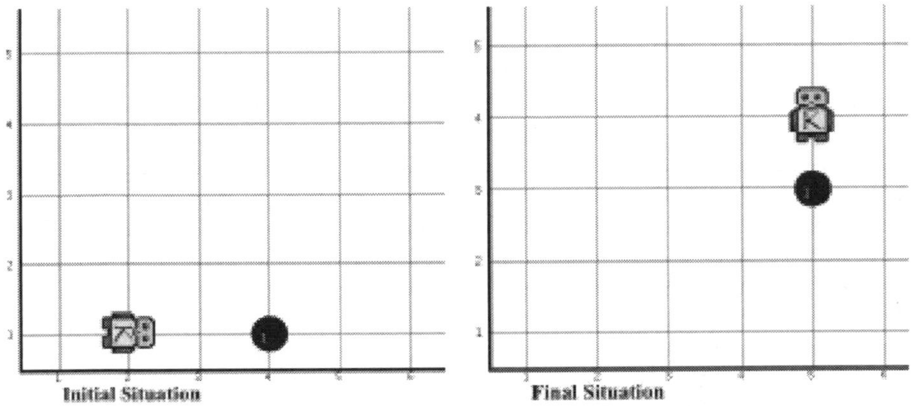

Figure 2-3 The Initial and Final Situations of Karel's task

The following program instructs karel to perform this task. The program uses all of the methods available to robots in the **UrRobot** class, a few new words from the robot programming vocabulary, and punctuation symbols such as the period and semicolon. We will first discuss karel's execution of this program, and then analyze the general structure of all robot programs.

```
import kareltherobot.*;

public class Tester implements Directions
{
        public static void main(String [] args)
        {
                UrRobot karel = new UrRobot(1, 2, East, 0);
                karel.move();
                karel.move();
                karel.pickBeeper();
                karel.move();
                karel.turnLeft();
                karel.move();
                karel.move();
                karel.putBeeper();
                karel.move();
                karel.turnOff();
        }
}
```

See Section 1 and 2 of the Appendix for more on the details of the above including the import statement.

We must note that this is not the only sequence of messages that will correctly perform the stated task. Although it is obvious and direct, this is just one of many sequences that will accomplish the task.

A set of messages to one or more robots is called a task. A task can be executed by the Java system. The first instruction in the main task block constructs the robot, associates the name **karel** with it, and delivers it, ready to run, from the factory to 1st Street and 2nd Avenue, facing east with no beepers in its beeper-bag. This instruction is not, technically speaking, a message since it is not addressed to any robot. This statement can be thought of as a delivery specification. It instructs the helicopter pilot how to set up the robot when it is delivered. The delivery specification also names the specific type or class of robot that we want delivered. Here we want an **UrRobot** .

The remaining lines of the main task block instruct karel how to carry out the task. These messages are sent to karel by the helicopter pilot, as described next.

2.6.1 Executing a Program

Before a program can be executed in a world, the program is read at the factory to make sure it has no errors. We will discuss errors later; for now, we will assume that our program is correct.

How is a program executed? A program execution is begun after the helicopter pilot delivers the robot to the required corner and sets it up according to the delivery specification. Here we require that the **UrRobot karel** be set up on 1st Street and 2nd Avenue, facing east, and with zero beepers in its beeper-bag. Then, for each additional command in the main task block, the pilot sends a corresponding electronic message to the robot named in that command. The message gives the instruction that the named robot is supposed to perform. These messages are relayed by the pilot to the robot through a special robot control satellite that hovers over the world. Since a robot can execute only one instruction at a time and since the satellite has a very limited communication capacity, only one message can be sent at a time. The pilot must wait for instruction completion before sending the next message. When the robot completes the current instruction, it sends a reply back to the pilot through the satellite indicating that the next message can be sent. Messages from the main task block are sent sequentially without omitting any messages in a strict top-to-bottom order. The pilot continues sending messages until either all messages in the main task block have been sent or the pilot attempts to send a message to a robot that has executed a **turnOff** or has performed an error shutoff.

It is also possible for robots to send messages to each other. When this occurs, the robot sending the message waits for the reply before continuing. This is to guarantee that the satellite communication channel is never overloaded. There is a subtle point here, however. The helicopter pilot only reads out the messages in the main task block. These messages contain the names of the robot's methods. The robot itself knows how to carry out the details of that method. We shall see how important this distinction is in the next chapter. A robot will only react to message sent specifically to it. This is important to remember when we have several robots.

To determine what a program does, we simulate, or *trace*, its execution. Simulating or tracing a robot program means that we must systematically execute the program exactly as the pilot and robots would, recording every action that takes place. We can simulate a robot program by using markers on a sheet of paper (representing robots and the world) or walking around on a rectangular grid. We simulate a robot program by following the sequence of messages in the order the pilot reads them to the robot. We will discuss tracing later, but in order to become proficient robot programmers, we must understand exactly how the pilot reads the program and the robot executes it. The ability to simulate a robot's behavior quickly and accurately is an important skill that we must acquire.

Let's follow a simulation of our program. In the following simulation **(1, 4)** means 1st Street and 4th Avenue. In the following annotation we explain exactly what state the robot is left in after the execution of the instruction. Note that the symbol // (two adjacent slash characters) is used in the simulation to introduce comments into our robot programs. Each comment begins with the // mark and continues to the end of the line. These comments are ignored by the pilot and by the robots; they are included only to aid our own understanding of the program. Here we use them to explain in detail each instruction as it will be executed. We note, however, that if the program is changed in any way, the comments are likely to become invalid.

```
public static void main(String [] args)
{
      UrRobot karel = new UrRobot(1, 2, East, 0);
                   // A new robot named karel is
                   // constructed and delivered to
                   // (1, 2), facing East. karel has
                   // no beepers in its beeper-bag.

      karel.move();            // karel moves east
                               // to (1, 3)
      karel.move();            // karel moves east
                               // to (1, 4)
      karel.pickBeeper();      // karel picks 1 beeper,
                               // 1 beeper in bag
      karel.move();            // karel moves east
                               // to (1, 5)
      karel.turnLeft();        // karel remains on
                               // (1, 5), faces North
      karel.move();            // karel moves north
                               // to (2, 5)
      karel.move;              // karel moves north
                               // to (3, 5)
      karel.putBeeper();       // karel puts 1 beeper
                               // down, now 0 beepers
                               // in bag
      karel.move();            // karel moves north
                               // to (4, 5)
      karel.turnOff();         // karel remains on
                               // (4, 5) facing North
                               // and shuts off
}
```

Karel is done and we have verified that our program is correct through simulation by tracing the execution of the program.

2.6.2 The Form of Robot Programs

Now that we have seen how a robot executes a program, let's explore the grammar rules of the robot programming language. The factory and pilots pay strict attention to grammar and punctuation rules, so our time is well spent carefully studying these rules. We start by dividing the symbols in a robot program into three groups. The first group consists of special symbols. It has members such as the punctuation marks like the semicolon, the braces { and } , and the period. The next group of symbols consists of names such as robot and class names, **karel** and **UrRobot** . We also use names to refer to instructions, like **putBeeper** and **turnLeft** . The third and last group of symbols consists of reserved words. We have already seen a few of these like **class** and **void**.

Reserved words are used to structure and organize the primitive instructions in the robot programming language. They are called reserved words because their use is reserved for their built-in purpose. These reserved words may not be reused for other purposes in a robot program, such as robot names. To make the reading of programs easier, we may write robot programs using both upper- and lowercase letters as well as the underscore character, but we must be consistent. For example, **void** is always spelled with all lowercase letters. The robot programming language is case-sensitive, meaning that the use of upper- and lowercase letters in a word must be consistent each time the word is used. If we use the word **Void** in a robot program it would refer to something else, perhaps the name of a robot.

Since robot programs need to be read by humans as well as robots, it is helpful to be able to put explanatory material into the program itself. The language therefore permits comments to be inserted into the text of the program. As we have seen in the foregoing program, a comment begins anywhere on a line with the special symbol // (two slash marks with no space between). The comment terminates only when the line does. Anything may follow the comment symbol on the same line.

Every robot program consists of a task to be completed by one or more robots. This main task block is normally included in a **main** method and is enclosed in curly brace punctuation marks. Notice that the opening brace must be matched eventually by a closing brace. Matching pairs of braces are called *delimiters*, because they mark, or delimit, the beginning and end of some important entity. Note that main is not a reserved word. It is just the name of a certain method known to the system.

If we needed specialized robots to perform various parts of the task, the class declarations of those robots would precede the task list, as would the definitions of any new instructions named in the class declarations. They could also be in separate files. We will go into this in detail in Chapter 3.

The main task block itself normally starts with a list of definitions, called declarations. In the following program we have only one declaration, which declares that the name **karel** will be used as the name of a robot in class **UrRobot** . Declarations introduce new names and indicate how they will be used in the rest of the program. The declarations of robot names always end with a semicolon. We could also declare names for several different robots, even robots of different classes. The declarations of robots can best be thought of as delivery specifications to the factory. They always contain information about how and where the robot should be placed in the world. They don't need to be at the beginning of a task, though we usually put them there. They do need to appear before we try to ask them to do anything. After all, we have to deliver a robot before we can ask it to do something.

Every program has one main task block. Each of the statements in the main task block is terminated by a semicolon. Most of the statements in the main task block are messages to the robots declared in the declaration list. The one exception here is the delivery instruction, which causes the factory to construct and deliver a new **UrRobot** named karel to 1st Street and 2nd Avenue (we always list streets first), facing east, with no beepers in its beeper-bag. When delivered, the robot is set up and ready to receive messages sent to it. Since robots are delivered by the factory in helicopters, we don't need to be concerned about walls in the world that might impede delivery to any corner. The helicopter will be able to fly over them.

We can send messagesto several different robots from the same main task block, so we need to specify which robot is to carry out each instruction. Thus, if we have a robot named karel and want it to move, we send the message **karel.move()** . This seems redundant here when there is only one robot, but it is required nevertheless. An instruction that causes a robot to perform one of its own instructions, such as move, is known as a message statement. The instruction named in a message statement (**move**) is called the message, and the robot (**karel**) is the receiver of the message. Messages are the means of getting a robot to execute an instruction.

Execution always begins with the first instruction of the main task block . Robots are not automatically shut down at the final closing brace in a program; the **turnOff** instruction should be used for that purpose. The closing brace marks the end of the instructions that will be executed. If we reach the end of the instructions in the main task block and any robot is still on because it hasn't yet executed a **turnOff** instruction, it means that at least one **turnOff** instruction has been omitted from the program. This is not an error, but turning off your robots when you are done with them is useful as their appearance will change to show you that they are done.

Observe that the program is nicely indented as well as commented. It is well organized and easy to read. This style of indenting, as well as the comments, is only for the benefit of human readers. The following program is just as easily executed as the previous program.

```
   public static void main(String [] args){  UrRobot karel =
new UrRobot(1,2, East,0); karel.move();
karel.move(); karel.pickBeeper(); karel.move();
karel.turnLeft(); karel.move(); karel.move();
karel.putBeeper(); karel.move(); karel.turnOff()};
```

As this example illustrates, the importance of adopting a programming style that is easy to read by humans cannot be overemphasized.

2.7 Error Shutoffs

When a robot is prevented from successfully completing the action associated with a message, it turns itself off. This action is known as an error shutoff, and the effect is equivalent to receiving a **turnOff** message. However, turning off is not the only way such a problem could be addressed. An alternative strategy could have the robot just ignore any message that cannot be executed successfully. Using this strategy the robot could continue executing the program as if it had never been required to execute the unsuccessful instruction.

To justify the choice of executing an error shutoff, rather than just ignoring messages in such situations, consider the following: Once an unexpected situation arises-one that prevents successful execution of an instruction-a robot probably will be unable to make further progress toward accomplishing the task. Continuing to execute a program under these circumstances will lead to an even greater discrepancy between what the programmer had intended for the robot to do and what it is actually doing. Consequently, the best strategy is to have the robot turn off as soon as the first inconsistency appears.

So far, we have seen three instructions that can cause error shutoffs: **move** , **pickBeeper** , and **putBeeper** . We must construct our programs carefully and ensure that the following conditions are always satisfied.

- A robot executes a **move** instruction only when the path is clear to the next corner immediately in front of it.
- A robot executes a **pickBeeper** instruction only when it is on the same corner as at least one beeper.
- A robot executes a **putBeeper** instruction only when the beeper-bag is not empty.

We can guarantee that these conditions are met if, before writing our program, we know the exact initial situation in which the robot will be placed.

2.8 Programming Errors

In this section we classify all programming errors into four broad categories. These categories are discussed using the analogy of a motorist with a task in the real world. It should help clarify the nature of each error type. You might ask, "Why spend so much time talking about errors when they should never occur?" The answer to this question is that programming requires an uncommon amount of precision, and although errors should not occur in principle, they occur excessively in practice. Therefore we must become adept at quickly finding and fixing errors by simulating our programs.

A lexical error occurs whenever the robot program contains a word that is not in its vocabulary. As an analogy, suppose that we are standing on a street in San Francisco and we are asked by a lost motorist, "How can I get to Portland, Oregon?" If we tell the motorist, "fsdt jkhpy hqngrpz fgssj sgr ghhgh grmplhms," we commit a lexical error. The motorist is unable to follow our instructions because it is impossible to decipher the words of which the instructions are composed. Similarly, the robot executing a program must understand each word in a program that it is asked to execute.

Here is a robot program with some lexical errors:

```
bublic static void main(String [] args)    // misspelled reserved word
{
  UrRobot karel(1, 2, East, 0) ; // missing new...
  karel.move();
  karel.mvoe();           // misspelled instruction
  karel.pick();           // unknown word
  karel.move();
  karel.turnright();      // unknown word
  karel.turn_left();      // unknown word
  karel.turnleft();       // unknown word
  Karel.move();           // unknown word
                          // (capitalizaton inconsistent with declaration)
}
```

The last two errors occur because the robot programming language is case-sensitive. The word turnLeft is not the same as turnleft, nor is karel the same as Karel.

Even if the pilot recognizes every word in a program, the program still might harbor a syntax error. This type of error occurs whenever we use incorrect grammar or incorrect punctuation. Going back to our lost motorist, we might reply, "for, Keep hundred. just miles going eight." Although the motorist recognizes each of these words individually, we have combined them in a senseless, convoluted manner. According to the rules of English grammar, the parts of speech are not in their correct positions. We discussed the grammar rules for basic robot programs in Section 2.6.2.

The following program contains no lexical errors, but it does have syntax errors.

```
UrRobot karel = new UrRobot(1,1,East,0);
       // declaration not in main task block
public static void main(String [] args)
  karel.move();                // missing brace
  move();                      // not addressed
                               // to any robot
  karel.pickBeeper;            // no ()
  karel move();                // missing period
  karel.turnLeft()             // missing semicolon
  karel.move();
  karel.move();
  karel.putBeeper();
  karel.move();
};                             // extra semicolon
  karel.turnOff()              // message outside
                               // task block and
                               // missing semicolon
```

If our program contains lexical or syntax errors, the factory will discover them when our program is checked there. In both cases, the factory has no conception of what we meant to say; therefore, it does not try to correct our errors. Instead, the factory informs us of the detected errors and doesn't build the robot. This action is not an error shutoff, for in this case the robot never has a chance to begin to execute the program. While discussing the next two categories of errors, we will assume that the factory finds no lexical or syntax errors in our program, so it builds the robot and the pilot delivers it and begins to execute the program.

The third error category is called an execution error. Unlike lexical and syntax errors, which are detected at the factory, the pilot can only detect these errors while the program is running or during a simulation of its execution. Execution errors occur whenever a robot in the world is unable to execute an instruction successfully and is forced to perform an error shutoff. Returning to our motorist, who is trying to drive from San Francisco to Portland, we might say, "Just keep going for eight hundred miles." But if the motorist happens to be facing west at the time, and takes our directions literally, the motorist would reach the Pacific Ocean after traveling only a few miles. At this point, the motorist would halt, realizing that he or she cannot follow our instructions to completion.

Likewise, a robot turns off if asked to execute an instruction that it cannot execute successfully. Instructing a robot to **move** when the front is blocked, to **pickBeeper** on a corner that has no beeper, and to **putBeeper** when the beeper-bag is empty are examples of execution errors, and each one results in an error shutoff.

The final error class is the most insidious, because pilots, the factory, and robots cannot detect this type of error when it occurs. We label this category of error an intent error. An intent error occurs whenever the program successfully terminates but does not successfully complete the task. Suppose our motorist is facing south when we say, "Just keep going for eight hundred miles." Even though these instructions can be successfully followed to completion, the motorist will end up somewhere in Mexico, rather than Oregon.

Here is an example of an intent error in a robot program: Beginning in the situation shown in Figure 2-4, karel is to pick up the beeper, move it one block to the north, put the beeper down, move one more block to the north, and **turnOff** .

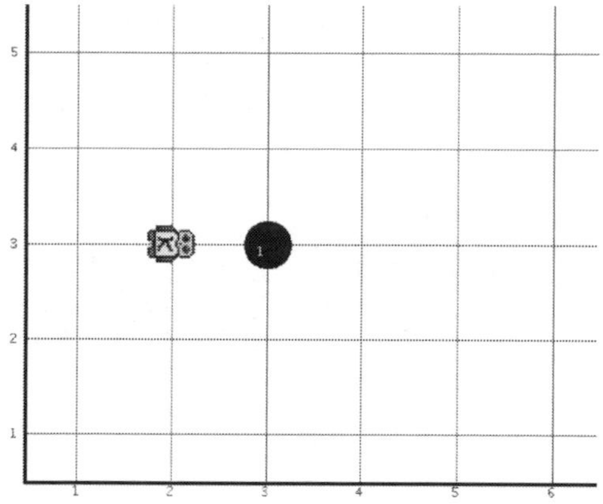

Figure 2-4 Karel's Initial Situation

```
public static void main(String [] args)
{ UrRobot karel = new UrRobot(3, 2, East, 0);
  karel.move();
  karel.pickBeeper();
  karel.move();
  karel.turnLeft();
  karel.putBeeper();
  karel.move();
  karel.turnOff();
}
```

There are no lexical, syntax, or execution errors in this program. As far as karel and the helicopter pilot are concerned, when the **turnOff** is executed, everything is perfect. However, look at the task and look at the program. What is the error? The task is to move the beeper one block to the north, yet karel moved the beeper one block to the east. The intent was a northerly move, but the final result was an easterly move. The program does not satisfy the requirements of the stated task and thus contains an error of intent.

Remember that a robot does not understand the task for which we have programmed it. All that the robot can do is execute the instructions corresponding to messages we have sent it in our program. Thus, there is no way for a robot to know that the program did not accomplish what we intended. Similarly, the pilot has no way to know what we intended. He or she only knows what is actually written in the program itself.

2.8.1 Bugs and Debugging

In programming jargon, all types of errors are known as bugs. There are many apocryphal stories about the origin of this term. In one story the term bug is said to have been originated by telephone company engineers to refer to the source of random noises transmitted by their electronic communications circuits. Another story originated with the Harvard Mark I Computer and Grace Murray Hopper, later Admiral. The computer was producing incorrect answers, and when engineers took it apart trying to locate the problem, they found a dead moth caught between the contacts of a relay, causing the malfunction: the first computer bug. Other stories abound, so perhaps we shall never know the true entomology of this word.

Perhaps the term bug became popular in programming because it saved the egos of programmers. Instead of admitting that their programs were full of errors, they could say that their programs had bugs in them. Actually, the metaphor is apt; bugs are hard to find, and although a located bug is frequently easy to fix, it is difficult to ensure that all bugs have been found and removed from a program. Debugging is the name that programmers give to the activity of removing errors from a program.

2.9 A Task for Two Robots

We are not restricted to using only a single robot to perform a task. We can have as many as we like. We shall see in later chapters that robots can communicate in sophisticated ways. For now, here is a simple task for two robots.

Karel is at 3rd Street and 1st Avenue on a corner with a beeper, facing East. Carl is at the origin facing East. Karel should carry the beeper to carl and put it down. Carl should then pick it up and carry it to 1st Street and 3rd Avenue. The beeper should be placed on this corner. Both robots should face East at the end.

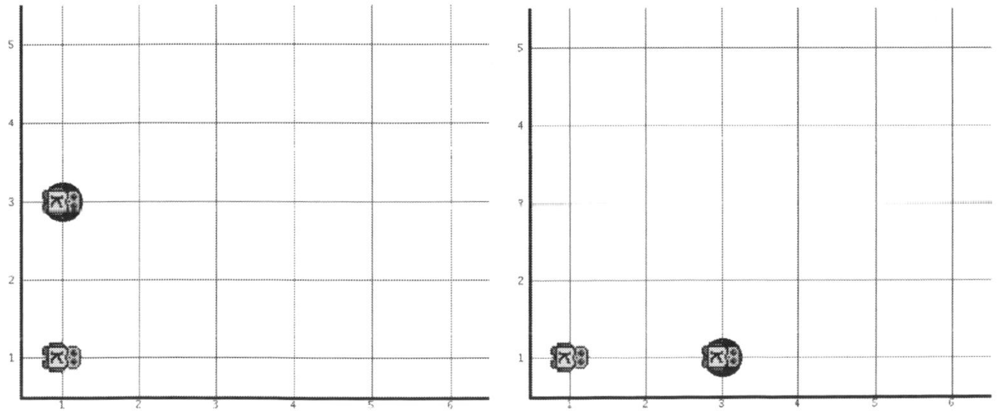

Figure 2-5. Initial and Final Situations for the Two Robot Task

```
 public static void main(String [] args)
{       UrRobot karel = new UrRobot(3, 1, East, 0);
        UrRobot carl  = new UrRobot(1, 1, East, 0);

        karel.pickBeeper();
        karel.turnLeft();
        karel.turnLeft();
        karel.turnLeft();
        karel.move();
        karel.move();
        karel.turnLeft();
        karel.putBeeper();
        carl.pickBeeper();
        carl.move();
        carl.move();
        carl.putBeeper();
        karel.turnOff();
        carl.turnOff();
}
```

2.10 An infinity of Beepers

We note for completeness, though we can't use the information yet, that a robot can be delivered with infinitely many beepers in its beeper-bag. If such a robot puts down a beeper or picks a beeper, the number of beepers in the beeper-bag does not change. It is still infinity.

UrRobot karel = new UrRobot(3, 2, East, infinity);

We will use this information in later chapters. It is also possible, though rare, for a corner to contain an infinite number of beepers. Since programs are finite, however, there is no way to put down or pick up an infinite number of beepers.

2.11 Some Terminology

Robots are examples of programming constructs called **objects**. Objects have two capabilities: they **do** things and they **remember** things. The things that robots do are move, pickBeeper, etc. We will learn some things about remembering in Chapter 4 and later. We ask an object to do something by sending it a message. We can also ask an object something about what it has remembered with a message. Beepers and walls in the robot world are not objects, however. You can't send them messages. As a person, you are something like an object. You can receive messages. You can do things. You can remember things. You respond to the messages you receive.

We refer to Robots using names. These names are called **variables**. This is because they can vary. A name can refer to different robots at different times, just as in your world, the name karel can refer to different people at different times. Sometimes a robot (and in general, an object) needs to refer to itself. When you refer to yourself you probably use a special "name", like "me." Likewise any robot can refer to itself with the special name "this".

2.12 Important Ideas From This Chapter

object
variable
bug
method
message
lexical error
syntax error
execution error
intent error
class
this

2.13 Problem Set

The purpose of this problem set is to test your knowledge of the form and content of simple robot programs. The programs you are required to write are long but not complicated. Concentrate on writing grammatically correct, pleasingly styled programs. Refer back to the program and discussion in Section 2.6 for rules and examples of correct grammar and punctuation. Each of these problems requires a single robot of the **UrRobot** class. In each case we assume it will be named karel. This is not required, however, and you are, in general, free to name your robots with other names. Verify that each program is correct by simulating karel's actions in the appropriate initial situation.

1. Start a robot in the initial situation illustrated in Figure 2-6 and simulate the execution of the following program. Karel's task is to find the beeper, pick it up, and then turn itself off. Draw a map of the final situation, stating whether an error occurs. If an execution or intent error does occur, explain how you would correct the program. This program has no lexical or syntactic errors.

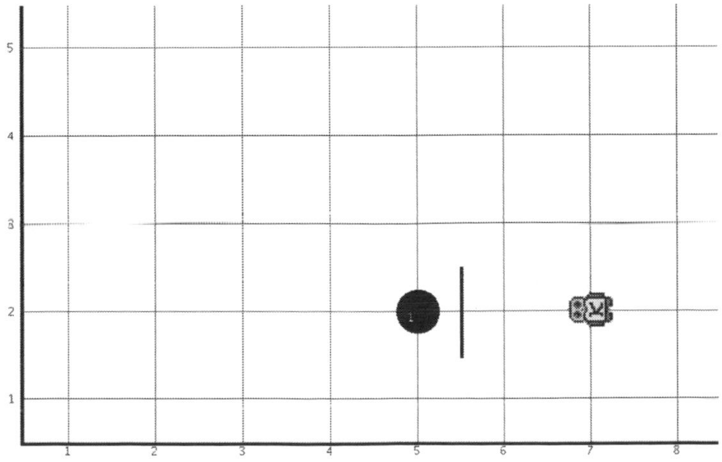

Figure 2-6: Initial Situation for Problem 1

```
public static void main(String [] args)
{   UrRobot karel = new UrRobot(2, 7, West, 0);
    karel.move();
    karel.turnLeft();
    karel.turnLeft();
    karel.move();
    karel.turnLeft();
    karel.move();
    karel.turnLeft();
    karel.move();
    karel.pickBeeper();
    karel.turnOff();
 }
```

2. Carefully inspect the following program and correct all lexical and syntactic errors. Hint: There are nine errors. Three errors involve semicolons, two are syntactical, and two are lexical. (Yes, there are other errors too.) Confirm that each word is in an appropriate place and that it is a correctly spelled instruction name or reserved word. You may use the program in Problem 1 as a model for a lexically and syntactically correct program.

```
public static vpid main(String [] args)
{   UrRobot karel = new UrRobot(2,7, East, 0);
    karel.move();
    karel.move()
    karel.pickBeeper();
    karel.move;();
    karel.turnLeft();
    move();
    karel.move();
    karel.turnright;
    karel.putBeeper();
    karel.putBeeper();
    karel.turnOff
}
```

3. What is the smallest lexically and syntactically correct robot program?

4. In most cities and towns we can walk around the block by repeating the following actions four times: walk to the nearest intersection, turn either right or left (the same one each time)
If done correctly we will return to our original starting place. Program karel to walk around the block. Will your program succeed for the initial situation in Figure 2-7?

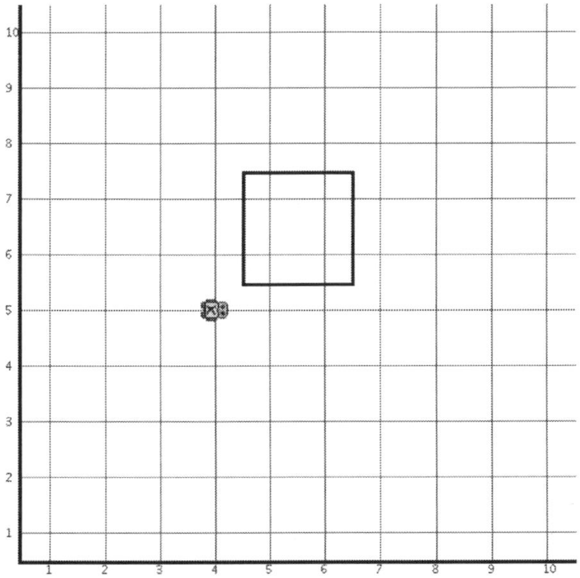

Figure 2-7 Initial Situation for the Walk Around the Block Task

5. Every morning karel is awakened in bed when the newspaper, represented by a beeper, is thrown on the front porch of the house. Program karel to retrieve the paper and bring it back to bed. The initial situation is given in Figure 2-8, and the final situation must have karel back in bed (same corner, same direction) with the newspaper.

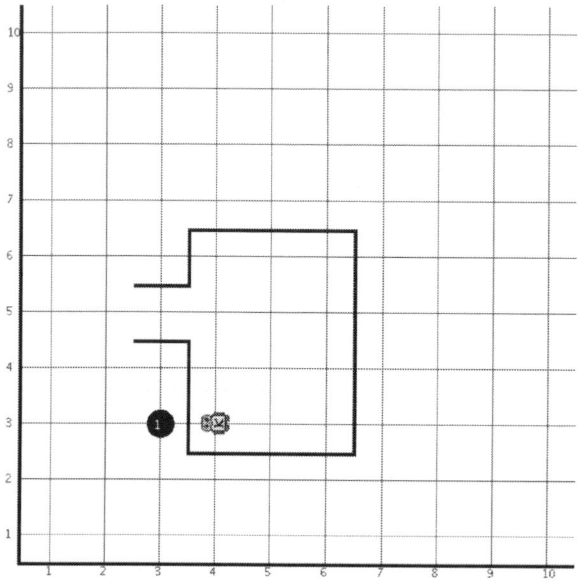

Figure 2-8: Initial Situation for the Newspaper Retrieval Task

6. The wall sections in Figure 2-9 represent a mountain (north is up). Program karel to climb the mountain and then plant a flag, represented by a beeper, on the summit; karel then must descend the other side of the mountain. Assume that karel starts with the flag-beeper in the beeper-bag. Remember that karel is not a super-robot who can leap to the top of the mountain, plant the flag, and then jump down in a single bound. As illustrated, karel must closely follow the mountain's face on the way up and down.

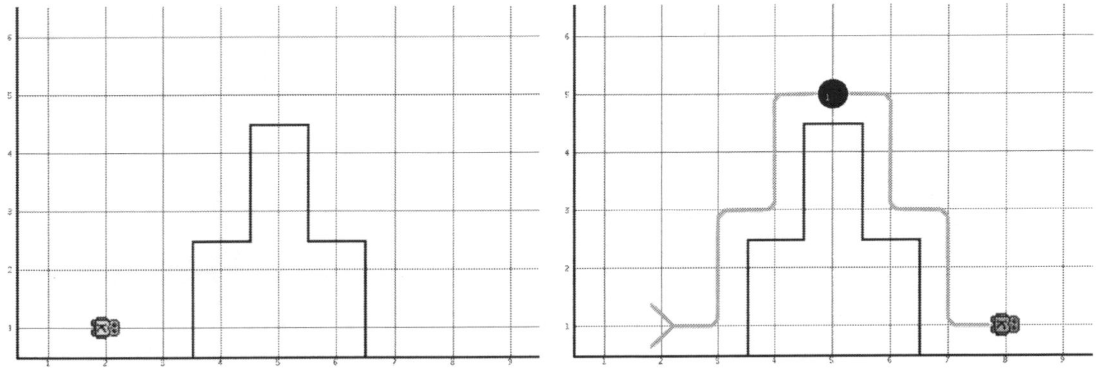

Figure 2-9: The Mountain Climbing Task

7. On the way home from the supermarket, karel's shopping bag ripped slightly at the bottom, leaking a few expensive items. These groceries are represented by -you guessed it- beepers. The initial situation, when karel discovered the leak, is represented in Figure 2-10. Program karel to pick up all the dropped items and then return to the starting position.

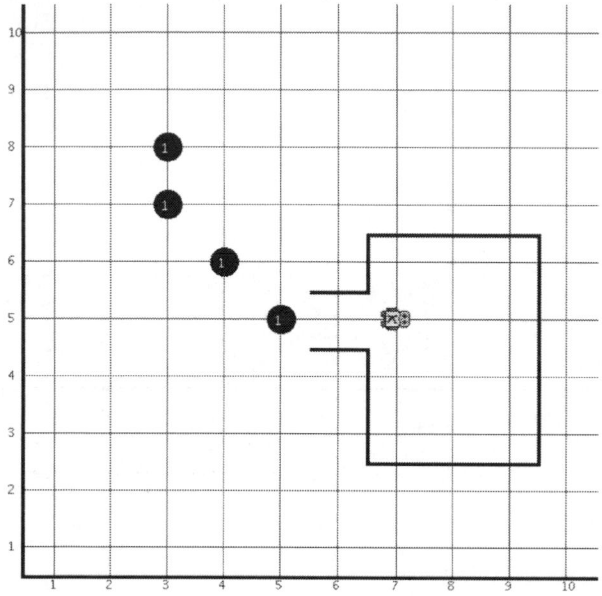

Figure 2-10 Initial Situation for the Grocery Pickup Task

8. Write a program that instructs karel to rearrange the beeper pattern as shown in Figure 2-11.

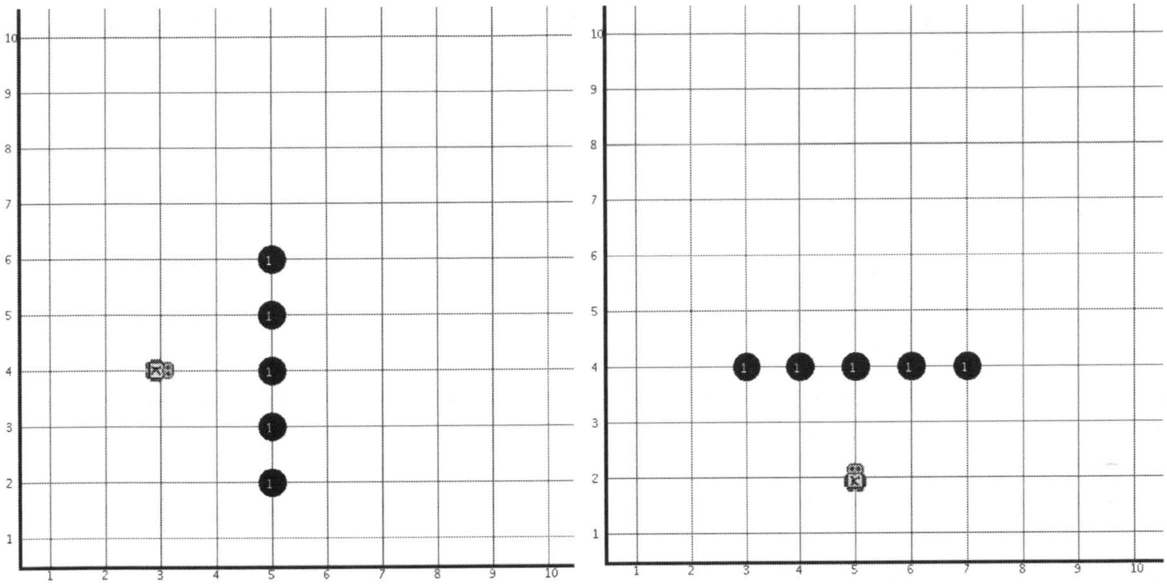

Figure 2-11 The Rearrange the Beepers Task

9. Karel is practicing for the Robot Olympics. One of karel's events is the shuttle race. The shuttle race requires karel to move around two beepers in a figure 8 pattern. Write a program that instructs karel to walk a figure 8 pattern as fast as possible (fast implies as few instructions as possible). Karel must stop in the same place it starts and must be facing the same direction.

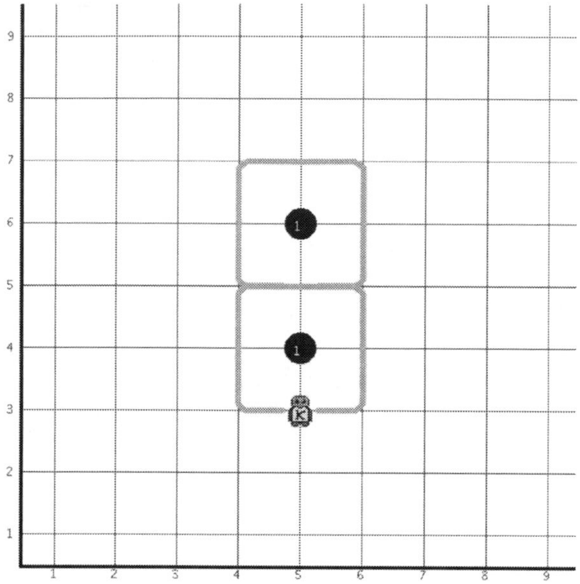

Figure 2-12 The Shuttle Race and karel's Figure 8 Path

10. Suppose we want a robot named karel to move from the origin to the intersection of 100'th street and 100'th avenue. How many different programs can we write to do this? What is the minimum number of instructions the robot will need to execute in order to carry this out? What is the minimum number of instructions you need to write (using just the knowledge gained from this chapter) in order to do it?

11. A robot named karel is at the origin facing North with one beeper in its beeper bag. Three blocks east of it is another robot named carl, facing East with no beepers. There are no wall sections or beepers in the world. Have karel walk to carl and give carl the beeper. Carl should then carry the beeper two blocks north and put it down. Both robots should then return to their original locations, facing the original directions.

12. How long would it take for a robot to put down an infinity of beepers?

13. If a robot named karel is on a corner with an infinite number of beepers and it picks one up, how many are left on the corner? How many are in the beeper-bag?

3 Extending the Robot Programming Language

This chapter explains the mechanics of specifying new classes of robots and adding new instructions to the robot vocabulary. It also discusses methods for planning, implementing, and testing our programs. The ability to extend the robot vocabulary combined with these techniques can simplify our work in writing robot programs.

3.1 Creating a More Natural Programming Language

In Chapter Two, we saw a robot perform a complex task. We also saw that it takes many messages to perform such a task. Writing so many messages is verbose and error prone.

Let's look at a particularly clumsy aspect of robot programming. Suppose that we need to program a robot to travel over vast distances. For example, assume that, starting at 3rd Avenue and 2nd Street, the robot must move east along 2nd Street for ten miles (a mile is eight blocks long), pick up a beeper, and then move another five miles north. Because a robot understands about moving *blocks* but not *miles,* we must translate our solution into instructions that move the robot one block at a time. This restriction forces us to write a program that contains 120 move messages. Although the conversion from miles to blocks is straightforward, it results in a very long and cumbersome program.

The crux of the problem is that we think in one language, but must program robots in another. Rather than make programmers the slaves of the machine, continually forced to translate their powerful ideas into the robot's primitive methods, Karel-Werke turned the tables and endowed robots with a simple mechanism to *learn* the definitions of new methods.

The robot programming language permits the robot programmer to specify new classes of robots. These class descriptions provide specifications of new robot instructions. Karel-Werke will then use the class descriptions to create robots able to interpret the new messages.

A robot's learning ability is quite limited. Karel-Werke builds each robot with a *dictionary* of useful method names and their definitions, but each definition must be built from simpler instructions that robots already understand. By providing robots with a dictionary of instructions that perform complex actions, we can build a robot vocabulary that corresponds more closely to our own. Given this mechanism, we can solve our programming problems using whatever instructions are natural to our way of thinking, and then we can provide robots with the definitions of these instructions.

We can define a **moveMile** instruction as eight **move** messages. Then, when a robot is told to moveMile in a program, it looks up the method definition associated with this message name and executes it. Now our unwieldy beeper-moving program can be written with a **moveMile** definition, containing eight **move** messages, and another 15 **moveMile** messages. This program, containing these 23 messages, would be quite an improvement over the original program, which needed more than 120 messages to accomplish the task.

Although both programs move the robot exactly the same distance, the smaller program is much easier to read and understand. In complicated problems, the ability to extend a robot's vocabulary makes the difference between understandable programs and unintelligible ones. We will explore in detail this extremely important definition mechanism in the next two sections.

3.2 A Mechanism that Defines New Classes of Robots

Back in Chapter 2 we saw the declaration of the primitive **UrRobot** class. Users of the robot language can also declare new classes of robots and the factory will be able to deliver them, just as it does the standard robots. To specify a new class of robots, we include a class specification in the declaration section at the beginning of our robot program. Isolated from a program, the general form of the specification is shown in the following template.

```
public class <new-class-name> extends <old-class-name>
{
  <list-of-new-methods>
}[3]
```

The class specification uses the reserved words **class** and **extends**, and the special symbols like braces to separate the various parts of the declaration. This general form includes elements delimited by angle brackets, < and >, which must be replaced with appropriate substitutions when we include a class specification in a robot program. Angle brackets are not part of the robot programming language, just a way we can set off locations in a program structure where actual language elements may appear. In this case, <new-class-name> must be replaced by a new name, not yet used in the program. This name can be built from upper and lower case letters, digits, and the underscore character, but must not match any other name in the program, nor the spelling of any reserved word. Names must also begin with a letter. The replacement for <old-class-name> is the name of an existing robot class, either UrRobot or one previously declared in the same program. New messages that apply to this class of robot will replace <list-of-new-methods>, and we will soon see how to define these new methods.

Suppose that we would like to solve the mile mover problem discussed in the introduction to this chapter. Suppose also that, in addition to the new capabilities, we want the robots of the new class to have all of the functionality of the standard UrRobot class. We can do so with a new class specification as follows.

```
import kareltherobot.*;
public class MileWalker extends UrRobot
{
        public void moveMile()
        {       ...     // instructions omitted for now
        }
}
```

The name of the new class of robots is **MileWalker**, which also names its main new capability. We also indicate, by giving the name of the **UrRobot** class following the word *extends*, that mile walkers are to have all of the capabilities of members of the **UrRobot** class. As a shorthand we say that **UrRobot** is the parent class of **MileWalker** or that **MileWalker** is a *subclass* of **UrRobot**. We also say that robots of the new class

[3] There are a few other things we can include in a robot class declaration. These will be introduced in future chapters.

inherit all the capabilities of the parent class. Therefore, mile walkers know how to move and turnLeft, just like members of the **UrRobot** class. They can also pick and put beepers and turn themselves off. In keeping with the Java convention, the name of the class begins with a capital letter, and since it is a catenation of words, each internal word also begins with a capital letter: MileWalker.

Here we have a list of only a single new method. Each method in the list is written with its definition in braces, and the detail of these will be shown just below. This specification says that when a robot in this class is first turned on it will be able to execute **moveMile** methods as well as all methods *inherited* from the **UrRobot** class.

We will see later that the names of instructions can be either new names or the names of methods already existing in the parent class. In this latter case we can give new meaning to methods as we shall see in section 3.7. Again, keeping with the Java convention, method names begin with a lower-case letter, but internal words begin with an upper-case letter: moveMile. You would do well to follow these conventions in your own programming as they make communication easier.

The methods of a class define what capabilities an object in that class has. They also define what messages you can send to such an object. Don't confuse the two, however. The message is how you "talk" to an object. The method is what it does when it gets a message. Different objects can have different methods associated with a given message as we shall see.

The class declaration introduces the names of new robot methods, but we have not yet explained how they are to be carried out. In the next section we will see how to define the new capabilities.

3.3 Defining the New Methods

As we declare a new robot class we need to define all of the new instructions introduced in it. These definitions are part of the class declaration in the declaration part of the robot program. The form of an instruction definition is as follows.

```
public void <method_name> ()
{
  <list_of_instructions>
}
```

As we see, we begin with the reserved words **public** and **void**. We have to give the name of the method we are defining, of course. Between the brace delimiters, we give a list of instructions, similar to a main task block, that tells a robot of this class how to carry out the new method. This list of instructions delimited by braces is called a *block* in the robot programming vocabulary. Again, every instruction in the list is terminated by a semicolon. For example, our **moveMile** method in the **MileWalker** class would be written within that class as shown below. Most of the instructions in the list of instructions will be messages.

```
import kareltherobot.*;
public class MileWalker extends UrRobot
{
        public void moveMile()
        {
```

```
                move();
                move();
                move();
                move();
                move();
                move();
                move();
                move();
        }

        // Required constructor omitted. See Section 4 of the Appendix.
        . . .
}
```

Actually, you also need a constructor in MileWalker. See Section 4 of the Appendix.

This block is like a main task block, but it is also different, since the messages in it are not prefaced here with the name of any robot. The reason for the difference is that in the main task block, we need to tell some particular robot to carry out an instruction, so we say something like **karel.move( )** to get a robot named **karel** to move. Here, however, a robot of the **MileWalker** class will eventually carry out this instruction when it is sent a **moveMile** message. The robot will carry out this instruction list itself. Since it is moving itself and not another robot, we don't need to give a robot's name here. If we really wanted to, we could use the name **this,** as in **this.move().**

The language could have been designed so that robots were *required* to refer to themselves with a special reserved word like **this**, in which case the move instructions in the above could be replaced by **this.move()**, but this is not required. It makes the language more concise. "this" means "this robot."

If we have a **MileWalker** named **lisa**, we can get it to walk a mile with either

```
lisa.moveMile();
```

or

```
lisa.move();
lisa.move();
lisa.move();
lisa.move();
lisa.move();
lisa.move();
lisa.move();
lisa.move();
```

In the former case, **lisa** will **move** itself eight times upon receiving the single **moveMile** message.

The complete robot program for the above is

```
import kareltherobot.*;

public class MileWalker extends UrRobot
{
	public MileWalker (int street, int avenue, Direction direction,
	   int beepers)
	{	super(street, avenue, direction, beepers);
	}

	public void moveMile()
	{
		move();
		move();
		move();
		move();
		move();
		move();
		move();
		move();
	}

	public static void main(String [] args)
	{	MileWalker lisa = new MileWalker (3, 2, East, 0);
				// Declare a new MileWalker lisa.

		lisa.moveMile();
		lisa.moveMile();
		lisa.moveMile();
		lisa.moveMile();
		lisa.moveMile();
		lisa.moveMile();
		lisa.moveMile();
		lisa.moveMile();
		lisa.moveMile();
		lisa.moveMile();
		lisa.pickBeeper();
		lisa.turnLeft();
		lisa.moveMile();
		lisa.moveMile();
		lisa.moveMile();
		lisa.moveMile();
		lisa.moveMile();
		lisa.turnOff();
	}
}
```

Here the static main method is within this same class. Actually it can be in any class in your program.

We can now give a better definition of the word program. A program both is a description of the objects that will be used (the classes) and a description of what we want those objects to actually do. Prior to the example above, the programs have been a bit incomplete since much is hidden in the definition of UrRobot, for example. Here, however, we see both the description of a new class of robots (objects) and the task we want them to perform.

Notice that having a moveFiveMiles instruction here would be useful. Contemplate writing the program without defining any new instructions. It requires 122 messages to be sent to the robot. This is not hard to write with a good text editor, but once it is written, it is tedious to verify that it has exactly the right number of move commands.

The usual form of a constructor is shown in the MileWalker class above. The constructor has the same name as the class, and for robot classes normally has four "parameters": the street and avenue, the direction faced initially, and the initial number of beepers. This is the Java definition that is required so that our "delivery specification" makes sense in the main task block.

```
public MileWalker(int street, int avenue, Direction direction,
    int beepers)
{       super(street, avenue, direction, beepers);
}
```

Within each pair of parameters the first word gives the kind of thing that will be used; here int or Direction. In Java, int means an integer value. Direction is actually another class, defining a different kind of object: a Direction object with possible values North, South, East, and West.
You need a constructor like the above in every robot class you write.

3.4 The Meaning and Correctness Of New Methods

A robot is a machine, a device completely devoid of intelligence. This is something that robot programmers must never forget. The robot does not "understand" what we "mean" when we write a program. It does exactly what we "say"-there is no room for interpretation. A robot class declaration is a description to the robot factory that tells it how to construct robots of this class. At the robot factory the entire declaration part of any robot program is read and examined for errors. As part of the manufacturing and delivery process the robots arc given the definitions of each of the new methods of their class. Each robot stores the definitions of the methods in its own dictionary of methods. Thus, when we tell a robot of the MileWalker class to moveMile, it receives the message, consults its dictionary to see how it must respond, and then carries out the required actions. The helicopter pilot does not have to read this part of the program when setting up robots for delivery since the robot already knows how to moveMile.

In a robot's world, just because we define a new method named moveMile, it doesn't necessarily mean that the instruction really moves the robot one mile. For example, there is nothing that prevents using the following method definition

```
public void moveMile()
{       move();
        move();
        move();
        move();
        move();
        move();
}
```

According to robot programming rules of grammar, this is a perfectly legal definition for it contains neither lexical nor syntax errors. However, by defining moveMile this way, we tell a robot that executing a moveMile instruction is equivalent to executing six move instructions. The robot does not understand what a moveMile method is supposed to accomplish; its only conception of a moveMile instruction is the definition we provide. Consequently, any new method we define may contain an intent error, as this example shows.

Besides intent errors, a new method can cause execution errors if it is defined by using primitive instructions that can cause error shutoffs. Can this incorrect definition of moveMile ever cause an error shutoff? The answer is yes, because we might encounter a wall before we completed six moves. However, it is possible to write a set of instructions for a robot to execute in which it would seem that nothing is wrong with this version of moveMile. Thus we might gain false confidence in this incorrect method and be very surprised when it fails us later. This example is somewhat trivial because the error is obvious. With a more complex defined method, we must take care to write a definition that really accomplishes what its name implies. The name specifies what the method is intended to do, and the definition specifies how the method does what the name implies. The two must match exactly, if we are to understand what our programs mean. If not, one or both must be changed.

When simulating a robot's execution of a defined method, we must adhere to the rules that the robot uses to execute these instructions. Robots execute a defined method by performing the actions associated with its definition. Do not try to shortcut this process by doing what the method *name* means because the robot does not know what a defined method means; the robot knows only how it is defined. We must recognize the significance of this distinction and learn to interpret robot programs as literally as the robot does. The meaning of names is supposed to help a human reader understand a program. If the actual instructions defining the meaning of a name are at variance with the meaning of the name, it is easy to be misled.

3.5 Defining New Methods in a Program

In this section we display a complete robot program that uses the method definition mechanism. We will first trace the execution of the program (recall that tracing is just simulating the execution of the methods in the order that a robot does). We will then discuss the general form of programs that use the new method definition mechanism. The task is shown below in Figure 3-1: it must pick up each beeper in the world while climbing the stairs. Following these figures is a program that correctly instructs a robot to accomplish the task.

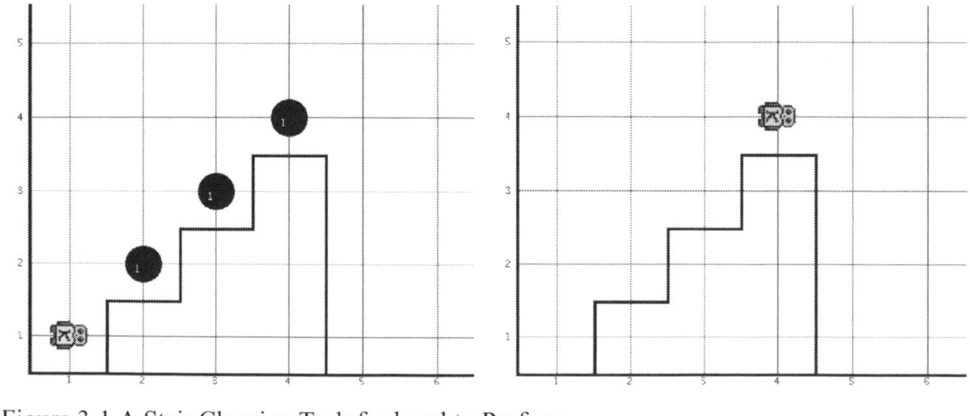

Figure 3-1 A Stair Cleaning Task for karel to Perform

```
import kareltherobot.*;

public class StairSweeper extends UrRobot
{
        public StairSweeper(int street, int avenue, Direction direction,
           int beepers)
        {       super(street, avenue, direction, beepers);
        }

        public void turnRight()
        {
                turnLeft();
                turnLeft();
                turnLeft();
        }

        public void climbStair()
        {
                turnLeft();
                move();
                turnRight();
                move();
        }

        public static void main(String [] args)
        {       StairSweeper alex = new StairSweeper(1, 1, East, 0);

                alex.climbStair();
                alex.pickBeeper();
                alex.climbStair();
                alex.pickBeeper();
                alex.climbStair();
                alex.pickBeeper();
                alex.turnOff();
        }
}
```

Next, we provide an annotated version of the same program that numbers each instruction and message in the order in which it is executed, starting with the delivery specification instruction #0.

```
public class StairSweeper extends UrRobot
{       ...
        public void turnRight()
        {// to here from       #4,     #13 or  #22
                turnLeft();    #5 or   #14 or  #23
                turnLeft();    #6 or   #15 or  #24
                turnLeft();    #7 or   #16 or  #25
        }//   return to        #4      #13     #22
```

```
        public void climbStair()
        {// to here from        #1,       #10, or #19
                turnLeft();     #2        #11      #20
                move();         #3        #12      #21
                turnRight();    #4        #13      #22
                move();         #8        #17      #26
        }//     return to       #1        #10      #19


        public static void main(String [] args)
        {       StairSweeper alex = new StairSweeper(1, 1, East, 0);   #0

                alex.climbStair();                                     #1
                alex.pickBeeper();                                     #9
                alex.climbStair();                                     #10
                alex.pickBeeper();                                     #18
                alex.climbStair();                                     #19
                alex.pickBeeper();                                     #27
                alex.turnOff();                                        #28
        }
}
```

To verify that this program is correct, we trace the execution of it, carefully simulating the execution of the instructions. Only one instruction can be executed at a time in the robot world. When a program is executing, we call the current instruction the "focus of execution. When the helicopter pilot starts to execute a program, the focus is initially on the first instruction within the main task block.

In this sample program the initial focus is the climbStair message, which is annotated as #1. The climbStair message is sent through the satellite to the robot alex. When alex receives this message, the focus of execution passes from the pilot to alex. The pilot, who must wait until the instruction has been completed, is very careful to remember where he or she was in the program when the climbStair message was sent. Alex, upon receiving this message, consults its list of dictionary entries and goes to the definition of climbStair. In the sample program the new execution point is annotated as "to here from #1".

Alex focuses on the list of instructions defining the new method, climbStair, and encounters a turnLeft message (marked as #2). Alex trains the focus of execution on the turnLeft message, executes it, and then focuses on #3, move. Alex executes this move and focuses on #4, turnRight. Since this is not a primitive instruction, alex must retrieve its definition from its dictionary. It then focuses on the instruction list from the definition of turnRight and executes the three turnLeft instructions, # 5, #6, and #7. Having completed the execution of the turnRight method, alex now returns its focus to the place in which the turnRight message occurred within climbStair. Alex shifts focus to #8 and executes the move. After alex performs this move it is finished executing the method climbStair so it yields execution back to the pilot since it has completely carried out the task required by the message climbStair. The focus of execution returns to the place in the program marked #1, and the pilot sends alex the pickBeeper message that is marked #9. With this message, the focus of execution is again passed from pilot to robot. Alex also interprets and carries out this pickBeeper instruction and yields focus back to the pilot at #10. The pilot then sends alex another climbStair message. Alex repeats this same sequence of steps a second time for this climb-stair message marked #10 and the pickBeeper that follows. It is then repeated yet again for the third climbStair and pickBeeper messages. Alex is finally instructed to execute the turnOff instruction, after which the program's execution is complete.

Notice that a method definition can become alex's focus from any place in the program that sends alex that message. The pilot and the robot must always remember the place in the program where they were when the focus changes. This allows the execution to return to its correct place and continue executing the program. It is important for us to understand that no complex rules are needed to execute a program containing new methods. Tracing the execution of this program was a bit tedious because each step is small and simple, but alex is not equipped to understand anything more complicated. Alex can follow a very simple set of rules that tell it how to execute a program. Yet we can use these simple rules, coupled with every robot's willingness to follow them, to command the robot to perform complicated tasks.

We should now understand how the helicopter pilot and the robots work together to execute a program that includes the method definition mechanism. We next turn our attention toward program form, and we make the following observations about the stair-cleaning program.

* The names defined within a robot class, including the names of the parent class and the parent of the parent, etc. (collectively called *ancestors*), are called the *dictionary* of the class.

* The declaration of UrRobot does not need to be included in your robot programs, since it is "factory standard." Any other class that you need to define must be completely written in the declaration part, along with the definitions of all of its methods. We will soon see a shorthand method that we can use to make the writing of this dictionary much easier.

* Each instruction in a block is terminated by a semicolon. The definition of a new method is not. Neither is the main task block.

* The class definitions of your robot classes are normally placed in separate files where the name of the file is the same as the name of the class, with .java appended to the end. So the StairSweeper class would appear in a file named StairSweeper.java. The main method can be in this class or not. In fact, main can be in a class of its own that is not a robot class at all. We shall see this later. Section 3 of the Appendix says how you can compile and execute your robot programs.

The class dictionary entries are not permanent and the world does not remember any definitions from program to program. Each time we write a robot program, we must include a complete set of all dictionary entries required in that program. They can be spread over several files, however.

3.6 Modifying Inherited Methods

Earlier in this chapter we built the class **MileWalker** that gave robots the ability to walk a mile at a time. Notice that they retained their ability to walk a block at a time as well. Sometimes we want to build a class in which some previously defined instruction is redefined to have a new meaning. For example, suppose we had a problem in which a robot always needed to move by miles, but never by blocks. In this case it would be an advantage to create a class with a new definition of the **move** instruction so that when a robot in this class was told to **move**, it would move a mile. This is easily done.

```
import kareltherobot.*;

public class MileMover extends UrRobot
{       public void move()
        {       super.move();
                super.move();
                super.move();
                super.move();
                super.move();
                super.move();
                super.move();
                super.move();
        }

        public MileMover(int street, int avenue, Direction direction,
           int beepers)
        {       super(street, avenue, direction, beepers);
        }

        . . .

}
```

We say that the new definition of **move** in this class overrides the original definition inherited from the class UrRobot. We now have a problem, since to move a mile we need to be able to move eight blocks, but we are defining **move** to mean move a mile here. Therefore, we can't just say **move** eight times because that is **this** instruction. (See Problem 19.) Instead, we need to indicate that we want to use the original, or overridden, instruction, **move**, from class UrRobot. We can do this since UrRobot is the parent class. We just need to preface the move message with the keyword super and a period. It gives us a way to specify a particular method from the parent class.

Note that in Java, if we override a public method we must do so with a public method. All of the methods defined in UrRobot are public, so if, as above, we want to override move, we must mark it as public. In fact you should generally mark your methods as public unless there is a reason not to. See Section 3.8.2 for more on the visibility of methods.

Now if we complete the above program with

```
public static void main(String [] args)
{       MileMover karel = new MileMover(5, 2, North, 0);
        karel.move();
        karel.pickBeeper();
        karel.move();
        karel.putBeeper();
        karel.turnOff();
}
```

Karel will find the beeper at (13, 2) and will leave it at (21, 2).

Notice now that if we had several different robots in the same program and we sent each of them the same messages, they might each respond differently to those messages. In particular, a **MileWalker** only moves a block when told to **move**, while a **MileMover**, moves a mile.

3.7 An Ungrammatical Program

Before reading this section, quickly look at the small program in the example below, and see if you can find a syntax error.

```
import kareltherobot.*;

public class BigStepper extends UrRobot
{
	public void longMove()
		move();
		move();
		move();
	}

	public static void main(String [] args)
	{	BigStepper tony(5, 2, North, 0);
		tony.longMove();
		tony.turnLeft();
		tony.turnOff();
	}
}
```

This example illustrates the common programming mistake of omitting necessary braces around a block. The program is nicely indented, but the indentation is misleading. The definition of longMove appears to define the instruction correctly, but we have omitted the opening brace of the pair that should enclose the three move instructions. Did you spot the mistake? And did you find the other error in this example? Finding the syntax error is not easy, because the indentation makes it look correct to us.

The factory reads the declaration part of a program and the main task block of the program to check for lexical and syntax errors. A reader (human or otherwise) discovers syntax errors by checking "meaningful" components of the program and checking for proper grammar and punctuation. Examples of meaningful components are class declarations, method definitions, and the main task block. In effect we verify the meaningful components separately. Let us illustrate how the factory finds the mistake in the program above using this examination. Remember that the factory only reads the program's words and is not influenced by our indentation.

The factory examines the new robot class declaration. It has a name, a parent class, and a list of features. The punctuation all checks out as well. Then it sees the class name and method name in the instruction definition. It then looks for a block to include with the definition, but doesn't find the opening brace. Instead it finds a name. So the factory tells us that a syntax error has occurred. In summary, forgetting to use necessary braces around a block can lead to syntax errors.

We are rapidly becoming experts at analyzing programs. Given a robot program, we should now be able to detect grammar and punctuation errors quickly. We should also be able to simulate programs efficiently.

Nevertheless, the other side of the programming coin, constructing programs, may still seem a little bit magical. The next few sections take a first step toward demystifying this process.

3.8 Tools for Designing and Writing Robot Programs

Designing solutions for problems and writing robot programs involve problem solving. One model[4] describes problem solving as a process that has four activities: definition of the problem, planning the solution, implementing the plan, and analyzing the solution.

The initial definition of the problem is presented when we are provided figures of the initial and final situations. Once we examine these situations and understand what task a robot must perform, we begin to plan, implement and analyze a solution. This section examines techniques for planning, implementing and analyzing robot programs. By combining these techniques with the new class and instruction mechanism, we can develop solutions that are easy to read and understand.

As we develop and write programs that solve robot problems, these three guidelines must be followed:

* our programs must be easy to read and understand,

* our programs must be easy to debug, and

* our programs must be easy to modify to solve variations of the original task.

3.8.1 Stepwise Refinement-a Technique for Planning, Implementing, and Analyzing Robot Programs

In this section, we will discuss stepwise refinement, a method we can use to construct robot programs. This method addresses the problem of how we can naturally write concise programs that are correct, simple to read, and easy to understand.

It may appear natural to define all the new classes and methods that we will need for a task first, and then write the program using these instructions. But how can we know what robots and which new instructions are needed before we write the program? Stepwise refinement tells us first to write the program using any robots and instruction names we desire, and then define these robots and their instructions. That is, we write the sequence of messages in the main task block first, and then we write the definitions of the new instruction names used within this block. Finally, we assemble these separate pieces into a complete program.

We will explore this process more concretely by writing a program for the task shown in Figure 3-2. These situations represent a harvesting task that requires a robot to pick up a rectangular field of beepers.

---

[4] G. Polya, How to Solve It, Princeton University Press, 1945, 1973.

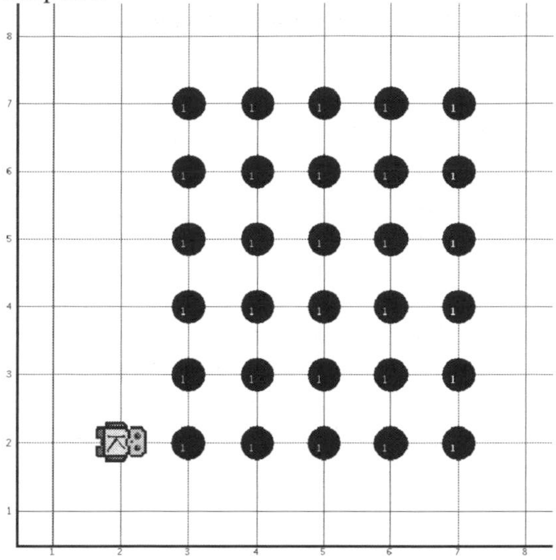

Initial Situation

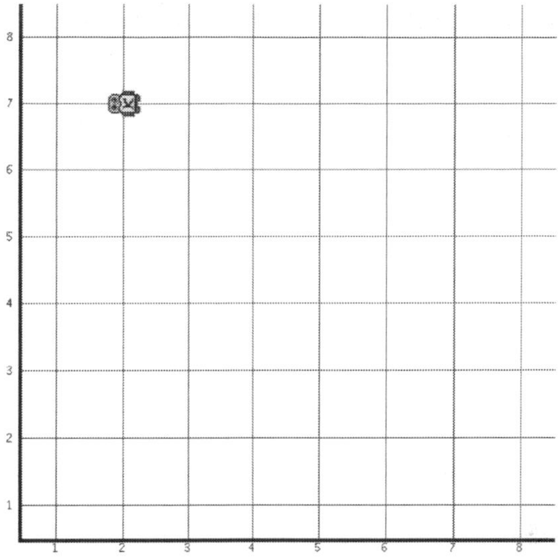

Final Situation

Figure 3-2 The Harvest Task

Our first step is to develop an overall plan to guide us in writing a robot program that allows karel to perform the task. Planning is probably best done as a group activity. Sharing ideas in a group allows members to present different plans that can be thoughtfully examined for strengths and weaknesses. Even if we are working alone, we can think in a question and answer pattern such as the following.

Question: How many robots do we need to perfrom this task?

Answer: We could do it with one robot that walks back and forth over all of the rows to be harvested, or we could do it with a team of robots.

Question: How many shall we use?

Answer: Let's try it with just one robot named mark, for now.

Question: How can mark pick a row?

Answer: Mark could move west to east across the southern most unpicked row of beepers, picking each beeper as it moves.

Question: How can mark pick the entire field?

Answer: Mark could turn around and move back to the western side of the field, move north one block, face east, and repeat the actions listed above. Mark could do this for each row of beepers in the field. Since mark is not standing on a beeper we will move it to the first beeper before starting to harvest the first row.

If this idea seems like it might work, our next step is to write out the main task block of the program using English-like new message names. We briefly move from planning to implementing our plan. Even though this is done on paper, we should still concentrate on correct syntax and proper indenting to reduce errors when we copy our program into the computer. Suppose we call the class of the new robot by the name **Harvester**.

```
public static void main(String [] args)
{       Harvester mark = new Harvester(2, 2, East, 0);
        mark.move();
        mark.harvestOneRow();
        mark.returnToStart();
        mark.moveNorthOneBlock();
        mark.harvestOneRow();
        mark.returnToStart();
        mark.moveNorthOneBlock();
        mark.harvestOneRow();
        mark.returnToStart;
        mark.moveNorthOneBlock();
        mark.harvestOneRow();
        mark.returnToStart();
        mark.moveNorthOneBlock();
        mark.harvestOneRow();
        mark.returnToStart();
        mark.moveNorthOneBlock();
        mark.harvestOneRow();
        mark.returnToStart();
        mark.turnOff();
}
```

Notice that what we have really done here is to design a new class of robot that can perform three new messages. We can think of a robot class as a mechanism for creating service providers; the robots. These robots, an example of objects in object-oriented programming, provide specific services when sent messages requesting the service. Here we seem to require three different services, harvestOneRow, returnToStart, and moveNorthOneBlock, beyond the basic services that all UrRobots can provide.

Before we continue with this plan and begin to work on the new instructions, harvestOneRow, returnToStart and moveNorthOneBlock, we should analyze our original plan looking at its strengths and weaknesses. We are asking if we are requesting the <u>right</u> services. Our analysis might proceed as follows.

Question: What are the strengths of this plan?

Answer: The plan takes advantage of the new instruction mechanism and it allows mark to harvest the beepers.

Question: What are the weaknesses of the plan?

Answer: Mark makes some "empty" trips.

Question: What are these empty trips?

Answer: Mark returns to the starting point on the row that was just harvested.

Question: Why are these bad?

ANSWER: Because robots (and computers) are valuable resources that should generally be used efficiently. Some tasks must be done "on time" if solving them is to confer any benefit. Moreover, programmer time is very valuable.

Question: Can mark pick more beepers on the way back?

Answer: Instead of harvesting only one row and then turning around and returning to the start, mark can harvest one row, move north one street and come back to the west harvesting a second row. Mark can then move one street north to begin the entire process over for the next two rows. If mark repeats these steps two more times the entire field of beepers will be harvested.

Again we analyze this new plan for its strengths and weaknesses.

Question: What advantage does this offer over the first plan?

Answer: Mark makes only six trips across the field instead of twelve. There are no empty trips.

Question: What are the weaknesses of this new plan?

Answer: None that we can see as long as there are an even number of rows.

When we are planning solutions, we should be very critical and not just accept the first plan as the best. We now have two different plans and you can probably think of several more. Let's avoid the empty trips and implement the second plan.

```
public static void main(String [] args)
{       Harvester mark = new Harvester(2, 2, East, 0);
        mark.move();
        mark.harvestTwoRows();
        mark.positionForNextHarvest();
        mark.harvestTwoRows();
        mark.positionForNextHarvest();
        mark.harvestTwoRows();
        mark.move();
        mark.turnOff();
}
```

Let us commit to this plan. We must now begin to think about planning the new instructions harvestTwoRows and positionForNextHarvest.

3.8.2 The Second Step-Planning harvestTwoRows and positionForNextHarvest

Our plan contains two subtasks: one harvests two rows and the other positions mark to harvest two more rows. The planning of these two subtasks must be just as thorough as the planning was for the overall task. Let's begin with harvestTwoRows.

Question: What does harvestTwoRows do?

Answer: harvestTwoRows must harvest two rows of beepers. One will be harvested as mark travels east and the second will be harvested as mark returns to the west.

Question: What does mark have to do?

Answer: Mark must pick beepers and move as it travels east. At the end of the row of beepers, mark must move north one block, face west, and return to the western edge of the field picking beepers as it travels west.

Continuing to use English-like message names, we can now implement this part of the plan.

```
public class Harvester extends UrRobot
{
        public void  harvestTwoRows()
        {
                harvestOneRowMovingEast();
                goNorthToNextRow();
                harvestOneRowMovingWest();
        }
        ...
}
```

We analyze this plan as before looking for strengths and weaknesses.

Question: What are the strengths of this plan?

Answer: It seems to solve the problem.

Question: What are the weaknesses of this plan?

Answer: Possibly one-we have two different instructions that harvest a single row of beepers.

Question: Do we really need two different harvesting instructions?

Answer: We need one for going east and one for going west.

Question: Do we really need a separate instruction for each direction?

Answer: Harvesting is just a series of pickBeepers and moves. The direction mark is moving does not matter. If we plan goToNextRow carefully, we can use one instruction to harvest a row of beepers when mark is going east and the same instruction for going west.

Our analysis shows us that we can reuse a single dictionary entry (harvestOneRow) instead of defining two similar instructions, making our program smaller. Here is the new implementation.

```
public void harvestTwoRows()
{
        // Before executing this, the robot should be facing East,
        //      on the first beeper of the current row.
        harvestOneRow();
        goToNextRow();
        harvestOneRow();
}
```

The comment written in this method is called a *precondition*. In order to guarantee that the method does what it is supposed to do, any message naming this method must first guarantee that the precondition is true. Otherwise the method may not carry us toward our goal. It is very important to notice when preconditions are needed and to include them in your methods. Note that we could also deduce a *postcondition* here. When the precondition is true beforehand, the method will leave the robot facing West, but one block North of where it started. It is often useful to state these in your methods as well.

Let's now plan positionForNextHarvest.

Question: What does the positionForNextHarvest instruction do?

Answer: This instruction is used when mark is on the western side of the beeper field. It moves the robot north one block and faces mark east in position to harvest two more rows of beepers.

Question: What does mark have to do?

Answer: Mark must turn right to face north, move one block and turn right to face east. We implement this instruction as follows.

```
public class Harvester extends UrRobot
{
    ...
    public void positionForNextHarvest()
    {
            // Before executing this, the robot should be facing West,
            //   on the last corner of the current row.
            turnRight();
            move();
            turnRight();
    }
```

```
        public void turnRight()
        {
                turnLeft();
                turnLeft();
                turnLeft();
        }
        ...
}
```

We should analyze this instruction to see if it works properly. Since it seems to work correctly, we are ready to continue our planning and in the process define more new instructions.

3.8.3 The Third Step-Planning harvestOneRow and goToNextRow

We now focus our efforts on harvestOneRow and finally goToNextRow.

Question: What does harvestOneRow do?

Answer: Starting on the first beeper and facing the correct direction, mark must harvest each of the corners that it encounters, stopping on the location of the last beeper in the row.

Question: What does mark have to do?

Answer: Mark must execute a sequence of harvestCorner and move instructions to pick all five beepers in the row.

Question: How does mark harvest a single corner?

Answer: Mark must execute a pickBeeper instruction.

Question: Will this method appear in a message in the main task block?

Answer: Probably not. It is just a helper.

We can implement harvestOneRow and harvestCorner as follows.

```
public class Harvester extends UrRobot
{
        ...
        public void  harvestOneRow()
        {
                harvestCorner();
                move();
                harvestCorner();
                move();
                harvestCorner();
                move();
                harvestCorner();
                move();
                harvestCorner();
        }

        public void  harvestCorner()
        {
                pickBeeper();
        }
        ...
}
```

We again simulate the instruction and it seems to work. We now address the instruction, goToNextRow.

Question: What does goToNextRow do?

Answer: This instruction moves mark northward one block to the next row.

Question: Didn't we do that already? Why can't we use positionForNextHarvest?[5]

Answer: It will not work properly. When we use positionForNextHarvest, mark must be facing West. Mark is now facing East so positionForNextHarvest will not work.

Question: What does mark have to do?

Answer: Mark must turn left to face North, move one block, and turn left to face West.

The following is the implementation of this new instruction.

[5] At this point you should simulate the instruction positionForNextHarvest on paper. Start with mark facing west and see where the robot is when you finish simulating the instruction.

```
public class Harvester extends UrRobot
{
        ...
        public void  goToNextRow()
        {
                // Before executing this, the robot should be facing East,
                //   on the last corner of the current row.
                turnLeft();
                move();
                turnLeft();
        }
        ...
}
```

We can use simulation to analyze this instruction and show that it is correct and our program is done.

Notice that some of our methods have preconditions. This means that the user (whoever sends the message) must guarantee that the precondition is true. If not, the program will not behave correctly. However, the wise programmer can limit the possible damage here, by making such methods harder to use by the unwary programmer (including herself). Note that harvestOneRow and goToNextRow are not intended to be used in the main task block at all, but are really just here to help us decompose the solution sensibly. Java will let us make them private instead of public so that they can be used only within this class, rather than throughout the program. Java actually has several forms of "visibility," though we will use only public and private. Here goToNextRow might better be changed to be a private method. Then we only need to worry about the precondition while we write this class, since it can't be seen (or abused) elsewhere in a larger program. While less important, perhaps, other helper methods should also normally be made private. This makes the class simpler for others to use, since there are fewer options and the intent of the class is usually clearer.

3.8.4 The Final Step-Verifying That the Complete Program is Correct

Since we have spread this program out over several pages, we print it here so you will find it easier to read and study. We have changed the visibility of some of the methods to be conistent with the discussion at the end of Section 3.8.3.

```
import kareltherobot.*;

public class Harvester extends UrRobot
{
        public Harvester(int street, int avenue,
           Direction direction, int beepers)
        {       super(street, avenue, direction, beepers);
        }

        public void harvestTwoRows()
        {       // Before executing this, the robot should be facing East,
                //      on the first beeper of the current row.
                harvestOneRow();
                goToNextRow();
                harvestOneRow();
```

```
    }

    public void positionForNextHarvest()
    {       // Before executing this, the robot should be facing West,
            //   on the last corner of the current row.
            turnRight();
            move();
            turnRight();
    }

    private void turnRight()
    {       turnLeft();
            turnLeft();
            turnLeft();
    }

    private void  harvestOneRow()
    {       harvestCorner();
            move();
            harvestCorner();
            move();
            harvestCorner();
            move();
            harvestCorner();
            move();
            harvestCorner();
    }

    private void  harvestCorner()
    {       pickBeeper();
    }

    private void  goToNextRow()
    {       // Before executing this, the robot should be facing East,
            //   on the last corner of the current row.
            turnLeft();
            move();
            turnLeft();
    }

    public static void main(String [] args)
    {       Harvester mark = new Harvester(2, 2, East, 0);
            mark.move();
            mark.harvestTwoRows();
            mark.positionForNextHarvest();
            mark.harvestTwoRows();
            mark.positionForNextHarvest();
            mark.harvestTwoRows();
            mark.move();
            mark.turnOff();
    }
}
```

We are not done. We have used simulation to analyze the individual instructions in the program to see if they work correctly. We have not examined how they work in concert as one large robot program. We must now simulate mark's execution of the entire program to demonstrate that all the parts work correctly to be sure the program is correct. We may have relied on some invalid assumptions when writing the instructions that move mark between rows, or we may discover another error in our planning or implementing; maybe our analysis was wrong. A skeptical attitude toward the correctness of our programs will put us in the correct frame of mind for trying to verify them.

Stepwise refinement blends the problem solving activities of planning, implementing and analyzing into the programming process. It is a powerful programming technique and can shorten the time required to write correct robot programs.

3.9 Advantages of Using New Instructions

It is useful to divide a program into a small set of instructions, even if these instructions are executed only once. New instructions nicely structure programs, and English words and phrases make programs more understandable; they help convey the intent of the program. Read back through the programs we have just written and see if you can find any place where they are confusing or difficult to understand.

We could, of course, use a different plan to solve the above (or any) problem. It is useful to think in terms of services required. For example, in the harvester example above, it might be useful to think of harvestField as a service. Fulfillment of this service would result in harvesting of an entire field, as the name suggests. We could easily add this feature to the Harvester class. Its implementation could be all of the statements of the main task block above except the first and last. It would also be possible to create a new class, say FieldHarvester, that adds just this new instruction, and that is derived from the Harvester class above.

```
import kareltherobot.*;

public class FieldHarvester extends Harvester
{
	public FieldHarvester(int street, int avenue,
	   Direction direction, int beepers)
	{	super(street, avenue, direction, beepers);
	}

	public void harvestField()
	{	move();
		harvestTwoRows();
		positionForNextHarvest();
		harvestTwoRows();
		positionForNextHarvest();
		harvestTwoRows();
		move();
	}
```

```
        public static void main(String [] args)
        {       FieldHarvester jim = new FieldHarvester(2, 2, East, 0);
                jim.harvestField();
                jim.turnOff();
        }
}
```

To use this new class we can include its definition as well as the definition of the Harvester class in a single file. However, to do this, only one of the classes can be public and this one must contain the main task block.

Another way to do this efficiently is to take advantage of the fact that a Java (hence robot) program can be spread over several files. Suppose that we put the above definition in a file named "FieldHarvester.java" and put the definitions of the Harvester class in another different file "Harvester.java." Either or both or neither could contain a main task block. We could actually specify a task within a different file, say "Task.java" that contains only the following lines. Separating our robot definitions into separate files makes it easier to reuse them in other programs.

```
import kareltherobot.*;

public class Task implements Directions
{
        public static void main(String [] args)
        {       FieldHarvester tony = new FieldHarvester(2, 2, East, 0);
                tony.harvestField();
                tony.turnOff();
        }
}
```

The first line tell the factory to include everything in the kareltherobot package into this program, including all of your robot classes. You will need to either include all three files in the javac compile instruction or include all three in your project if you use an IDE (integrated development environment.) See the appendix for more on the mechanics of executing programs.

We discuss "implements Directions" in Section 4.2. It is required here since it is where East is actually defined.

3.9.1 Avoiding Errors

Many novices think that all of this planning, analyzing, tracing, and simulating of programs as shown in the previous sections takes too much time. What really takes time is correcting mistakes. These mistakes fall into two broad categories:

- Planning mistakes (execution and intent errors) happen when we write a program without a well-thought-out plan and can waste a lot of programming time. They are usually difficult to fix because large segments of the program may have to be modified or discarded. Careful planning and thorough analysis of the plan can help us avoid planning mistakes.

- Programming mistakes (lexical and syntax errors) happen when we actually write the program. They can be spelling, punctuation, or other similar errors. If we write the entire program without testing it, we will undoubtedly have many errors to correct, some of which may be multiple instances of the same mistake. Writing the program in slices will both reduce the overall number of errors introduced at any one time and may prevent multiple occurrences of the same mistake (e.g., we discover a misspelling of a new instruction name). Practice helps of course. It also helps NOT to abbreviate the names we give things but to spell them out completely. Typing is not what makes programming hard, but understanding. Using real and informative names helps a lot with this. Often when you abbreviate you forget just how you spelled something and spend more time looking up your spellings than the time you spend typing them out completely.

Stepwise refinement is a tool that allows us to plan, analyze and implement our plans in a way that should lead to a robot program containing a minimum of errors.

3.9.2 Future Modifications

Earlier in this chapter we said we must write programs that are easy to read and understand, easy to debug, and easy to modify. The robot's world can be readily changed and we must be able to modify existing programs to keep the robot out of trouble. It can be much simpler and takes less time to modify an existing program to perform a slightly different task than to write a completely new one. Below are two situations that differ somewhat from the Harvester task.

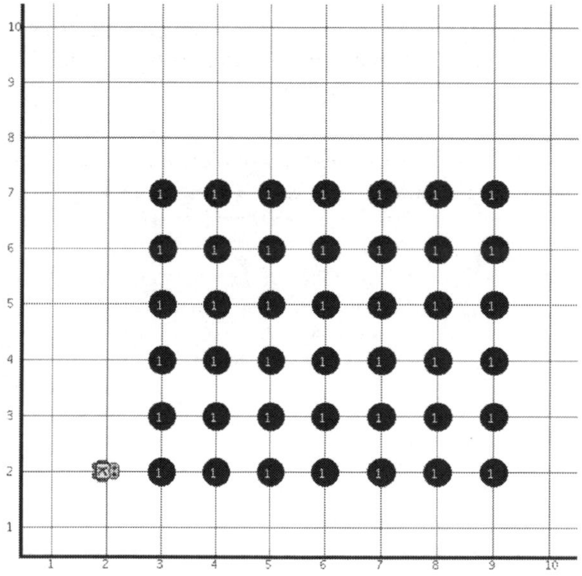

Figure 3.3 a. Longer rows

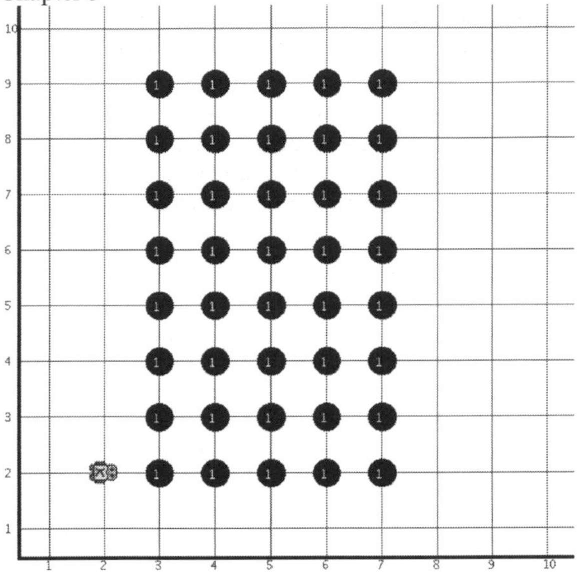

Figure 3.3 b. More rows

How difficult would it be to modify our Harvester class and the program containing it to accomplish the new beeper harvesting tasks? The second problem is easy to solve; we just add two new lines to the original main task block to solve the new task! We don't need any changes to the Harvester class itself.

What about the first problem? The change here is very different from the change in the first one since we have to pick up an additional beeper in each row. The use of new instructions allows us to quickly find where we need to make the change. There is only one instruction that actually picks up any beepers. We make a simple change to harvestOneRow as follows,

```
public void harvestOneRow()
{
        harvestCorner();
        move();
        harvestCorner();
        move();
        harvestCorner();
        move();
        harvestCorner();
        move();
        harvestCorner();
        move();                     // Add these two
        harvestCorner();            // new messages
}
```

This change to the Harvester class is fine provided that we will not need to solve the original problem in the future. It is truly advantageous here to leave the Harvester class unchanged and create a new class, Long_Harvester that contains this modified harvestOneRow instruction.

```
import kareltherobot.*;
public class Long_Harvester extends Harvester
{
        public void  harvestOneRow()
        {
                super.harvestOneRow();
                    // Execute the inherited instruction
                move();                     // Add these two
                harvestCorner();            // new messages
        }
}
```

The use of new instructions also simplifies finding and fixing intent errors. This is especially true if the instructions are short and can be easily understood. Suppose our robot makes a wrong turn and tries to pick up a beeper from the wrong place. Where is the error? If we use new instructions to write our program, and each new instruction performs one specific task (e.g., positionForNextHarvest) or controls a set of related tasks (e.g., harvestTwoRows), then we can usually determine the probable location of the error.

3.9.3 A Program Without New instructions

Below is a program that attempts to solve the original beeper planting problem with only primitive instructions. Examine the program and ask the same questions we have just explored.

- Where would we change the program to solve the first modified situation?

- Where would we change the program to solve the second modified situation?

- Suppose mark makes a wrong turn while planting the beepers. Where would we first look to correct the error?

As an example, find the single error that we included in this program.

```
public static void main(String [] args)
{       UrRobot mark = new UrRobot(2, 2, East, 0);
        mark.move();
        mark.pickBeeper();
        mark.move();
        mark.pickBeeper();
        mark.move();
        mark.pickBeeper();
        mark.move();
        mark.pickBeeper();
        mark.move();
        mark.pickBeeper();
        mark.turnLeft();
```

```
        mark.move();
        mark.turnLeft();
        mark.pickBeeper();
        mark.move();
        mark.pickBeeper();
        mark.move();
        mark.pickBeeper();
        mark.move();
        mark.pickBeeper();
        mark.move();
        mark.pickBeeper();
        mark.turnRight();
        mark.move();
        mark.turnRight();
        mark.pickBeeper();
        mark.move();
        mark.pickBeeper();
        mark.move();
        mark.pickBeeper();
        mark.move();
        mark.pickBeeper();
        mark.move();
        mark.pickBeeper();
        mark.turnRight();
        mark.move();
        mark.turnLeft();
        mark.pickBeeper();
        mark.move();
        mark.pickBeeper();
        mark.move();
        mark.pickBeeper();
        mark.move();
        mark.pickBeeper();
        mark.move();
        mark.pickBeeper();
        mark.turnLeft();
        mark.move();
        mark.turnLeft();
        mark.pickBeeper();
        mark.move();
        mark.pickBeeper();
        mark.move();
        mark.pickBeeper();
        mark.move();
        mark.pickBeeper();
        mark.move();
        mark.pickBeeper();
        mark.move();
        mark.turnOff();
}
```

Long lists of messages such as this may correctly solve a problem but they are very difficult to read and understand. They are also very difficult to debug and modify.

3.10 Writing Understandable Programs

Writing understandable programs is as important as writing correct ones; some say that it is even more important. They argue that most programs initially have a few errors, and understandable programs are easier to debug. Good programmers are distinguished from bad ones by their ability to write clear and concise programs that someone else can read and quickly understand. What makes a program easy to understand? We present two criteria.

* A good program is the simple composition of easily understandable parts. Each part of the programs we just wrote can be understood by itself. Even without a detailed understanding of the parts, the plans that the programs use to accomplish their respective tasks are easy to understand.

* Dividing a program (or a large method definition) into small, easy to understand pieces is not enough. We must also make sure to name our new methods properly. These names provide a description, possibly the only description, of what the method does. Imagine what the previous programs would look like if for each meaningful method name we had used a name like firstInstruction or doItNow. The robot programming language allows us to choose any method names we want, but with this freedom comes the responsibility to select accurate and descriptive names.

It is much easier to verify or debug a program that contains new methods. The following two facts support this claim.

* New methods can be independently tested. When writing a program, we should hand simulate each method immediately after it is written, until we are convinced that it is correct. Then we can forget how the method works and just remember what the method does. Remembering should be easy, if we name the method accurately. This is easiest if the method does only one thing.

* New methods impose a structure on our programs, and we can use this structure to help us find bugs. When debugging a program, we should first find which of the new methods is malfunctioning. Then we can concentrate on debugging that method, ignoring the other parts of our program, which are irrelevant to the bug.

Thus we see that there is an interesting psychological phenomenon related to the robot method definition mechanism. Because the human brain can focus on only a limited amount of information at any one time, the ability to ignore details that are no longer relevant is a great aid to program writing and debugging.

To help make our new method definitions understandable, we should also keep their lengths within a reasonable range. A good rule of thumb is that definitions should rarely exceed five to ten instructions. This limit leaves us enough room to write a meaningful method, but restrains us from cramming too much detail into any one definition. If a method's size exceeds this limit, we should try to divide it naturally into a set of smaller instructions.

This rule applies to the number of messages written within the main task block too. Most novice programmers tend to write method definitions that are too large. It is better to write many small, well-named methods, instead of a few oversized definitions.

If a new method that we write can only be executed correctly in a certain situation, then we should include comments in the definition explaining what those conditions are. For example, an method that always picks up a beeper should indicate in a comment where that beeper must appear. For example:

```
public void moveAndPick() // from class Walker
// Requires a beeper on the next corner in front.
{       move();
        pickBeeper();
}
```

Writing understandable programs with new methods and using the technique of stepwise refinement can reduce the number of errors we make and the amount of time we spend writing robot programs. The real goal, however, is to write *beautiful* programs; programs that other programmers read with enjoyment and we read with satisfaction.

3.11 Important Ideas From This Chapter

subclass
override
extends
stepwise refinement
precondition
postcondition
visibility (public and private)

3.12 Problem Set

The problems in this section require defining new methods for a robot named karel, or writing complete programs that include such new methods. Concentrate on writing well-structured programs, built from naturally descriptive new methods. Practice using stepwise refinement and freely define any new methods that you need. If you find yourself continually writing the same sequence of messages, it is a sure sign that you need to define that sequence as a new method. Carefully check for syntax errors in your program, and simulate karel's execution of each program to verify that it is correct.

Paradoxically, the programs in this problem set will be among the largest you will write. The instructions covered in the next chapters are so powerful that we will find that complex tasks can be solved with programs comprising a small number of these potent instructions.

1. Write appropriate definitions for the following new methods: (1) moveMile, remembering that miles are 8 blocks long; (2) moveBackward, which moves karel one block backward, but leaves it facing the same

direction, and (3) moveKiloMile, which moves karel 1000 miles forward. This last problem is difficult but a fairly short solution does exist. You may use the moveMile message in this problem without redefining it. Can any of these methods cause an error shutoff when it is executed?

2. Karel sometimes works as a pin-setter in a bowling alley. Write a program that instructs karel to transform the initial situation in Figure 3-4 into the final situation. Karel starts this task with ten beepers in its beeper-bag.

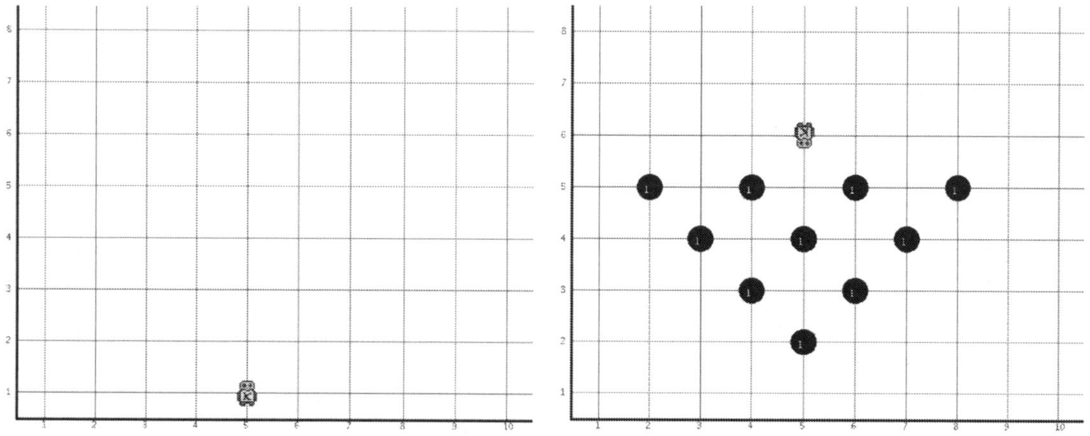

Figure 3-4 A Pin-Setting Task

3. Rewrite the harvesting program using a different stepwise refinement.

4. Figure 3-5 illustrates a field of beepers that karel planted one night after a baseball game. Write a program that harvests all these beepers. Hint: this task is not too different from the harvesting example. If you see the correspondence between these two harvesting tasks, you should be able to develop a program for this task that is similar to the original harvesting program.

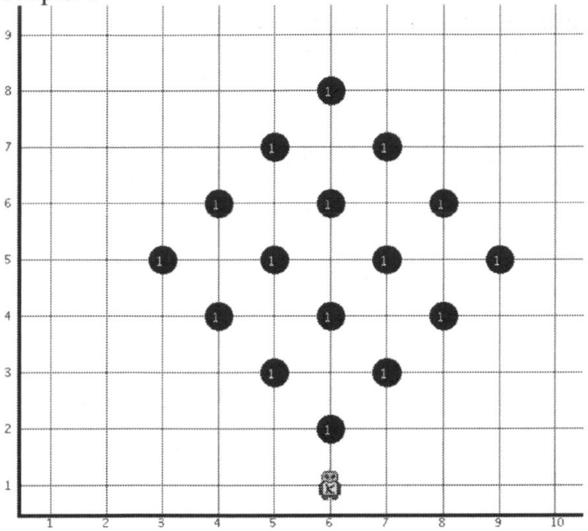

Figure 3-5 Another Harvesting Task

5. Karel wants to send greetings to the other inhabitants of the universe, so the robot needs to plant a field of beepers that broadcasts the message to alien astronomers. Program karel to plant the message of beepers shown in Figure 3-6. You may choose karel's starting position.

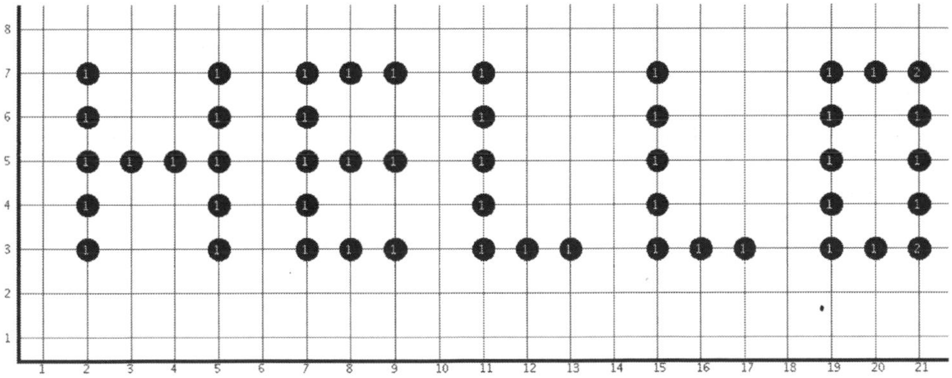

Figure 3-6 A Message for Alien Astronomers

6. Karel has received a contract from NASA (the National Aeronautics and Space Administration of the United States) to display the correct time for astronauts to read as they orbit above karel's world. The time must be displayed digitally and must fit in the situation shown in Figure 3.7. You may choose the size and shape of the digits. The program must allow you to change the time quickly so karel can rapidly update the display. For practice, display the time 10 : 52.

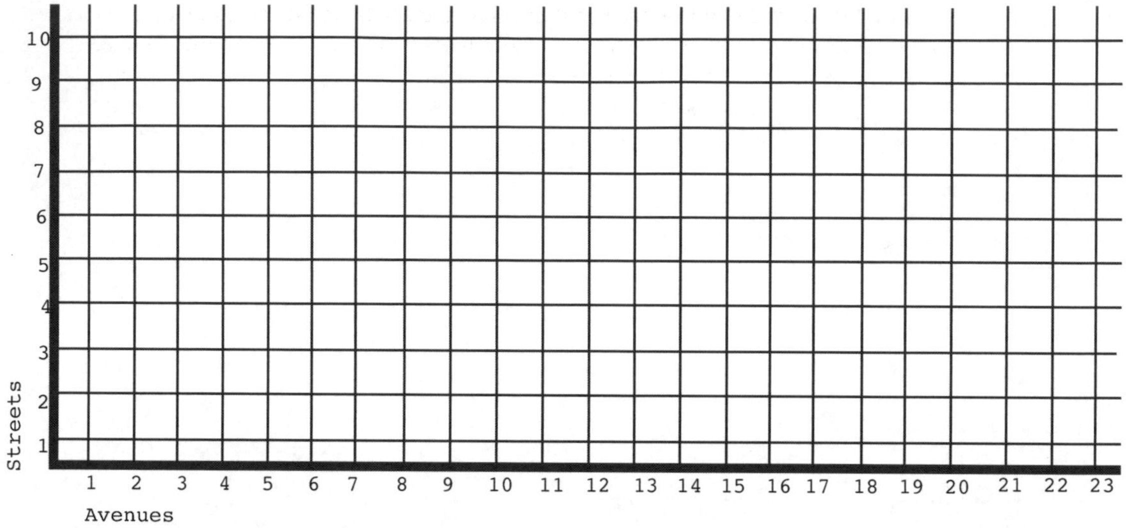

Figure 3-7 A Digital Clock

7. Karel has taken a part time job as a gardener. Karel's specialty is planting beepers. Karel's current task is to plant one and only one beeper on each corner around the "+" shaped wall arrangement as shown in the situation in Figure 3-8.

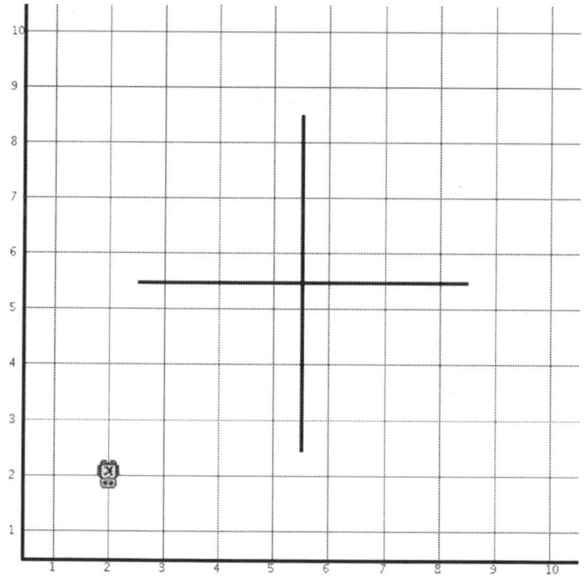

Figure 3-8 A Gardening Task

8. Karel got bored with gardening, so the robot decided to try a different part time job. The robot now installs carpets (made from beepers) in buildings in its world. Write a program that instructs karel to install a carpet in the building shown in Figure 3-9. There must be no "lumps" in the carpet so be sure that karel places one and only one beeper on each intersection in the room.

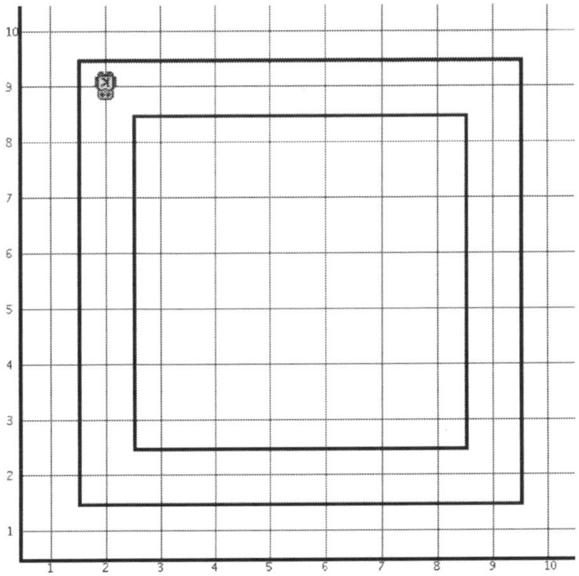

Figure 3-9 A Carpet Task

9. Program karel to arrange beepers as shown in the final situation given in Figure 3-10. Karel has exactly twelve beepers in its beeper bag. You may start karel on any convenient corner.

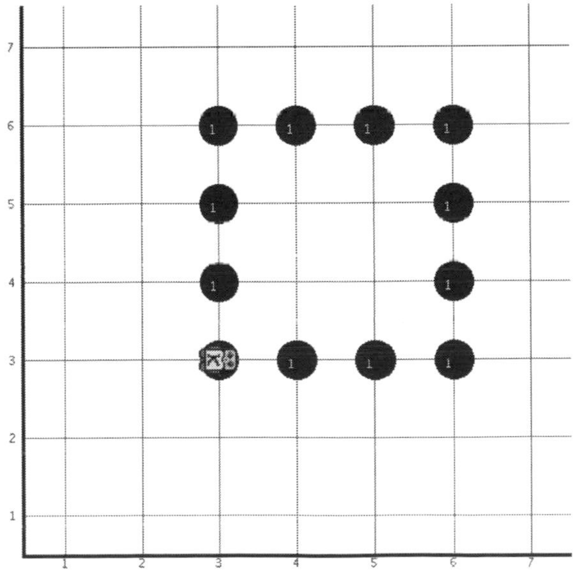

Figure 3-10 A Box of Beepers

10. Give a specification for a class where a) the new robots have all of the capabilities of robots in class UrRobot, and b) they can also execute method pickAPair, which will cause such a robot to pick up two beepers (if available) from the current corner. Call this new class PickAPairRobot. Give the specification for this new class in the robot programming language.

11. Suppose we define an method in some robot class like this.

```
public void move()
{
  super.move();
  move();
}
```

What will happen if we send our robot such a message? If you want to test this, start your robot facing West or South. What is the meaning of the move instruction within this method?

12. Read Problem 2.13-10 of Chapter 2 again. How short a program can you write now to carry out this task, using knowledge from this chapter?

13. Why is it important that programs be easily readable by people?

14. How can we achieve the goal of writing readable programs?

4 Polymorphism

This chapter explains the consequences of specifying new classes of robots and some objects that are not robots. Objects in different classes can behave differently when sent the same messages. This is called polymorphism. Each robot or other object behaves according to the definition of its own class.

When you build a new robot class you really want to keep it simple. Each class should define objects that do one task and do it well. As we have seen, it may be necessary to define several methods in that class to carry out the task, but we should be able to name the overall task or service that the robot class is supposed to provide. Suppose that we have two tasks to do, however. How do we handle that? One way is to have two classes, one for each task and then use a robot from each class to perform each task. This implies more than one robot in a program, of course.

4.1 Robot Teams

In this section we will introduce a very different problem-solving method. Instead of solving a problem with a single robot, suppose we have a team of robots cooperate in the task.

For example, the beeper harvesting task could be quite easily done by three robots each sent the message harvestTwoRows, if we position them appropriately two blocks apart. The first robot would harvest two rows, then the next robot would harvest the next two rows, etc. The main task block would look like the following.

```
public static void main(String [] args)
{ Harvester karel = new Harvester(2, 2, East, 0);
  Harvester kristin = new Harvester(4, 2, East, 0);
  Harvester matt = new Harvester(6, 2, East, 0);

  karel.move();
  karel.harvestTwoRows();
  karel.turnOff();
  kristin.move();
  kristin.harvestTwoRows();
  kristin.turnOff();
  matt.move();
  matt.harvestTwoRows();
  matt.turnOff();
}
```

The problem could also be solved by six robots, of course.

We could also intersperse the operations of the three robots if we wished, rather than have one complete its task before the other makes any move:

```
public static void main(String [] args)
{ Harvester karel = new Harvester(2, 2, East, 0);
  Harvester kristin = new Harvester(4, 2, East, 0);
  Harvester matt = new Harvester(6, 2, East, 0);

  karel.move();
  kristin.move();
  matt.move();
  karel.harvestTwoRows();
  kristin.harvestTwoRows();
  matt.harvestTwoRows();
  karel.turnOff();
  kristin.turnOff();
  matt.turnOff();
}
```

However, if we are happy to have one robot complete its task before the next begins, we can solve this in a more interesting way. We don't actually need to use three different names to refer to the three robots. We can let an existing name refer to another robot. The names of robots are called "references" for this reason. They are also called variables since their values can vary, or change, as the program proceeds as we see now.

```
public static void main(String [] args)
{ Harvester karel = new Harvester(2, 2, East, 0);
  karel.move();
  karel.harvestTwoRows();
  karel.turnOff();

  karel = new Harvester(4, 2, East, 0);
  karel.move();
  karel.harvestTwoRows();
  karel.turnOff();

  karel = new Harvester(6, 2, East, 0);
  karel.move();
  karel.harvestTwoRows();
  karel.turnOff();

}
```

There is one subtle difference here. We only declare the name karel once in the first statement of the task block when we say

```
Harvester karel
```

In this same line we also *initialize* this reference to a new robot at corner (2, 2). Then later we give this same reference a new value (*initialize* its value) by creating a new robot at (4, 2), etc. The old robot to which the name karel referred is, in a sense, discarded. We still have a team of robots, but we only need one name. We do the same in the world of people, by the way. There are several people named Karel in the real world, and who the name refers to depends on context. It is the same in the robot world.

In fact, we can separate the notion of reference declaration and robot creation, perhaps by replacing the first statement in the main task block above with the following two statements. We use the special value *null* to indicate that a reference to a robot doesn't refer to any robot at all.

```
Harvester karel = null; // Declare a reference
karel = new Harvester(2, 2, East, 0);
        // Create a robot to which karel will refer.
```

We can have a given reference refer to different robots at different times, and, conversely, we can have different names refer to the same robot at the same time. It is, therefore, good to separate two concepts in your mind: that of the name of a robot (a reference to a robot) and that of the robot itself (a robot, of course). These ideas will be explored later.

When we change the object to which a reference points we call it **assignment**. We use assignment to have the program remember things using reference variables like the name karel above. We use the = operator to indicate assignment, though it is also used when we declare a new variable and initialize the value. The concept of initialization is slightly different, but not so much that it matters here.

Finally, we note that if you reach a situation in which there is no reference at all to some object, then there is no way to reconstruct a reference. The object, perhaps a robot, passes out of your program's control. A system component called the "garbage collector" will return the resources that the object uses to the "factory."

In the above we had several robots, but they were all of the same class. We can have teams in which there are several different kinds of robots as well.

4.2 Similar Tasks

Sometimes we want to do several tasks, but the tasks are very similar. How can we build the classes to take advantage of the common parts of the task and yet distinguish the specific differences?

Often we use inheritance to solve this problem. After all, we have seen several kinds of robots already and all have a move method. We didn't need to write that method in all the classes, only in those in which move should do something different than the version inherited from UrRobot. We can do more, however.

Here is a task for a team of robots. Suppose we want to lay down beepers in a field that has five rows and four columns. Suppose that we want the odd numbered rows (first, third, and fifth) to have two beepers on each corner and we want the other rows to have three beepers on each corner.

One good way to solve this is to have two different kinds of robots: TwoRowLayers and ThreeRowLayers. A two-row layer will put down two beepers on each corner that it vists while laying beepers and a three-row layer will put three instead.

However, it is good to recognize that these two kinds of robots are very similar in their overall behavior, only differing in one aspect of their behavior. In particular, we will have a method called layBeepers that implements the way a robot lays down a full row of beepers. This will be identical in both our new classes, since each will lay a row of the same length. This method will call another method called putBeepers, that will be different in each of our classes. It will put down two beepers when received by a TwoRowLayer, and three when received by a ThreeRowLayer. However, if we write layBeepers twice, once in each class, we will be wasting effort. Worse, if the problem changes to one that requires rows of length five instead of four, we have two places to change the program. If we change only one of them the program will be broken, but it may not be immediately obvious why, especially if we have left the problem alone for a few days before modifying it.

We can capture the commonality of their behavior in a special class called an *abstract* class. An abstract class is one that the robot factory never actually manufactures, but uses as a kind of template for the construction of more specialized robots.

```
public abstract class BeeperLayer extends UrRobot
{
     public abstract void putBeepers();

     public void layBeepers()
     {    move();
          putBeepers();
          move();
          putBeepers();
          move();
          putBeepers();
          move();
          putBeepers();
          move();
          turnOff();
     }

     public BeeperLayer(int street, int avenue,
        Direction direction, int beepers)
     {    super(street, avenue, direction, beepers);
     }
}
```

Here we define BeeperLayer as such a class. We give it a new layBeepers method in which we describe laying down a row of length four. For each corner we visit (other than the starting corner) we execute putBeepers(). This is a new method defined in this class, but not given any definition here. The putBeepers method is called an abstract method and it must be marked abstract as we see here. Only an abstract class can have an abstract method, but abstract classes can have ordinary methods as well, as we also see above.

In effect an abstract class is a template with a hole (putBeepers) that can be filled for a specific use. One of the advantages of object-oriented programming is that it permits something called "reuse." Note that an abstract class provides a general framework via its non-abstract methods for something to occur, and lets you fill (reuse) the holes in the template in different ways for different purposes. This idea of reusing the holes in a basic structure is very important and powerful. Here is an analogy that might be helpful in understanding abstract classes. Suppose you want to build a home music system from various components. Suppose you have decided on all the elements except the amplifier. You can purchase and even assemble the other components, though they won't be very useful yet. However, the standards adopted by manufacturers assure you that whichever amplifier you later buy will plug properly into the rest of your system. Your skeleton system is something like an abstract class, not usable in itself, but very usable when extended.

Since we didn't give a definition to putBeepers, a robot of this type wouldn't know what to do when given this message, so the factory doesn't make any of these. It is useful, however, as a partial specification of other classes that extend this one. These extensions are not abstract and they will give a definition for putBeepers, while also inheriting layBeepers. Thus, any new subclasses automatically have the same version of layBeepers, even if we need to modify it in the future. Next we see two such classes.

```
public class TwoRowLayer extends BeeperLayer
{ public void putBeepers()
  {       putBeeper();
          putBeeper();
  }
… // constructor omitted
}

public class ThreeRowLayer extends BeeperLayer
{ public void putBeepers()
  {       putBeeper();
          putBeeper();
          putBeeper();
  }
… // constructor omitted
}
```

Each of these two classes extends BeeperLayer and so has the same layBeepers method. The layBeepers method calls putBeepers. We will declare a robot reference named lisa to be of type BeeperLayer (an abstract class) and will let this name refer alternately to a succession of two- and three-row layers. The reason why the name lisa (of class BeeperLayer) can refer to a robot of a class that extends this class is that each such extension class defines robots that in a very real sense "are" members of the class that is extended. In other words a TwoRowLayer really is a BeeperLayer and a ThreeRowLayer really is a BeeperLayer. Note the subtle distinction here. We can have variables (names) of type BeeperLayer, but no objects of this type. Instead, such a variable will refer to an object that extends BeeperLayer. This is just our usual meaning of inheritance, by the way. Nothing new is added by this, except that we defer the definition of some methods to subclasses. A class that is not abstract is sometimes called *concrete,* but that is not a special Robot programming (or Java) word.

```
public static void main(String [] args)
{ BeeperLayer lisa = null;
  lisa = new TwoRowLayer(1, 3 ,East, infinity);
  lisa.layBeepers();
  lisa = new ThreeRowLayer(2, 3, East, infinity);
  lisa.layBeepers();
  lisa = new TwoRowLayer(3, 3, East, infinity);
  lisa.layBeepers();
  lisa = new ThreeRowLayer(4, 3, East, infinity);
  lisa.layBeepers();
  lisa = new TwoRowLayer(5, 3, East, infinity);
  lisa.layBeepers();
}
```

Each time the name lisa refers to a two-row layer it puts two beepers at each corner on which it is asked (within layBeepers) to putBeepers, and each time it refers to a three-row layer it puts three beepers on each corner. Again, this is just like the situation with people. If I know two people named Bill and I say to each "Bill, move." and one of the Bills always moves slowly and the other always moves quickly, then I can expect them to act in their usual way. Even if I refer to them with a generic name, they will likely behave as they always do: "Friend, move." And not that it isn't the *name* that moves, but, rather, the person (object) to which the name refers.

Notice that starting with the second assignment here, each time we make an assignment we let the name lisa refer to a different robot. This means that no name at all refers to the previous robot. We can no longer send instructions to a robot if we have no reference to it. The robot factory will know that this is the case and collect the unusable robot back using its garbage collector. The resources it uses will be recycled.

The fact that each robot always interprets each message it gets, directly or indirectly, in terms of the program defined by its own class, is called polymorphism. It is impossible to make a robot behave differently than the definition of its class, no matter what reference is used to refer to it. While it is not important to minimize the number of names used in a program, understanding polymorphism is fundamental. You will see later, perhaps only after leaving the robot world for true Java programming, that we often use a name to refer to different variables at different times and that we just as often refer to a given robot by different names at different parts of a large program. The key to understanding is to simply remember that it is the robot itself, not the name by which we refer to it, that determines what is done when a message is received.

Finally in this section we should look at what it is that makes programs easy to understand and to modify. Often we have the choice, when designing a program, to have a single robot perform a complex task or to have a team of robots each performing some part of that task. Which is to be preferred? In the extreme, it is possible to build a single robot class that will solve all of the problems in this book--a super-super-super-duper-robot. Should we do that, or should we build a lot of simpler classes each of which solves a single task?

The answer to the above is clear to those who have had to live with large programs. Large programs are usually written to solve significant problems. Such programs take a significant amount of time and money to develop and the problems that they solve are usually ever changing. This is due to the fact that the organizations that want the programs are continually evolving. Yesterday's problems are usually similar to tomorrow's problems but they are seldom identical. This means that programs must change and adapt to the problems they intend to solve.

Because of the way people think, it is difficult to understand and modify large programs. This is largely because of the amount of detail in them. It is therefore useful if they are built out of small and easy to understand parts. The implication of this for robot programming is that you will be building better skills if you build small robot classes with a single, simple to understand purpose, rather than a large, complicated, do everything class that can solve all problems. With the small classes you can choose a set of robots to perform much of a complex task and write other simple classes to perform the rest, rather than to have to understand all of the interconnections in a complex class. This is similar to what we learned in the previous chapter. Small methods are better than big ones. The same is true for classes. We will see this again in Section 4.4.

Polymorphism also helps us here, since it means that when we design a robot to perform a certain simple task we can be assured that it will always perform that task when sent a message, independent of how that message reaches it. If we design our classes well, our robots will be trustworthy. We can also use polymorphism as we did above to factor out the common behavior of a set of classes into a superclass, like BeeperLayer, that may be abstract or not.

4.3 Choreographers

There is an even more interesting way to carry out some complex tasks if we let one robot coordinate the actions of some others. For this plan to work we need at least two different kinds of robots. One kind of robot will be called a Choreographer, because it directs the others, which can be ordinary, standard issue UrRobot robots. The trick here is that the Choreographer will set up the others and then will guarantee that they mimic the actions of the Choreographer.

For this to work, the Choreographer needs to know the names of the other robots and have complete control over them, so we will make these names *private* names of the Choreographer itself. We have not seen this feature of the robot programming language previously. Rather than declare robots in the main task block, we can define robot names within a new class. Robots declared like this will be available as helpers to robots of the class being declared, but may not be used by other robots or in the main task block. This is because the names of the helper robots will be private to the robot of the new class.

This also brings up the second major feature of objects. Objects can **do** things. For example, robots can move. But objects can also **remember** things. So a Choreographer can remember the names of its helpers. The things that robots, and objects in general, can do are represented by its methods, like turnLeft. The things that objects remember are called its **instance variables** or **fields**. When one robot remembers the name of another, it sets up a (one way) association between the robots. A Choreographer will know who its helpers are, but the helper may not know the Choreographer. Usually human associations are two way, of course, but it is not the same with robots.

Our Choreographer will also need to override all of the Robot methods so that, for example, if we tell the Choreographer to move, that it can direct the others to move as well. Below we show just the interface of this class so that we can see it all at once. Note that within the class definition we define two robots. These two robots will be helpers for our Choreographer robot.

```
public class Choreographer extends UrRobot
{
      private UrRobot lisa = new UrRobot(4,2,East,0);
      // the first helper robot
      private UrRobot tony = new UrRobot(6,2,East,0);
         // the second helper robot
      public void harvest(){...}
      public void harvestARow(){...}
      public void harvestCorner(){...}
      public void move(){...}
      public void pickBeeper(){...}
      public void turnLeft(){...}
      public void turnOff(){...}

      public Choreographer(...){...}
}
```

Here is the main task block for our program.

```
public static void main(String [] args)
{       Choreographer karel = new Choreographer(2, 2, East, 0);
        karel.harvest();
        karel.turnOff();
}
```

Here is the complete Choreographer class, with some annotations.

```
public class Choreographer extends UrRobot
{
        private UrRobot lisa = new UrRobot(4,2,East,0);
            // the first helper robot
        private UrRobot tony = new UrRobot(6,2,East,0);
            // the second helper robot
```

Robots or other variables defined within a class are called *instance variables* for they are associated with each instance (robot) that is created. Each Choreographer, if we have several, will have its own helpers. They are normally private. They are therefore only available within the class. If other programs outside this class could manipulate these helpers, then the Choreographer couldn't determine accurately what they do.

Harvest and harvestARow are similar to what we have seen before.

```
public void harvest()
{
        harvestARow();
        turnLeft();
        move();
        turnLeft();
        harvestARow();
}

public void harvestARow()
{       move();
        harvestCorner();
        move();
        harvestCorner();
        move();
        harvestCorner();
        move();
        harvestCorner();
        move();
        harvestCorner();
        move();
}
```

```
        public void harvestCorner()
        {
                pickBeeper();
        }
```

The key to making a choreographer and its team work together is in redefining the inherited methods. The other methods are very similar to each other. We show only move here.

```
        public void  move()
        {       super.move();
                lisa.move();
                tony.move();
        }
```

Each of the other methods first executes the inherited instruction of the same name and then sends the message to the two helper robots.

```
        ... // similar to the move method
}
```

Notice that when asked to move, the Choreographer robot (here karel) first executes the inherited move instruction to move itself. It then sends move messages to the two helpers, which are only UrRobots, so they don't affect any other robots. This means that whenever karel moves, each of its helpers also moves "automatically." The same will be true for the pickBeeper, turnLeft, and turnOff instructions. When a robot sends a message to another robot, the message passes from the sender of the message through the satelite to the other robot. The sender must then wait for the completion of the instruction by the robot it sent the message to before it can resume its own execution.

Be sure to trace the execution of this program. Notice that the order of execution of this solution is very different from the solutions given in Section 3.8 or 4.1.

The reader may consider what would happen here if the helper robots were not simply UrRobots but were instead robots of some other class with new move methods of their own. The results can be very interesting. The choreographer would ask each helper to move and the helper would, of course, do what it was programmed to do when asked to move, which might be quite complex.

4.4 Object Oriented Design -- Clients and Servers

In section 3.8 we learned a useful technique for designing a single class. We learned to ask what services (methods) are needed from that class and designing complex tasks as a decomposition into simpler tasks. Now we are going to look at design from a broader perspective. Here we will learn to recognize that we may need several classes of robots to carry out some task, and these robots may need to cooperate in some way. We will discuss only the design issues, leaving implementation until we have seen some more powerful ideas.

Suppose that we want to build a robot house as shown in Figure 4-1. Houses will be built of beepers, of course. In the real world, house building is a moderately complex task that is usually done by a team of builders, each with his or her own specialty. Perhaps it should be the same in the robot world.

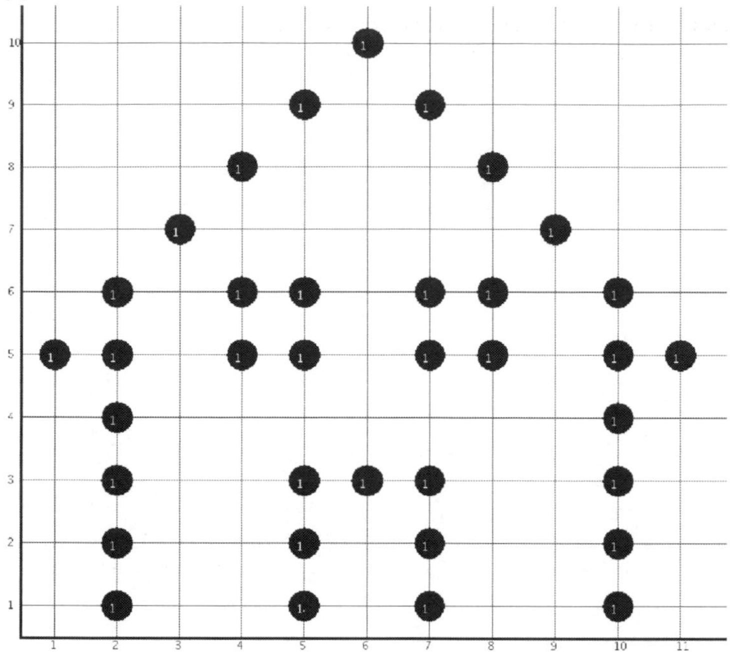

Figure 4-1 A House Building Task.

If you look back at some of our earlier examples, you will find that there are really two kinds of instructions. The first kind of instruction, such as **harvestTwoRows** in the Harvester class is meant to be used in the main task block. The other kind, like **goToNextRow**, is meant primarily to be used internally, as part of problem decomposition. For example, the instruction **goToNextRow** is unlikely to be used except from within other instructions. The first kind of instruction is meant to be public and defines in some way what the robot is intended to do. If we think of a robot as a *server*, then its *client* (the main task block, or perhaps another robot) will send it a message with one of its public instructions. The client is one who requests a service from a server. A Harvester robot provides a harvesting service. Its client requests that service. The place to begin design is with the public services and the servers that provide them. The server robot itself will then, perhaps, execute other instructions to provide the service. We can use successive refinement to help design the other instructions that help the server carry out its service.

The easiest way to get a house built is to call on the services of a **Contractor**, who will assemble some appropriate team to build our house. We tell the contractor robot **buildHouse** and somehow the job gets done. The client doesn't especially care how the contractor carries out the task as long as the result (including the price) are acceptable. (Here the costs are low, since robots don't need to send their children to college.) Notice that we have just given the preliminary design for a class, the Contractor class, with one public method: **buildHouse**. We may discover the need for more methods and for more classes as well. We also know that we will probably need only a single robot of the Contractor class. Let's name it kristin, to have a working name.

Now we examine the task from kristin's standpoint. What does it need to do to build a house? One possibility is to place all of the beepers itself. But another way is to use specialist robots to handle well-defined parts of the house: for example, walls, the roof, and the doors and windows. Kristin will **delegate** the work to other robots. Well, since we want the walls to be made of bricks (beeper-bricks, that is), we should call on the services of one or more **Mason** robots. The doors and windows could be built by a **Carpenter** robot, and the roof built by a **Roofer** robot.

The **Contractor**, kristin, needs to be able to gather this team, so we need another method for this. While it could be called by the client, it probably should be called internally by the contractor itself when it is ready to begin construction. Kristin also needs to be able to get the team to the construction site. We will want a new Contractor method **getherTeam**.

Focusing, then, on the smaller jobs, the **Mason** robot should be able to respond to a **buildWall** message. The contractor can show the mason where the walls are to be built. Similarly, the **Roofer** should be able to respond to **makeRoof**, and the **Carpenter** robots should know the messages **makeDoor** and **makeWindow**. We might go a step farther with the roofer and decide that it would be helpful to make the two gables of the roof separately. So we would also want a Roofer to be able to **makeLeftGable** and **makeRightGable.**

However, we can also make the following assumption. Each specialized worker robot knows how to do its own task and also knows the names of the tasks and subtasks that it must do. If the contractor simpy tells it to getToWork, then it already knows what it should do. Therefore, we can factor out this common behavior into a Java interface named Worker.

```
public interface Worker
{        public void getToWork();
}
```

A Java interface is used to introduce a protocol that some objects must follow without any restrictions on how the protocol should be implemented. It defines a set of public method names (and parameters when necessary) that we would like to use elsewhere for some objects. A class can *implement* (not extend) one or more interfaces. Doing so gives it the requirement of implementing all of the methods named in all the interfaces. Also, an interface can define many methods, not just one as we have here.

Unlike abstract classes, interfaces never contain any implementations of methods (and no constructors). They may define constant values, however, though we haven't introduced that concept yet. On the other hand, a class can implement several interfaces, but can only extend one class (even if it is an abstract class). In effect, an interface is "all holes" while an abstract class has some holes and usually some additional structure. An interface is purely a way for objects to agree on how they will communicate. In the music system analogy we used earlier, an interface is like the agreements that component manufacturers made on how to connect various things together.

For our robots, if we implement an interface, such as Worker, we will also need to extend one of the robot classes, such as UrRobot. Like classes, interfaces are usually put into their own files with the name of the interface and .java appended to the end: Worker.java here. In this case, the interface should be marked public and should be in the same package as the one you are working in: kareltherobot.

There is an interface named Directions already defined in the Karel J Robot system. It is where the constants North, East, South, West (and infinity) are defined. The class of North, etc., is Direction, however, without an s on the end. UrRobot implements this interface, so our robots know about the various directions. If you write non-robot classes that need to use these words, you will need to "implement Directions" as we did in Section 3.9.
By way of analogy, a class is like a blueprint for an object (robot, for example), containg information about how to build it. An interface is like a user's manual, showing how it can be used, but not built.

The classes then implement this interface and provide an implementation of the new method. Here we show outlines of the new methods. Each class implements getToWork in a different way. We also mark each method telling whether it is public or private. A public method may be called from anywhere that the robot is known. A private method may only be called within the class definition of the robot itself. Private methods are "helper" methods to carry out the public services.

```
public class Mason extends UrRobot implements Worker
{
  public void getToWork()
  {      buildWall();
         ...
         buildWall();
  }
```

```
private void buildWall()
  {
          ...
  }
}

public class Carpenter extends UrRobot implements Worker
{
  public void getToWork()
  {       makeWindow();
          ...
          makeWindow();
          ...
          makeDoor();
  }

  private void makeWindow()
  {
          ...
  }

  private void makeDoor()
  {
          ...
  }
}

public class Roofer extends UrRobot implements Worker
{
  public void getToWork()
  {       makeRoof();
  }

  private void makeRoof()
  {
          makeLeftGable();
          makeRightGable();
  }

  private makeLeftGable()
  {
          ...
  }

  private makeRightGable()
  {
          ...
  }
}
// Constructors omitted from all of the above
```

This gives us an outline for the helper classes. Let's look again at the Contractor class. Since the team of builders is assembled by the contractor it must know their names. Therefore, it would be useful if the names of the helpers were declared as private names in the Contractor class itself, rather than global names. This will also effectively prevent the client of the contractor from telling the workers directly what to do.

```
class Contractor extends UrRobot
{
  private Mason kenMason = new Mason(1,1,E,??);
  private Roofer  sueRoofer = new Roofer(...);
  private Carpenter lindaCarpenter = new Carpenter(...);

  private void gatherTeam()
  {
  ...// messages here for initial positioning of the team.
  }

  public void buildHouse()
  {       gatherTeam();
          kenMason.getToWork();
          sueRoofer.getToWork();
          lindaCarpenter.getToWork();
  }
}

public static void main(String [] args)
{         Contractor kristin = new Contractor(1, 1, East, 0);
          kristin.buildHouse();
          kristin.turnOff();
}
```

Note that the Contractor kristin is a server. Its client is the main task block which delivers messages to it. But note also that kristin is a client of the three helpers since they provide services (wall services . . .) to kristin. In fact, it is relatively common in the real world for clients and servers to be mutually bound. For example, doctors provide medical services to grocers who provide food marketing services to doctors.

In object-oriented programming, this idea of one object delegating part of its task to other ojbects is very important. When one bit of code asks an object to perform some action or retrieve some information, the receiver of the message will often delegate the work to another object. In this world, that object could be another robot, or something else entirely as we shall see. Delegation in this way helps us break up a large program into small, understandable, parts. And, of course, delegation models what happens in the real world. It is nearly the same in the object-oriented world. Delegation is a big idea. One object carries out part of its task by asking another to do something for it.

A reference variable in Java is a name that is defined to have some object type (here a robot type). For example, we have often used the name karel as a reference and above we used kenMason, etc. There are some rules that you need to know about references that will also help you understand polymorphism. The first rule is that if a reference is declared to be of a particular class then it can also refer to (point to) an object of that class or any subclass. So a robot karel declared to be a UrRobot reference can actually point to a MileWalker object if we like. The object that is referred to is always and ever a MileWalker if it is created with new MileWalker(...) independent of which reference points to it. However, if a variable of type UrRobot points to a MileWalker object, then the only messages we can send to the object are UrRobot messages. Otherwise, the Java system will give us an error since it can't verify that the program is correct. Variables and parameters can also be given interface types (rather than class types). In this case, the variable can refer to any object whose class implements that interface. Again, in this case the only message we can send to the object will be one defined in the interface.

There is a way to loosen these rules (i.e., casting) that will be introduced later.

Finally, you can declare a reference to have an abstract class type. In this case the reference must necessarily point to an object of some concrete subclass, since it is impossible to create an object from an abstract class. How an object behaves, however, depends on the actual object itself, and not on the reference we use to point to it. Objects never change their type, but can be referred to by variables of different types at different times.

4.5 Using Polymorphism

Here is a simple problem. Suppose we have a bunch of robots, one on each corner of a street (say first street) from some avenue to some avenue farther on and we want to ask each robot to put down one beeper. We want to write a program that will work no matter how many robots there are. To make it explicit, suppose there is a robot on first street on every corner between the origin and 10'th avenue. Each robot has one beeper and we want to ask them all to put down their beeper. We want to build a set of classes to solve this problem in such a way that it doesn't matter how many robots there are. In other words, the same program should work if we have robots between first and 20'th avenues instead. The idea is that most of the robots will put down a beeper and then pass the same message to the next robot. The last one won't pass the message on, since there are no more.

To do this we need at least two classes of robots, one for each behavior. However, as usual with polymorphism, we will try to factor out the common behavior of our classes into an interface or abstract superclass. In this case we will call this interface BeeperPutter and it will define one method: distributeBeepers. For most of the robots this method will cause the robot that receives the message to put down its own beeper and then send the same message to its neighbor robot. One of the robots will be different, however, and it will simply put down its beeper and nothing else. However, in order to see the effect we will also have each robot move off its corner after it puts down its beeper so that we can see the beepers.

```
public interface BeeperPutter
{     public void distributeBeepers();
}
```

We will have two classes that implement this interface as mentioned above. The simplest kind of a BeeperPutter doesn't have any neighbor to pass any message to, but still must be able to put down a beeper and move. It simply implements BeeperPutter and implements the required distributeBeepers method. In this case it just puts its own beeper and moves off of its original corner.

```
public class NoNeighbor extends UrRobot implements BeeperPutter
{	public void distributeBeepers()
	{	putBeeper();
		move();
	}

	public NoNeighbor(int street, int avenue,
	   Direction direction, int beepers)
	{	super(street, avenue, direction, beepers);
	}
}
```

On the other hand, the NeighborTalker robots remember a reference to another robot and they will pass the distributeBeepers message to this robot after they have placed their own beeper and moved.

```
public class NeighborTalker extends UrRobot implements BeeperPutter
{
	private BeeperPutter neighbor = null;

	public void distributeBeepers()
	{  putBeeper();
	   move();
	   neighbor.distributeBeepers();
	}
```

Here we have an example of a robot remembering something. A NeighborTalker remembers a reference to another robot: its neighbor. We shall see below how the constructor is used to get the NeighborTalker to remember a specific robot. It will remember it in its own instance variable called neighbor. Each NeighborTalker can remember a different neighbor. The neighbor *instance variable*, or *field*, becomes part of each robot of this kind. This instance variable is just a reference to some other BeeperPutter, like a local nickname. Note that the Karel Werke must build in this ability to reference another robot. Not only that, when you create such a robot we want the one that it will reference to exist beforehand. Then the other robot can be given as part of the delivery specification of the one you create with *new*.

Notice, however that we didn't define the neighbor robot in the above, we just declared the name by which the neighbor would be known. We need to give this reference a value, however, and we will do this with a new constructor. Sometimes we need to send additional information when we create a robot or send it a message. This extra information is called a parameter to a constructor or a method. Parameters can have any type; a robot class type for example.

You have experience with parameters in your ordinary dealings in the world. Suppose you go to the post office. You want to "send a message" buyStamps to the postal worker. Since there are many kinds of stamps, you can either have a separate message for each kind, or use a parameter to make the distinction. Moreover, even if you use a diffferent message for each kind of stamp (buyFirstClassStamps, etc.) you still need to say how many you want. These are parameters: postalWorker.buyStamps(FirstClass, 20); or postalWorker.buyFirstClasStamps(20);

In this case we want to tell a NeighborTalker which other robot (a BeeperPutter, actually) will be its neighbor when we create it. This other robot is the one that this one will tell to put down a beeper after it puts down its own. Here is a constructor that we can use to accomplish this.

```
public NeighborTalker(int street, int avenue,
   Direction direction, int beepers, BeeperPutter aRobot)
{       super(street, avenue, direction, beepers);
        neighbor = aRobot;
}
```

Note that we first invoke the super construction to create the UrRobot and then we save the parameter with name aRobot in the neighbor field of this robot using an assignment statement. This assignment just makes the neighbor reference refer to the BeeperPutter we are naming aRobot here. The name aRobot is itself a reference to some robot that is specified in the delivery specification. We have been using parameters all along, of course, in out constructors. Here we just use an additional one. Methods can have parameters as well as we shall soon see.

Note that the field *neighbor* is known only within the robots of class NeighborTalker and can be referenced from any of the methods. But if we create several NeighborTalker robots, then each will have the ability to reference a different robot via its neighbor field. The reference field is built into each robot separately. When the constructor references neighbor as above, it is setting the reference for the robot being created at that moment.

On the other hand, the parameter name aRobot is known only within the constructor itself since that is where it is declared. It is called *local* to the constructor. Parameter names are local to the constructor or method in which they occur.

Now we are ready to use the above classes. We define a set of NeighborTalker robots and one NoNeighbor. We let each of the NeighborTalkers know which robot we want to designate as its neighbor by naming some BeeperPutter as the argument matched with the extra parameter in the delivery specification. Notice that most of the Neighbor Talkers have another NeighborTalker for a neighbor. This is legal since a NeighborTalker is a BeeperPutter which was the robot class of the parameter to rememberNeighbor. However, one of the NeighborTalkers is given the NoNeighbor as in the delivery specification. This is also legal, since a NoNeighbor is also a BeeperPutter.

Then all we need to do is tell the first robot to distributeBeepers. It will place its own beeper and pass the same message to its neighbor, which in this case is another NeighborTalker. Thus the neighbor will do the same, putting a beeper and passing the message to ITS neighbor, and so on down the line until a NoNeighbor gets the same message. This one will put the beeper and will not pass on any message so the process stops. (Each robot also moves, of course.)

```
public static void main(String [] args)
{	BeeperPutter aRobot = new NoNeighbor(1, 1, North, 1);
	aRobot = new NeighborTalker(1, 2, North, 1, aRobot);
	aRobot = new NeighborTalker(1, 3, North, 1, aRobot);
	aRobot = new NeighborTalker(1, 4, North, 1, aRobot);
	aRobot = new NeighborTalker(1, 5, North, 1, aRobot);

	aRobot.distributeBeepers();
}
```

The interesting thing is that it doesn't matter how many of the NeighborTalker robots we put before the final NoNeighbor robot. All of the robots will place their beepers and the process will be stopped only when the distributeBeepers message is finally sent to the NoNeighbor robot. (It also doesn't really matter where the robots are. We positioned them along first street simply for convenience.)

The above code might be confusing the first time you encounter it. Note that we have declared only one reference variable (whose type is the interface BeeperPutter). Since it has an interface type we can make it refer to any robot whose class implements that interface, here either a NoNeighbor or a NeighborTalker. In the first statement of main we declare the name and initialize the variable to refer to a new NoNeighbor robot. In the second line the name *aRobot* appears twice, once on the left side of the assignment operator, =, and once as a parameter to the NeighborTalker constructor. How can this be? Note that before we can assign something to the aRobot variable on the left side, that object must exist. It exists because it is created on the right, so here we must process the right side of the = before the left side. Not only that, but the parameters themselves are all evaluated before the constructor's execution begins. Therefore, the current value of the reference *aRobot* is used, and that is the object created in the first statement. Thus the new robot is made to point to the first one, and then the name, which up to now has been pointing to the first one, is made to point to the second. Likewise in the third statement, the new robot is initialized to point to the second and the name is made to point to the newly created third robot. There are actually two rules at work here. The first is that parameter values are evaluated before the constructor or method is executed, using current values. The second rule is that the right hand sides of assignments are evaluated before the assignments to the left side variables are made.

The reader should note that we have been passing parameters all along in the robot language. We have only seen it in the construction statements for new robots, however. Parameters are used to pass information into a method so that it may tailor its behavior more finely. We shall see later in this chapter that it is also possible for a method to return information to the client that sent the message so that it can get feedback on what the message accomplished.

The careful reader will also have noted that we constructed a specific number of robots here. It didn't matter in the operation how many it was, but we knew when we wrote the program how many it would be. In Chapter 6 we shall see a way to avoid even this limitation.

When we define a new parameter we give it a type and a local name. Later when we use the constructor or method with the new parameter, we match some value, called an *argument*, with the parameter. The type must match, so here we can only use a BeeperPutter for the argument value. If, as here, there are several parameters, they must match in order, number, and type.

> The purpose of a constructor is actually more than just to deliver an object. More important is to guarantee that the object (here a robot) can be used immediately: that it is *properly* and *completely* constructed. When you define a class you are really giving the definition of a set of objects that the class can create. It is a template that the factory uses to create objects of that kind. These objects may have certain requirements. Here we require that the neighbors field actually refer to a BeeperPutter. If it does not, and remains null, then trying to send a message to neighbors will result in an intent error: a NullPointerException, technically. Normally this will halt our program. To avoid this we say that the NeighborTalker class has an *object invariant* that it must maintain. This is just a statement that must be true whenever we have such a robot and it must hold throughout its life. Here the invariant is the statement that the neighbor refers to an actual BeeperPutter, rather than remaining null. The job of the constructor is really to establish all object invariants. While technically the word invariant means "doesn't vary," in practice it means "is always true." So the job of the constructor is to make all invariants true. The other public methods then keep them true.
>
> Actually we don't do a very good job of it here, since the delivery statement could in fact specify *null* for the argument. We will think about this more in the future. It is possible to do a better job here.

4.6 Still More on Polymorphism -- Strategy and Delegation

So far, the only objects we have seen have been robots, UrRobots and the robots we have built. Beepers and walls are not objects because they don't have behavior, other than implicitly. In order to take advantage of polymorphism you want to have lots of objects of different kinds. Here we will introduce some new kinds of objects that are not even robots, but they can be helpful to robots. We will also learn a bit more about Java as we go along.

When we look back at section 4.2 we notice that we used two types (classes) of robots and several robot objects. We called them all by the same name, lisa, but there were still several objects. We did that to get different behavior. Different objects can perform different behaviors when sent the same message. That is the main message of polymorphism. Now we want to try something different and have the same robot behave differently at different times -- polymorphically. To do this we use a simple idea called "delegation." A robot can delegate one of its behaviors to another object. We did something like this with the Contractor robot earlier in this chapter, which delegated the building tasks to its helpers which were other robots. Here the object we delegate to won't be another robot, however, but a special kind of object called a Strategy.

You probably use strategies yourself when you do things: play games for example. A smart player will change strategies when she learns that the current one is not effective. This happens in both active games (basketball) and mental games (golf, Clue, ...). To be useful, strategies need to be somewhat interchangable, as well as flexible. You probably use a strategy to do your homework, in fact. Some strategies are more effective than others, also. Some common homework strategies are "As early as possible," and "As late as possible." I've even heard of a "Don't bother" strategy. In the robot world, as in ours, a strategy is something you use. The strategy is used to do something. We will capture strategies in objects and what they do in methods. By having a robot employ different strategies at different times, it will behave differently at diffferent times. For example, we could have a robot with a turn method, where sending the turn message causes the robot to turn left sometimes and the same message causes it to turn right at other times, by employing different strategies. Let's see how to do this.

First note that objects model things. Some objects model things like robots that seem concrete. Other objects can model things of pure thought, like strategies. Objects can model almost anything you can think of.

Strategy is not built in to the robot infrastructure, however. It is something you define and create yourself. There can be several kinds of strategies and several kinds of delegation also. We will explore only a simple case.

We will use a Java interface to define what we mean here by a strategy.

```
public interface Strategy
{
        public void doIt(UrRobot which);
}
```

This just defines what strategies "look like", without defining any strategies themselves. A strategy will, indirectly, form the body of one of our methods. A class can implement this interface, but to do so it should implement the doIt method of the Strategy interface (otherwise it would be abstract). And note that the doIt method of any strategy will require a parameter of type UrRobot when we define it and an argument of type UrRobot (or a more specific kind) when we invoke the method. Within any doIt method it will be possible to send messages to this UrRobot object.

For starters, it will be useful to have a strategy that does nothing.

```
public class NullStrategy implements Strategy
{
  public void doIt(UrRobot which)
  {
        // nothing
  }
}
```

Not very interesting, of course, but certainly simple. This is a concrete class, but it is not a robot class. It defines objects, but not robots since we don't extend UrRobot. Classes may implement zero or more interfaces. When they implement an interface, they must define the methods declared by the interface. In NullStrategy we implement the doIt method by giving it an empty body. Note that the parameter list must match that of the interface exactly.

This doIt method has a UrRobot parameter named *which*. The intent is to use the body of the method to do something with the robot referred to by the name *which* by sending it some messages.

Now we will see how to use a strategy. Let's create a special kind of BeeperLayer called a StrategyLayer.

```
public class StrategyLayer extends BeeperLayer
{
  public StrategyLayer(int street, int avenue,
     Direction direction, int beepers, Strategy strategy)
  {       super(street, avenue, direction, beepers);
          myStrategy = strategy;
  }

  public void putBeepers()
  {
          myStrategy.doIt(this);
  }

  private Strategy myStrategy = null;
}
```

There are a few things to note here. First is that we have a new parameter in our constructor. When we create a StrategyLayer we need to give it a Strategy object as well as the usual arguments, so the strategy must be created before the StrategyLayer robot is created. Note that the reference to the super (super class constructor) must begin the constructor. The StrategyLayer will remember this object in its instance variable myStrategy. Most important, is that when we call putBeepers the StrategyLayer will delegate the action performed to whatever Strategy it currently has. In other words, when you ask a StrategyLayer to putBeepers, the StrategyLayer in turn asks its myStrategy to doIt. This is delegation. You can think of the StrategyLayer object as a client of the Strategy in this interaction, and the Strategy as a server. Object interactions always have this basic client-server character to them. The sender of any message is the client, and the receiver is the server.

When this doIt message is sent to the strategy, the robot also sends a reference to itself as the parameter. The idea, is that the strategy will send other messages to this robot, almost as if the robot had sent messages to itself.

Now it gets interesting. Suppose we create a TwoBeeperStrategy as follows.

```
public class TwoBeeperStrategy implements Strategy
{
  public void doIt(UrRobot aRobot)
  {
          aRobot.putBeeper();
          aRobot.putBeeper();
  }
}
```

Now we can create something that behaves like a TwoRowLayer from the StrategyLayer class with just

```
lisa = new StrategyLayer(1, 3, East, infinity, new
TwoBeeperStrategy());
```

A simple shorthand was used here also. Instead of declaring a variable to refer to the strategy, we just created it where the argument to the StrategyLayer's constructor requried a strategy. We could have expanded this as

```
Strategy twoRow = new TwoBeeperStrategy();
BeeperLayer lisa = new StrategyLayer(1, 3, East, infinity,
  twoRow);
```

However, if we don't otherwise need to refer to the strategy, there is no need for the reference variable. We can just create a new strategy wherever a strategy is needed, without providing it a name.

Similarly we could create another StrategyLayer using a similar ThreeBeeperStrategy. However, we can do something much more interesting, which is to show StrategyLayers how to change their strategy as the program executes. Suppose we give the StrategyLayer class a new method:

```
public void setStrategy(Strategy strategy)
{      myStrategy = strategy;
}
```

The = operator in this method is assignment, which we have seen earlier in the chapter, and it is the means by which we get an object to remember something. We assign a new value to one of its instance variables. This just says that the robot will remember a new value in its myStrategy field. The new value to be remembered is provided by the parameter of the method. If it was already remembering another strategy when this occurs, it will forget that strategy and now remember this one instead. Actually, assignment was used in the constructor of StrategyLayer as well.

Then a strategy object can have its strategy changed whenever we like. It might even be advantageous to change the rest of the class slightly to make maximum use of this new feature.

```
public class StrategyLayer extends BeeperLayer
{
  public StrategyLayer(int street, int avenue,
     Direction direction, int beepers)
  {       super(street, avenue, direction, beepers);
  }

  public void setStrategy(Strategy strategy)
  {       myStrategy = strategy;
  }

  public void putBeepers()
  {
          myStrategy.doIt(this);
  }

  private Strategy myStrategy = new NullStrategy();
}
```

Now we create a new StrategyLayer with a NullStrategy for is initial strategy and have a simpler constructor. When we ask it to putBeepers, it does nothing at all unless we give it a new strategy. However, we can give it any strategy we like. For example

```
BeeperLayer lisa = new StrategyLayer(3, 4, East, infinity);
lisa.setStrategy(new TwoBeeperStrategy());
lisa.layBeepers();
...
lisa.setStrategy(new ThreeBeeperStrategy());
lisa.layBeepers();
...
```

In the above, it might be advantageous to actually name the two strategies. Since each strategy object might be needed more than once in the program. If lisa wants to go back to the two beeper strategy at the end of the above, then having a name for the one we created means that we can just reuse it and don't need to create another.

At any given time, lisa is delegating the putBeepers action to whichever strategy object it holds. It does this by simply sending the doIt message to the strategy. The strategy objects behave polymorphically, each doing what it was designed to do. The lisa robot doesn't need to know what kind of strategy it is, just that it does implement the Strategy interface so that the doIt method can behave polymorphically. And note that it is an invariant of BeeperLayers that they have a valid strategy.

Here we have had strategies only for putting down beepers. You could, however, also have strategies for moving, or for doing complicated combinations of things. All you need in order to make things useful is some way to change the strategy as needed. Here we used a setStrategy method, but there are other interesting ways as well.

For example, a robot can alternate between two known strategies. Suppose we want a robot that will walk around a rectangle that is three blocks long in one direction and two blocks long in the other. I'm sure you could write this easily, but here is another way that might give you some ideas about the possibilities of strategies.

```
public class BlockWalker extends UrRobot
{
  public BlockWalker(int street, int avenue,
     Direction direction, int beepers)
  {
         super(street, avenue, direction, beepers);
  }

  public void walkASide()
  {
         myStrategy.doIt(this);
         swapStrategies();
  }

  private void swapStrategies()
  {
         Strategy tempStrategy = myStrategy;
         myStrategy = otherStrategy;
         otherStrategy = tempStrategy;
  }
```

```
        private Strategy myStrategy = new ThreeBlockStrategy();
        private Strategy otherStrategy = new TwoBlockStrategy();

    }
```

Such a robot starts out with a ThreeBlockStrategy as the one it will delegate to. (I assume you can write the ThreeBlockStrategy and the TwoBlockStrategy classes.) However, whenever it is asked to walkASide, it not only performs that strategy, it also replaces that strategy with the other one it is remembering, while also remembering the current one as if it were the other. Think about why swapStrategies requires three assignments and cannot be done in two. For example, if you had two very large, fragile, and valuable objects, one in each hand and you wanted to swap them with each hand holding the other object, it would be helpful to have a third hand.

Now, if we set a BlockWalker, say john, down in the world and execute

```
john.walkASide();
john.turnLeft();
john.walkASide();
john.turnLeft();
john.walkASide();
john.turnLeft();
john.walkASide();
john.turnLeft();
```

then it will walk around a block that is three blocks in one direction and two in the other. We say that the BlockWalker changes its **state** each time it executes walkASide and its current state is the strategy it will use the next time it is asked to walkASide. The state of an object is both what it remembers and what situation it finds itself in in the world at the moment.

There is a bit of a problem, however. All of this works quite nicely if you want to use just the methods of UrRobot in your strategies. However, it is of most use when you apply it using actions of your own classes. If you look back at the TwoBeeperStrategy, for example, we see that it just uses putBeeper which is defined in UrRobot. However, suppose that we wanted to write a strategy that used methods from Harvester in the previous chapter.

```
public void doIt(UrRobot aRobot)
{
        aRobot.putBeeper();
        aRobot.harvestTwoRows();
        aRobot.putBeeper();
}
```

This doesn't work, because harvestTwoRows is not a method of UrRobot and the declaration of doIt requires a parameter of type UrRobot. Well, a Harvester is, in fact, an UrRobot, but not all UrRobots are Harvesters. All the language procesor (compiler) knows is that the local declaration says UrRobot, so all it will let us do is send messages defined in that class. Unfortunately we can't just change the declaration, since then the method signature doesn't match that of the Strategy interface. The signature of a method includes the name as well as the types of its parameters in the order they were defined. We require exact matches of signature when we implement an interface or override a method.

There are two possible solutions to the dilemma. First, there is nothing magic about how we wrote the Strategy interface. If we have a problem that deals primarily with harvesters and expect that we will want to call methods of Harvester from the strategies, then we could write a different interface, say HarvesterStrategy, that has a different method (or set of methods) defined in the interface. We would then require these instead by having Harvester named in the parameter instead of UrRobot.

On the other hand, if we do want to use this general Strategy framework, then not all is lost. If you can be sure, from your own analysis of the program, that your new Strategy class will be used only with Harvester robots, then you can slightly modify the second message in the above to tell the compiler of your belief.

```
public void doIt(UrRobot aRobot)
{
        aRobot.putBeeper();
        ((Harvester)aRobot).harvestTwoRows();
        aRobot.putBeeper();
}
```

This is called a "cast." A cast assures the compiler that only Harvesters should appear here. Actually the part **(Harvester)aRobot** is the cast. The parentheses are required. The extra parentheses in the above use are necessary since it is the aRobot that we want the compiler to consider as a Harvester (instead of the more general UrRobot of the declaration), and not the entire expression that follows (aRobot.harvestTwoRows()), which is void in this case anyway. Note that casts are checked by Java. If you cast in error, your program is broken (intent error) but the error will be caught when it runs and this is executed. You will then be told you have a ClassCastException and you will need to think about why you cast in error and fix it.

It is important to remember that a cast does not change the type of anything. Nor can it make an otherwise incorrect program correct. It just assures the compiler that you know more about what is going on here than can reasonably be inferred from reading the current statement. In this case you know that *aRobot* really refers to a Harvester, not something more general, in spite of the declaration of the parameter as UrRobot.

4.7 Java Enumerations and More on Strategies

Now that we know how to use a strategy and how to change a strategy, let's try something fun. Imagine a situation like this. Suppose we have a Spy robot that has an initial set of clues (a Strategy) to move somewhere. When it does that it meets another Accomplice robot on the final corner and gets a set of clues (another Strategy) from the accomplice. It takes that Strategy for its own and follows it, which should take it to another corner with another Accomplice. This can be repeated for as many steps as you like. The very last Strategy will direct the original Spy to some treasure, say. We can do most of this now, except the handoff. Up until now, if a robot wants to exchange things, beepers or strategies, with another, it must know the name of the other, but this would be bad practice for spies.

When a robot arrives on a corner there will be a **collection** of other robots on the same corner. Usually this collection is empty. But not always. When the spy arrives on the corner with the accomplice the collection will not be empty since it will contain the accomplice. We can ask about this collection using any robot's neighbors() method. This method will give us information about all the other robots on the same corner. The neighbors method is part of UrRobot, but we have not yet referred to it.

So far all of our methods have been void methods, meaning that they do not return information. They represent actions: things robots do. Now we need to look at the other situation. Recall that some objects remember things. Sometimes a user (client) of that object may want some of the information remembered by another object. This new kind of method is used to obtain it. When the method is defined, it tells what kind of information it provides.

The neighbors method in the UrRobot class looks like this:

```
public Enumeration neighbors()
{ ...
}
```

So the neighbors method returns an object to us of type Enumeration.

Objects **do** things and objects **remember** things. So we have void methods, sometimes called "procedural" so that we can ask an object to do something. We also have these other methods (called "functional") that we use to ask an object to return information of some kind to us. These are also called *accessors*. An object can simply remember this information, it can compute it as needed (which, in fact, is what happens in this case) or it can ask another object (delegation again) for the information that it will then return to the message sender.

Enumerations are defined as part of the Java language libraries in a package called java.util (for utilities). To make use of this, your program should put an import statement at the beginning, just after your own package statement:

```
import kareltherobot.*;
import java.util.Enumeration;
```

This will make it easy to use Enumerations. Without the import statement you would need to say java.util.Enumeration whenever we use the term. With the import statement, Enumeration is sufficient.

The Enumeration interface is defined in java.util like this:

```
public interface Enumeration
{
        public Object nextElement();
        public boolean hasMoreElements();
}
```

We will discuss the second of these methods in the next two chapters, but for now we focus on the nextElement method of an enumeration. Notice that the nextElement method of an Enumeration returns Objects. This means that whenever we send the nextElement message to an Enumeration we get an Object back. The idea is that an Enumeration remembers a collection of things (objects) and gives us one of them when we ask it for its nextElement.

When a collection is not empty, and has not been completely enumerated already, an enumeration's nextElement() will give us an element (the next one) from the collection. Calling the method in any other situation is an (intent) error and will result in a NoSuchElementException. This will generally halt your program and you will need to fix it.

In general, we "enumerate" a collection by creating an Enumeration over it, and then sending the nextElement message to the enumeration several times. The number of times must be less than or equal to the size of the collection. We will see later how hasMoreElements helps with this.

The UrRobot class defines a method, neighbors(), that returns an Enumeration over the robots on the same corner as the one that executes it, though the one executing it will NOT be part of the collection or the Enumeration. So a better way to say it is that neighbors() is an enumeration over the *other* robots on the same corner. If we can be sure that there *is* another robot on the same corner, then we can safely call nextElement() of such an enumeration at least once.

But if a robot executes its neighbors() method on a corner with no robots we will get an Enumeration over an empty collection and then the NoSuchElementException will occur the first time we send the enumeration a nextElement() message. If there is only one neighbor when we obtain the enumeration, then the error will occur if we send the nextElement() message a second time. (In Chapter 5 we will learn how to avoid the possible exception, and, in Chapter 6, how to process the entire collection using the enumeration.)

So, when our spy meets its accomplice on a corner, the spy can get a reference to the accomplice by executing

```
Enumeration myNeighbors  = this.neighbors();
Accomplice myAccomplice  = myNeighbors.nextElement();
```

Of course, the second instruction is an execution error if you are on a corner with no other robots. Actually, the second instruction above is a syntax error in Java in any case, since nextElement returns an Object and we are trying to remember the returned reference in a variable of type Accomplice (or some other, more specific robot type, if you like). To correct this we must assure the Java system that in this situation anything returned by nextElement will indeed be of the correct class. We do this with a cast.

```
Accomplice myAccomplice =
  (Accomplice)myNeighbors.nextElement();
```

But doing this also implies that you know the robot on the corner is an Accomplice, and that if there are several, that they are all Accomplices, since we don't know which of them will be returned by nextElement if there are several. Notice that Enumerations are objects and they have behavior. They also remember the collection over which they iterate, but that collection is invisible to us. Here the robot world keeps that information inside itself.

Let us put this together so that we can do our Spy's search. We need two classes. The Accomplice is simpler, so we write it first. It remembers some strategy and has a way to tell it to another robot who asks for it.

```
public class Accomplice extends UrRobot
{

  public Accomplice(int street, int avenue,
     Direction direction, int beepers, Strategy strategy)
  {
        super(street, avenue, direction, beepers);
        myStrategy = strategy;
  }

  public Strategy requestStrategy()
  {     return myStrategy;
  }

  private Strategy myStrategy = null;
}
```

Again, we see a method returning information. requestStrategy is a method that returns a Strategy.

Now we can create several strategy classes. One to direct the robot to turn left and then move three times, or whatever you want. That is easy and we leave it to you. Next we see how the Spy robot will use the accomplices.

```
public class Spy extends UrRobot
{
        public Spy(int street, int avenue, Direction direction,
             int beepers, Strategy initialStrategy)
        {
                super(street, avenue, direction, beepers);
                myStrategy = initialStrategy;
        }

        public void getNextClue()
        {
         // precondition. Robot must be on a corner with another robot.
                Enumeration neighbors = neighbors();
                Accomplice accomplice =
                        (Accomplice)neighbors.nextElement();
                myStrategy = accomplice.requestStrategy();
        }

        public void followStrategy()
        {
                myStrategy.doIt(this); // leaves you at next accomplice
        }

        private Strategy myStrategy = null;
}
```

When you create a Spy, you must give it the strategy that will let it find the first accomplice. Each accomplice will provide one that takes it to the next, and the last "clue" will take you to the final target. If we have already created and placed some accomplices and some strategies, including one called StartStrategy, we can then say.

```
Spy bernie = new Spy(1, 1, East, 0, new StartStrategy())
bernie.followStrategy();
bernie.getNextClue();
bernie.followStrategy();
bernie.getNextClue();
bernie.followStrategy();
bernie.getNextClue();
bernie.followStrategy();
```

Again we emphasize the relationship to polymorphism here and the meaning of the word. Put simply, all it really means is that each object knows what to do when it receives a proper message. You can't force an object to do something else. We can refer to different objects at different times in the same program by a single name, and the actual behavior of a message sent through that name to an object will depend on the object to which the name actually refers. This means that each object is in complete control of what it does, depending on its class and its current state. The behavior is under the control of the object and not the other program code that makes requests of the object.

Finally, note that once a robot has established a reference to its neighbor Enumeration, then all the robots can move off this corner without affecting the Enumeration. The robot that sent the neighbors() message has access to all of the robots that were neighbors at the point at which the message was sent. Thus, the Enumeration is like a snapshot of what was the state of that corner at that moment.

4.8 Decorators

Let's start writing such a Spy walk, considering what other tricks we might employ. Here is a simple situation. The Spy will start at the origin facing East. The first Accomplice will be three blocks to the East. The next will be three blocks East beyond the first. The third will be three blocks north of the second. Finally the "treasure" will be four blocks East of the last Accomplice. The Spy doesn't know all of this, of course, and only has a clue (Strategy) to reach the first. So the initial Strategy will be a ThreeStep.

```
public class ThreeStep implements Strategy
{
  public void doIt(UrRobot aRobot)
  {
          aRobot.move();
          aRobot.move();
          aRobot.move();
  }
}
```

Interestingly, we can use the same Strategy for that of the first Accomplice, so that simplifies our work a bit. We not only don't need another class, we can reuse the same ThreeStep object. That will get us to the second Accomplice on 1st street and 7th avenue. Since the Spy arrives here from the West, all it needs to do from here to find the nrext Accomplice is to turnLeft and then apply the ThreeStep strategy again, but there is no way for the Spy itself to know about the turn. It needs to be incorporated into another Strategy. We can write it simply, of course, but if we do so, we will be writing the same code (for three moves) a second time in the program.

We can, however, apply another technique that lets us modify a strategy's operation in a variety of ways without changing the code defined in the strategy. This works beyond strategies, by the way. We just employ it here for convenience. The new idea is called a Decorator. A Decorator makes something "nicer" without changing its character. Much like you decorate a cake or a house. The first thing to know about a strategy decorator is that it is itself a strategy. The second thing to know is that it knows about another strategy -- the one it decorates. It learns of this in its constructor. So here is a LeftTurnDecorator for strategies.

```
public class LeftTurnDecorator implements Strategy
{
  public LeftTurnDecorator(Strategy decorated)
  {
         myDecorated = decorated;
  }

  public void doIt(UrRobot aRobot)
  {
         aRobot.turnLeft();
         myDecorated.doIt(aRobot);
  }

  private Strategy myDecorated = null;
}
```

Remember that, as a Strategy, it must implement the doIt method. A strategy decorator does something somewhere in its doIt method and then sends the same doIt message to the strategy that it is decorating. So if we create a new strategy with

```
Strategy aStrategy = new LeftTurnDecorator(new ThreeStep());
```

then the resulting strategy is a decoration of a ThreeStep, and which also does a leftTurn before it executes the ThreeStep strategy, so it turns left and then moves three blocks. Employing this strategy in the second Accomplice will get us to the third. Note that two objects are created here; a new ThreeStep and a new LeftTurnDecorator.

We arrive at the third Accomplice from the South, so we need to turn right and then walk four blocks. Again this could be done with an entirely new class, but we could also again decorate a ThreeStep with another decorator that turns left three times **before** applying the decorated strategy and **then** moves once afterwards. This emphasizes that the decorator can do anything it wants, before *and* after sending the doIt message to the Strategy it decorates.

While the situation here is somewhat simplified, this works best when the basic strategies are somewhat complex and the modifications are quite simple. And note that the decorated strategy's doIt is executed in full. We don't modify it. We just create a new strategy that uses it: surrounds it, actually.

The key to a Decorator is that it decorates an object of some interface that it also implements. In other words, it remembers another object implementing some interface that also itself implements the same interface. Finally, some method of the interface is implemented by doing something and also sending the same message to the object it has remembered.

And it is important to remember that since a strategy decorator is itself a strategy it can itself be decorated by another StrategyDecorator. Quite complex behavior can be built up in parts from a sequence of decorators on a basic strategy. Each decorator can do some simple thing. When well done, decorators can also be generally useful. For example, our left turn decorator could be applied to other strategies than just walk strategies.

One way to think of decorators is as if the decorated object is *inside* the decorator. A message sent to it has to pass through the decorator to get to it. Likewise, if you have a strategy with an action method that returns a value, then that value has to pass back out through the decorator to get back to the original client. The decorator can make modifications both as the message passes in, and as the returned value passes back out. While this may not be a precisely accurate picture, it is helpful to pretend that it is.

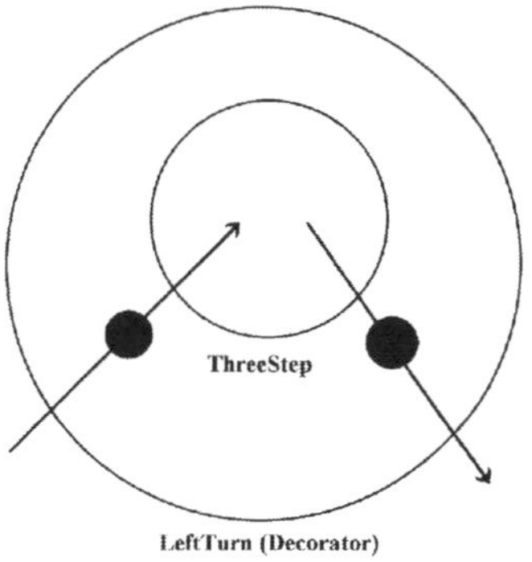

Figure 4.2 A Decorator and the Object it Decorates

Here the arrows represent a message moving through the decorator and the object it decorates, and the two bullet points are places where the decorator can make changes and additions.

4.9 Observers

In this section we will see another means of building and using robot teams. The idea is that a controller robot will perform some basic actions that will cause another controlled robot to automatically do something. We will also provide a flexible way for the controller robot to learn about the controlled robot. In general, the first robot could control several this way, but we will only show one. The controlling robot is called "observable" and the one controlled is called an "observer". This is because the one controlled does nothing until it *observes* the other doing the thing that causes it to carry out its action.

Actually, the common notion of the meaning of the word observer might be misleading here. Usually, the observed takes no action to cue the observer and may not even know of the existence of the observer. Imagine yourself at a sporting event in which your friend is a participant and you are a spectator. At various times you decide to take a picture of your friend in competition. This is the normal meaning, but not the one we intend here. Instead, imagine yourself at the same sporting event, but you have prearranged with your friend that you will only take her picture when she waves to you. So, the observed actually signals the observer. Note that you could arrange to do this for several friends at the same event. Likewise your friend could have the same arrangement with several observers.

First we need an agreement or "protocol" that the two robots can agree upon to set up their cooperation. We do this in the form of an interface that is implemented by the observer.

```
public interface RobotListener
{
  public void action();
}
```

Next we need a version of this that does nothing at all.

```
public class NullListener implements RobotListener
{
  public void action()
  {
          // nothing
  }
}
```

We will create a very simple example here, of a robot that just walks one block when the robot it is observing does the key thing that causes the action to occur.

```
public class WalkListener extends UrRobot implements RobotListener
{
  public WalkListener(int street, int avenue,
     Direction direction, int beepers)
  {
          super(street, avenue, direction, beepers);
  }

  public void action()
  {
          move();
  }
}
```

So, whenever such a robot is sent the action message, it just moves, but it could do anything you like. If you look carefully at the definition of RobotListener, you will notice that it doesn't actually require that a RobotListener be another Robot. This is intentional. Any object can observe a robot by implementing this interface. On the other hand, a WalkListener is an UrRobot that also observes another robot. However, it doesn't know which robot it observes and in fact, can observer many. We will see how next.

Now we will build a robot that can have one observer and whenever it picks up a beeper, it signals to its observer to do whatever action the observer is prepared to do. Note that the action performed by the observer (perhaps a WalkListener) is defined there, not here.

```
public class ObservablePicker extends UrRobot
{
  public ObservablePicker(int street, int avenue,
     Direction direction, int beepers)
  {
        super(street, avenue, direction beepers);
  }

  public void register(RobotListener listener)
  {
        myListener = listener;
  }

  public void pickBeeper()
  {
        super.pickBeeper();
        myListener.action();
  }

  private RobotListener myListener = new NullListener();
}
```

Again, note that the observable does not define the action of the observer, but only arranges for it to be executed. The register method is used to let an observable robot know who wants to observe it. Finally note that we protect against the possibility of forgetting to register any observer, by initializing myListener with one that does nothing. The pickBeeper method is overridden here to also signal our observer to perform its action.

We create such robots as follows.

```
WalkListener tom = new WalkListener(1, 1, North, 0);
ObservablePicker jerry = new ObservablePicker(2, 3, East, 0);
jerry.register(tom);
```

Now, whenever jerry picks a beeper, tom moves one block. An observable knows very little about its observer, only that it implements the action method. The observer knows nothing at all of the object it is observing. This "decoupling" between the definitions of the two robot classes allows for great flexibility. We can create complex observers. We can create complex observables. We can do both, independently. All that we need is an agreed upon method in the observer and a registration mechanism in the observable logically held together by an interface. In a sense, it is the interface that forms a glue between these two kinds of objects.

Observers, like strategies, can use any of the techniques we have discussed so far and will discuss later in the book. In particular, they can create additional robots and send them instructions. This can be used to create extremely complex behavior.

Java actually has something like our simple observers in its libraries but it is much more sophisticated there. In particular it permits an observable to have several observers. When you press a button in a Java interface, for example, an observer carries out the task defined for that button by the programmer of the interface.

4.10 Final Words on Polymorphism

Polymorphism is both simple and profound. Simply stated it just means that each robot (or object) does what it knows how to do when sent any message. However, the consequences of this are quite deep. In particular, it means that when you as a programmer send a message to a robot referred to by a reference, you don't know in general what will happen. You know the type of the reference, but perhaps not the type of the object it points to. You don't decide. The robot to which the reference points will decide. You might think you have a simple UrRobot, since the reference variable you use has that type, but the variable might point to a robot in some sub class of UrRobot instead. So even if you say something as simple as

```
myRobot.move();
```

you can't be sure what will happen. In particular, the following is legal

```
UrRobot mary = new MileMover();
```

in which case mary.move() will move a mile, rather than a block. Combining this with the ability to write a method that has a parameter of type UrRobot to which you can pass any robot type, and again with the possibility of changeable strategies in robots, means that what happens when you write a message, may not be precisely determinable from reading the program, but only from executing it. Moreover, the same variable can refer to different robots of different types at different times in the execution of the program.

This doesn't mean that all is chaos, however. What it does mean is that you need to give meaningful names to methods, and also guarantee that when that kind of robot receives that message, it will do the right thing for that kind of robot. Then, when some programmers decide to use that kind of robot, they can be assured that sending it a message will do the right thing, even if they don't know precisely what that will be. The main means of achieving this is to keep each class simple, make its name descriptive of what it does, and make it internally consistent and difficult to use incorrectly.

Perhaps even more important are two rules: one for interfaces and one for inheritance. When you define an interface you need to have a good idea about what the methods defined there mean logically, even though you don't implement them. When you do implement the interface in a class, make sure that your implementation of the methods is consistent with your logical meaning. If you do this consistently, then the interface will have a logical meaning that a programmer can depend upon, even though they don't know what code will be executed.

The rule for inheritance is a little more precise. Think of inheritance as meaning specialization. If class SpecialRobot extends class OrdinaryRobot, for example, make sure that logically speaking a special robot is really just a specialized kind of ordinary robot. So it wouldn't make sense for an IceSkaterRobot to extend Carpenter, for example, since ice skaters are not specialized carpenters, but a different kind of thing altogether. If you do this faithfully, then the logic of your program will match the rules of assignment in the language. Our shorthand for this is called the IS-A rule. Ask "IS-A skater a carpenter?" The answer is no, so skater classes should not be subclasses of any Carpenter class. On the other hand a "Carpenter IS-A UrRobot" and has all of its capabilities and more, so it is appropriate to make Carpenter a subclass of UrRobot. Not that a strategy is not a robot at all, but it is an object. If you create a class and don't specify what it extends, then it automatically extends the built-in Object class.

You may have noticed that we have been careful to initialize all of our instance fields when we declare them. This helps avoid problems. We have also used null strategies and listeners to make sure that every class that requires these has a default version available even if the user doesn't supply a more useful one. All of this is necessary to guarantee that every class you write can be guaranteed to **do the right thing** when used.

Finally, we note that we have two different kinds of decomposition of programs. Stepwise refinement takes a complex method and breaks it into simpler methods. Polymorphism, on the other hand, takes related tasks and puts them into different objects, perhaps strategies or similar things.

4.11 Important Ideas From This Chapter

polymorphism
abstract class
interface
import
delegation
strategy
null strategy
decorator
observer
client, server
observable
instance variable (field)
parameter
object invariant
enumeration
return value
IS-A

4.12 Problem Set

1. Re-do problem 3.12-5, but this time use five robots; one for each letter to be written. You may choose each robot's starting position.
2. Re-do problem 3.12-5, but this time use 5 robots; one for each street.
3. Re-do problem 3.12-5, but this time use 17 robots; one for each avenue.
4. Re-do Problem 3.12-6, using 5 robots, one for each digit and one for the colon.
5. Re-do Problem 3.12-7 with four robots. You may choose the starting positions of each robot.
6. Re-do Problem 3.12-7 with eight robots. You may choose the starting positions of each robot.
7. Re-do Problem 3.12-7 with a Choreographer and 3 helpers. You may choose the starting positions of each robot.
8. Solve the harvester problem of Chapter 3 again using a team of six robots. Each robot can harvest a single row.

9. There is a simpler kind of strategy in which the robot is not passed to the doIt method.

```
public interface Controller
{
        public void controlIt();
}
```

For this to work, however, the class that implements the interface needs to remember a robot on which it will act. One way to do this is to provide a constructor that is passed a robot, which is saved within the strategy object in a "myRobot" instance variable. When a controller is sent the controlIt message, it applies the strategy to its own saved robot. This is quite nice, except that such strategies can't be exchanged between robots as easily, since if a robot john passes its strategy to george, then the strategy still refers to john and so if george sends controlIt to the strategy, it will manipulate john and not george. This can be useful, actually, and makes george something like a choreographer or a contractor for john. This is why we called the interface Controller. Try to exploit this in a fun and interesting way.

See Controllers and Inner Classes in Section 5 of the Appendix.

10. What happens if a Spy chase causes a Spy to return to an Accomplice for the second time? Are there situations in which this is OK? Are there situations in which this is dangerous? Demonstrate each situation with a separate program for each.

11. Actually, it is possible for robots to adopt strategies of other robots even if the version of Problem 9 is used. Explain how. Write a program to test your ideas.

12. Write a beeper layer program, using strategies, that allows a single robot to place a beeper on every other corner of a 5 by 5 field. Do this by alternating strategies as you go along a single row, but starting each row with the "one beeper" strategy.

13. A class that implements an interface must implement the methods defined in that interface, but it can implement additional ones as well. Build three interesting controller classes. Give each one an additional method undoIt that will do just the opposite of the doIt method. The meaning of this is that if you doIt and then immediately undoIt, the robot using the strategy will return to its original location and orientation. Moreover, if it placed any beepers on the way, it will pick them up, etc. Note that if you do this correctly and if you apply (say) three strategies and then immediately undo each in the opposite order, they should all be undone.

14. Develop a set of rules that you can use to make writing undoIt methods easier. For example, how do you undo the following?

```
move();
move();
turnLeft();
move();
turnRight();
move();
turnLeft();
```

15. Write and test a new observer that normally sits on First street and Second avenue. Whenever its observable sends it an action message it leaves a beeper at the origin and returns to its original location.

16. Write and test an observable that signals its observer whenever it moves, puts a beeper, picks a beeper, or turns left.

17. Two Spy robots who don't know each other's name, meet on a pre arranged corner and exchange clues (Strategy objects). Each then follows the strategy it was given. Test this.

18. (hard). Revisit Problem 14. Will your rules still work if the programmer overrides some of the UrRobot primitives? Suppose, for example, that move has been defined as:

```
public void move()
{
        super.move();
        super.move();
        turnRight();
        super.move();
        turnLeft();
}
```

Would it also work if we had omitted the final turnLeft()? What do you need to do to fix this, so that undo still works in such a class?

19. A Contractor is standing at the origin with one Roofer, one Carpenter, and one Mason. The Contractor gives each of them a strategy telling where a house is supposed to be constructed and sends them off to build it. Write this program. It should be one strategy for all, probably. Note that the same Strategy object can be shared by all. (Why?)

20. Here is an example of a fairly common problem. You want an object to behave one way the first time it gets a message and a second way each time thereafter that it gets the same message. For example, suppose you want something like a beeper layer to lay down two beepers on each corner of the first row of a rectangular field, but three beepers on each corner of all the other rows. Use strategies to solve this so that the robot automatically changes its strategy at the right time.

21. Create a beeper laying robot that starts somewhere in the world with an infinite number of beepers in its beeper bag and begins to lay down beepers in a "left handed" spiral pattern until it eventually runs into one of the bounding walls. Use a strategy that you modify at each turn by adding a decorator. The idea is if you walk in one direction for a certain number of steps, turn left, and then walk in the new direction for one greater than the old number of steps, and repeat this over and over, you will walk in a widening spiral. At each step you lay down one beeper. Except for the fact that the robot must eventually come to one of the boundary walls, this would be an infinite program. This can be done with a single basic strategy class and a single decorator class, in addition to a robot that uses a strategy and knows just the right way to modify its own strategy. Hint. You many need a lot of objects, but only these few classes.

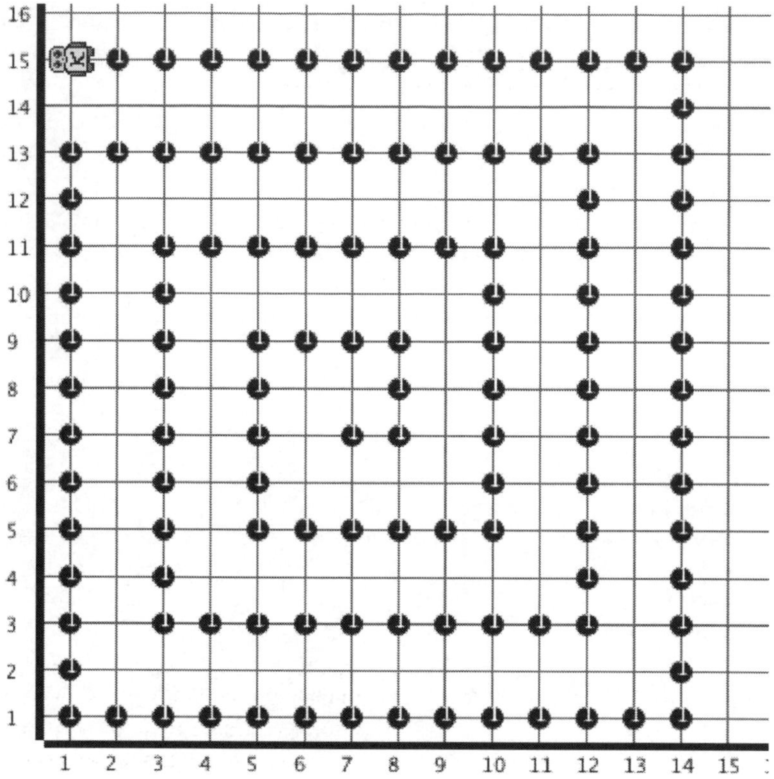

Figure 4.3 A Spiral Walk

22. Here we want to run a robot relay race using Observers. Imagine three robots at different avenues along first street. Starting from the West, the first two are observable robots and the last two are observers. Each observer observes the robot to its West. Note that the middle one both observes the one to the West and is observed by the one to its East. The robot to the West will carry a beeper to the one in the middle and then put it down and signal the one in the middle. When signaled, the one in the middle will pick up the beeper and carry it to the one to the east and put it down. It will then signal the one on that corner which will then pick up the beeper and carry it farther along. Suppose the robots start on first, fifth, and ninth avenues and the finish line is at thirteenth. Note that the robots should come from different classes. (How many classes are required? Would an abstract superclass help here? How much harder would it be to have four robots instead of three?)

5 Conditionally Executing Instructions

In the preceding chapters, a Robot's exact initial situation was known at the start of a task. When we wrote our programs, this information allowed karel to find beepers and avoid running into walls. However, these programs worked only in their specific initial situations. If a robot tried to execute one of these programs in a slightly different initial situation, the robot would almost certainly perform an error shutoff.

What a robot needs is the ability to survey its local environment and then decide from that information what to do next. The IF instructions are discussed in this chapter. There are two versions of the IF statement, the IF and the IF/ELSE. They provide robots with their decision ability. Both allow a robot to test its environment and, depending on the result of the test, decide which instruction to execute next. The IF instructions enable us to write much more general programs for our robots that accomplish the same task in a variety of similar, but different, initial situations. These instructions are especially suited for letting robots deal with things like walls and beepers that are not objects. If they were objects, we could interact with them polymorphically as we saw in the last chapter.

Robot programs contain several different kinds of instructions. The first, and most important, is the message to a robot. These messages are sent to robots, either by the pilot (when they appear in the main task block) or by another robot (when they occur in a method of some class). The action associated with this kind of instruction is defined by the corresponding method in the class of the robot to which the message is directed.

Another kind of instruction is the delivery specification, which is sent to the factory to construct a new robot and have the helicopter pilot deliver it.

The IF instruction is yet another different kind of instruction. It provides a way to structure the program itself. The rest of this chapter and the next are going to add to this list of kinds of instructions.

5.1 The IF Instruction

The IF instruction is the simpler of the two IF variants. It has the following general form.

```
if ( <test> )
{
    <instruction-list>
}
```

The IF instruction introduces the new reserved word **if** (spelled in lowercase). The reserved word **if** signals a program reader that an IF instruction is present, and the braces enclose a list of instructions. The<instruction-list> is known as the THEN clause of the instruction. We indent the IF instruction as shown, to highlight the fact that <instruction-list> is a component of the IF instruction. Note that we do not follow the right brace of an IF instruction with a semicolon. An IF instruction is not a message to any robot.

A robot executes the IF instruction by first checking whether <test> contained in the parentheses is true or false in the robot's current situation. If <test> is true, the robot executes <instruction-list>; if <test> is false, the robot skips <instruction-list>. In either case, the robot is then finished executing the entire IF instruction. For an example, let's look at the program fragment[1] below, which consists of an IF instruction followed by a move message. Assume that this fragment is contained in a method of some class. Some robot of that class will be executing the code[6].

```
if ( nextToABeeper())
{
        pickBeeper();
}
turnLeft();
```

When this IF instruction is executed by the robot, it first checks whether it is next to (on the same corner as) a beeper. If it finds that nextToABeeper is true, the robot executes the THEN clause, which instructs it to execute pickBeeper. The robot is now finished executing the IF instruction, and continues by executing the rest of the instructions, starting at the turnLeft message.

Now suppose that there are no beepers on the corner when the robot executes this program fragment. In this case nextToABeeper is false, so the robot does not execute the THEN clause. Instead, it skips directly to the turnLeft message and continues executing the program from there. The result of this second case is that the robot executes the IF instruction by doing nothing more than asking itself to check whether or not it is next to a beeper. An error shutoff cannot occur in either case because the robot executes the pickBeeper message only if it confirms the presence of at least one beeper on the corner.

It is also possible to use IF statements in the main task block, but here we must be careful to ask a particular robot about its state. We ask about a robot's state by sending messages, just as we ask robots to perform instructions using messages. If we want to know about the state of a particular robot we must send a message to that robot. When we don't name any robot at all, we are asking about the state of the robot actually executing the current instruction. Since the main task block is not a method of any particular robot, we must use a robot's name there.

```
if ( karel.nextToABeeper())
{
        karel.pickBeeper();
}
karel.turnLeft();
```

5.2 The Conditions That Robots Can Test

In Chapter 1 we briefly discussed the sensory capabilities of robots. We learned that a robot can see walls, hear beepers, determine which direction it is facing, and feel if there are any beepers in its beeper-bag or other robots on its current corner. The conditions that a robot can test are divided according to these same four categories.

---

[6] To conserve space, we often demonstrate a programming idea without writing a complete robot program or new method. Instead, we just write the necessary instruction, which is called a program fragment.

Below is a new class with several conditions that robots of this class can test. This class can serve as the parent class of many of your own classes for the remainder of your visit to karel's world. The class is so important, in fact, that the Karel-Werke makes its definition available to all robot purchasers. Therefore, you may use this class in the same way that you use UrRobot. You don't need to create it. Since these are the most common type of robot, the name of the class is simply Robot. These robots will be able to make good use of IF and other similar statements.

```
public class Robot extends UrRobot
{
        public boolean frontIsClear(){...}
        public boolean nextToABeeper(){...}
        public boolean nextToARobot(){...}
        public boolean facingNorth(){...}
        public boolean facingSouth(){...}
        public boolean facingEast(){...}
        public boolean facingWest(){...}
        public boolean anyBeepersInBeeperBag(){...}
}
```

The items in the instruction list name the tests that a robot of the Robot class may perform using its sensors. They return true or false values to the robot mechanism and so we mark them as **boolean**.[1] These methods are called *predicates*. They provide the means by which robots can be queried (or can query their own internal state) to decide whether certain conditions are true or false. On the other hand, actions like **move** and **turnOff** are flagged as **void** because the robot gets no feedback information from them. The word **void** indicates the absence of a returned value. In computer programming languages, parts of a program that have a value are called *expressions*. Expressions are usually associated with a *type*, giving the valid values of the expression. A predicate represents a *boolean expression*, meaning that its value is either **true** or **false**[7].

Robot programmers can create new predicates in their own classes, just as they can create new void methods.

Recall that robots have a microphone that they can use to listen and determine if there are any beepers present on their current corner. This action is activated by the nextToABeeper message. If a robot, say carol, is sent the message **`carol.nextToABeeper()`** it will activate the microphone, and will respond to the message with *true* or *false* and then turn the microphone off again. The state of the robot doesn't change, but the sender of the message will obtain information about the state of the robot. This information can be put to use by statements like the IF instruction and others in this and the next chapter. The nextToABeeper test is true when a robot is on the same corner as one or more beepers. A robot cannot hear beepers any farther away, and it cannot hear beepers that are in the sound proof beeper-bag.

The **nextToARobot** predicate is similar and returns whether or not there is another robot on the same corner. This predicate momentarily activates the robot's arm, which is used to feel about for other robots.

Remember that each robot has a TV camera for eyes, focused to detect a wall exactly one half of a block away to the front. This camera is facing directly ahead. The **frontIsClear** predicate tests this condition. If a robot needs to test if its right is clear, it will need to proceed by first turning to the right to check for the presence of a wall. It can then return to its original orientation by turning back to its left.

---

[7] Boolean methods are named after George Boole, one of the early developers of formal logic.

A robot consults its internal compass to decide what direction it is facing. Finally, a robot can test whether or not there are any beepers in the beeper-bag by probing it with the mechanical arm. This condition is returned by the **anyBeepersInBeeperBag** predicate.

We will often want both positive and negative forms of many predicates. For example, we would probably want a predicate frontIsBlocked as the negative form of frontIsClear. Only the positive forms are provided by the Robot class, however. To aid in the writing of such negative forms, we will rely on the logical negation operator. In English this is usually written **not**. In the robot programming language we use the *negation operator*, "!", for this. For example, we have nextToABeeper. If we also want "**not** nextToABeeper", what we write is "`! nextToABeeper()`". Any message evaluating a predicate can be "negated" by preceding it with the negation operator, "!" (sometimes called "bang"). Thus, if robot karel has beepers in its beeper-bag, then it could respond to the instruction

```
if (! karel.nextToABeeper())
{
//Read: "If it is not true that karel is next to a beeper . . . "
        karel.putBeeper();
}
```

Alternatively we could create our own subclass of the Robot class and provide a new predicate not_nextToABeeper, as shown in the next section. In this case we could use:

```
if ( karel.not_nextToABeeper())
{
        karel.putBeeper();
}
```

5.2.1 Writing New Predicates

While the eight predicates defined above are built into the language, the user can also write new predicates. Predicates return boolean values, **true** and **false**. Therefore, in the block of the definition of a new predicate we need to indicate what value is to be returned. For this we need a new kind of instruction: the RETURN instruction. The form of the RETURN instruction is the reserved word **return**, followed by an expression. In a boolean method the value of the expression must be true or false. RETURN instructions are only legal in predicates. They won't be used in ordinary (void) methods (in this book), nor in the main task block. Actually Java has other forms of the return instruction, but they are beyond the scope of this book.

We might want predicates that are negative forms of the Robot class predicates. They can be defined using the not operator. For example, in a class CheckerRobot, we might want the following as well as some others.

```
public class CheckerRobot extends Robot
{       public boolean frontIsBlocked()
        {       return ! frontIsClear();
        }
        ...
}
```

Then, when a CheckerRobot is asked if its frontIsBlocked, it executes the return instruction. To do this it must first evaluate the frontIsClear predicate, receiving an answer of either true or false. It then returns the negative of this because of the negation operator. Therefore, if frontIsClear returns **false**, and if this is negated, then frontIsBlocked returns **true**. We can similarly write not_nextToABeeper. We show just the predicate here. Of course, it has to be written within its class.

```
public boolean not_nextToABeeper()
{       return ! nextToABeeper();
}
```

We might also want to "extend" a robot's vision by providing a test for rightIsClear. This instruction is much more complicated since robots have no sensor to their right. One solution is to face towards the right so that the forward sensor may be used. However, we shouldn't leave the robot facing that new direction, since the name of the method, rightIsClear, doesn't seems to imply any change in direction. Therefore, we should be sure the robot faces the original direction before returning. Therefore, rightIsClear must execute turn instructions in addition to returning a value.

```
public boolean rightIsClear()
{       turnRight();
        if ( frontIsClear() )
        {       turnLeft();
                return true;
        }
        turnLeft();
        return false;
}
```

The return instruction immediately terminates the predicate it is contained within. Therefore, if frontIsClear is true then the robot will turn left and return true. This method will have then terminated (returned). It won't reach or execute the second *turnLeft* or the *return false* instruction. On the other hand, if the *frontIsClear* test returns false, then the robot skips the THEN clause, and so it executes the second *turnLeft* and the *return false* instruction. Notice that we were careful here to leave the robot facing the same direction that it was facing before this predicate was executed. Therefore the programmer using *rightIsClear* can ignore the fact that the robot executes turns in order to evaluate this predicate, since any turn is undone. We can say that the turn is "transparent" to the user. Said another way, rightIsClear is directionally invariant. Viewed from outside, the robot executing it faces the same direction after executing it as it did before.

Notice that in the rightIsClear method, if we reverse the order of the last two messages in the body, then the *return* instruction will be executed before the *turnLeft* (only when frontIsClear() is false of course). But since the return will terminate the predicate, we won't ever execute the *turnLeft*. This would be an intent error, since it wouldn't leave the robot facing the original direction as was intended.

5.3 Simple Examples of the IF Instruction

This section examines three new methods that use the IF instruction. During our discussion we will also discuss how IF instructions are checked for correctness.

5.3.1 The harvestOneRow Method

Let's give karel a new task similar to the harvesting task discussed in Section 3.8.1. Karel's new task still requires the robot to harvest the same size field, but this time there is no guarantee that a beeper is on each corner of the field. Because karel's original program for this task would cause an error shutoff when it tried to execute a pickBeeper on any barren corner, we must modify it to avoid executing illegal pickBeeper instructions. Karel must harvest a beeper only if it determines that one is present.

Knowing about the new IF instruction, we can now write a program for this slightly more general task. One sample initial situation is illustrated in Figure 5-1.

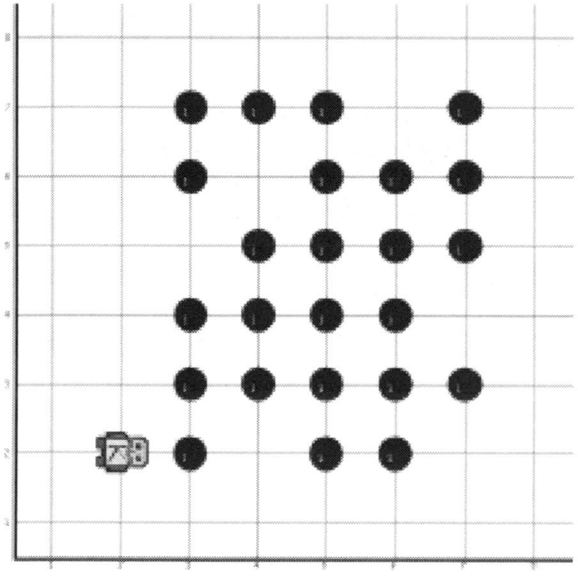

Figure 5-1: A Modified Harvest Task-not all corners have beepers

Please notice that this is only one of many possible initial situations. Our program must be able to harvest this size field (six by five) regardless of which corners have beepers and which corners do not.

Luckily for us, most of our previously written harvesting program can be reused -- another advantage of object-oriented programming with classes. All we need to do is to create a new version of the harvestCorner method in a new subclass of Harvester. The new version of harvestCorner only picks up a beeper if it knows there is one on the current corner. To do this we create a new class, SparseHarvester, whose parent class is Harvester. We will also, however, need to modify Harvester so that its parent class is Robot rather than UrRobot. With this change we can take advantage of the predicates defined in class Robot.

```
import kareltherobot.*;

public class SparseHarvester extends Harvester
{
        public void harvestCorner()
        {       if ( nextToABeeper() )
                {       pickBeeper();
                }
        }
}
```

5.3.2 The faceNorthIfFacingSouth Method

This section will demonstrate how we decide when to use the IF instruction and how we decide what condition we want a robot to check in <test>. As part of this and future discussions, let's assume we are planning and implementing the solution to a large problem where a robot named karel is on a treasure hunt for the "Lost Beeper Mine" which is a very large pile of beepers.

Let's further assume that we have developed an overall plan and are working on one small task within this plan. This task requires that karel face to the north only if it is currently facing south. In Chapter 3 we introduced a question and answer format to show how we might plan and analyze possible ways to solve a problem. The same format also works well in the implementing phase of problem solving.

Question: What does karel have to do?

Answer: Karel must turn to face north only if it is currently facing south.

Question: How many alternatives does the robot have to choose from?

Answer: Two.

Question: What are these alternatives?

Answer: Alternative #1 is to turn to the north if it is facing south. Alternative #2 is to do nothing if it is facing any other direction.

Question: What instruction can we use to allow karel to decide which alternative to choose?

Answer: The IF instruction allows karel to decide which alternative to choose.

Question: What test can karel use in the IF instruction?

Answer: Since karel is supposed to turn to the north only if it is facing to the south, the facingSouth test can be used.

Question: What does karel do if it is facing south?

Answer: Karel will turnLeft twice.

Question: What does karel do if it is not facing south?

Answer: Karel does nothing.

The thought process for implementing each instruction definition in our program must be as careful and detailed as it was when we were developing our original plan for the solution. Each step must be carefully analyzed for its strengths and weaknesses. If we ask a question and we cannot answer it satisfactorily, then either we have asked the wrong question or our plan for the instruction's definition is flawed. The longer we spend thinking about the implementation, the less time we will spend correcting errors. Having taken the time to analyze our answers, our instruction implementation looks like this. We assume here that we are building a new class, Prospector, of robots that can search for the Lost Beeper Mine.

```
public void faceNorthIfFacingSouth()
{       if  (facingSouth())
        {       turnLeft();
                turnLeft();
        }
}
```

5.3.3 The faceNorth Method

Here is a new problem to solve. Let's assume we are planning the definition of another part of the Lost Beeper Mine problem. We must implement an instruction definition that faces a robot north regardless of the direction it is currently facing. Using the question/answer format, we approach this solution by first thinking about karel's situation. Can we use the information about the direction karel is currently facing to solve the problem?

Question: What does karel have to do?

Answer: It must determine which direction it is facing to decide how many turnLefts to execute so it will be facing north.

Question: How many different alternatives does the robot have?

Answer: Karel has one alternative for each direction it could be facing. Therefore, it has four alternatives.

Question: What are these alternatives?

Answer: Alternative #1 facing north - do nothing.

Alternative #2 facing east - turn left once.

Alternative #3 facing south - turn left twice.

Alternative #4 facing west - turn left three times.

Question: What test(s) can karel use to decide which direction it is facing?

Answer: Karel can check to see if it is facingEast, facingSouth, facingWest--since karel does not have to do anything when it is facing north, we do not have to use that test.

We can use these questions and their answers to aid us in implementing the new method, faceNorth.

```
public void  faceNorth()
{       if (facingEast())
        {       turnLeft();
        }
        if (facingSouth())
        {       turnLeft();
                turnLeft();
        }
        if (facingWest())
        {       turnLeft();
                turnLeft();
                turnLeft();
        }
}
```

Compare this method to the set of questions preceding it. Did we ask all of the necessary questions? Did we answer them correctly? Trace this method for execution and simulate it four times, one for each direction karel could initially be facing. Does it work in all cases?

There is another way to solve this problem. Examine this set of questions.

Question: What does karel have to do?

Answer: Karel must turnLeft until it is facing north.

Question: How many alternatives does the robot have?

Answer: Two.

Question: What are they?

Answer: Alternative # 1 is to turnLeft if it is not facing north.

Alternative # 2 is to do nothing if it is already facing north.

Question: How can we use this information?

Answer: Karel can never be more than three turnLefts away from facing north so we can use a sequence of three IF instructions; each one will check to see if karel is not facingNorth. If the test is true, karel will turnLeft and be one turnLeft closer to facing north.

Question: What happens when karel starts out facing north?

Answer All three tests will be false and karel does nothing.

Question: What happens when karel is facing east?

Answer: The first test is true and karel executes a turnLeft. The remaining two tests are false and karel does nothing.

Question: What happens when karel is facing south?

Answer: The first two tests are true so karel executes two turnLefts. The third test is false and its THEN clause is skipped.

Question: What happens when karel is facing west?

Answer: All three tests will be true so karel will execute three turnLefts.

Here is our resulting new instruction.

```
public void faceNorth()
{       if ( ! facingNorth() )
        {       turnLeft();
        }
        if ( ! facingNorth() )
        {       turnLeft();
        }
        if ( ! facingNorth() )
        {       turnLeft();
        }
 }
```

Trace this instruction for execution and simulate it four times, one for each direction karel could initially be facing. Does it work in all cases?

The question must be asked as to which of these two faceNorth instructions is better. For now, either is perfectly acceptable.

5.3.4 Determining the correctness of the IF Instruction

Checking an IF instruction is similar to checking a dictionary entry, since both are "meaningful" components of a program. Both IF instructions and dictionary entries use reserved words and braces to separate their different parts. You check the IF instruction by first checking the <test>, making sure it is correct and contained in parentheses. You then check the instructions inside the braces. Finally, you check the entire IF instruction including its braces.

Study, for example, the version of captureTheBeeper that follows.

```
public void captureTheBeeper()
{       move();
        if (nextToABeeper())
        {       pickBeeper();
                turnAround();
        }
        move();
}
```

This definition contains three instructions: the first move, the IF and the second move. The move messages are terminated by semicolons, and the two messages inside the block of the IF are likewise terminated by semicolons. The predicate is correct and contained in parentheses and the braces for the IF correctly enclose the two messages. It seems OK. Notice, however, that it leaves us in one of two different places, facing in one of two different directions, depending on whether it finds a beeper or not. It might be important in some problems to avoid this difference since other instructions will be executed after this one. If we are not careful, the robot could wander away from the desired path. We try to be careful to pick a name for a method that describes all that the robot will do when executing it. We also generally try to leave the robot in the same state regardless of how it executes the instruction. The next instruction will help in this.

5.4 The IF/ELSE Instruction

In this section we discuss the second type of IF instruction built into the robot vocabulary. The IF/ELSE instruction is useful when, depending on the result of some test, a robot must execute one of two alternative instructions. The general form of the IF/ELSE is given below.

```
if ( <test> )
{
        <instruction-list-1>
}
else
{
        <instruction-list-2>
}
```

The form of the IF/ELSE is similar to the IF instruction, except that it includes an ELSE clause. Note the absence of a semicolon before the word else and at the end. A robot executes an IF/ELSE in much the same manner as an IF. It first determines whether <test> is true or false in the current situation. If <test> is true, the robot executes <instruction-list-1>; if <test> is false, it executes <instruction-list-2>. Thus, depending on its current situation, the robot executes either <instruction-list-1> or <instruction-list-2>, but not both. By the way, the first instruction list in an IF/ELSE instruction is called the *THEN clause* and the second instruction list is called the *ELSE clause*.

Let's look at a task that uses the IF/ELSE instruction. Suppose that we want to program a robot to run a one mile long hurdle race, where vertical wall sections represent hurdles. The hurdles are only one block high and are randomly placed between any two corners in the race course. One of the many possible race courses for this task is illustrated in Figure 5-2. Here we think of the world as being vertical with down being south. We require the robot to jump if, and only if, faced with a hurdle.

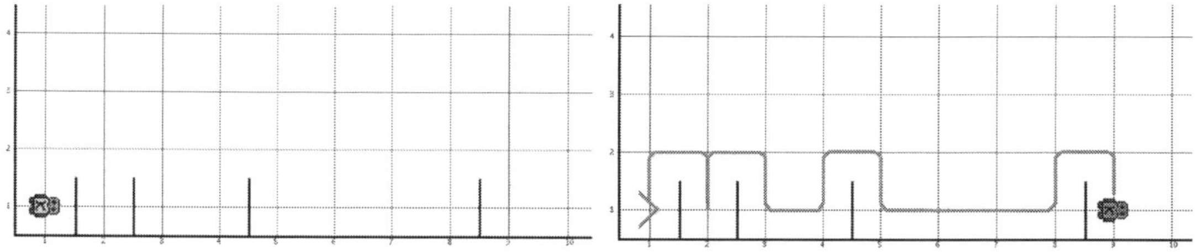

Figure 5-2: A Hurdle Jumping Race

The robot could easily run this race by jumping between every pair of corners, but although this strategy is simple to program, it doesn't meet the requirements. (Perhaps it would slow the robot down too much.) Instead, we must program the robot to move straight ahead when it can, and jump over hurdles only when it must. The program implementing this strategy consists of a main task block that contains eight raceStride messages followed by a turnOff. The definition of raceStride can be written using stepwise refinement as follows.

```
public class Racer extends Robot
{
        public void  raceStride()
        {
                if ( frontIsClear() )
                {       move();
                }
                else
                {       jumpHurdle();
                }
        }
        ...
}
```

We continue our refinement by writing jumpHurdle.

```
public void jumpHurdle()
{       jumpUp();
        move();
        glideDown();
}
```

Finally, we write jumpUp and glideDown, the methods needed to complete the definition of jumpHurdle.

```
public void jumpUp()
{       turnLeft();
        move();
        turnRight();
}
```

and

```
public void glideDown()
{       turnRight();
        move();
        turnLeft();
}
```

To verify that these methods are correct, complete and assemble the program. Then simulate a Racer robot running the race in Figure 5-2.

5.5 Nested IF Instructions

Although we have seen many IF instructions, we have ignored an entire class of complex IF'S. These are known as nested IF instructions because they are written with an IF instruction nested inside the THEN or ELSE clause of another IF. No new execution rules are needed to simulate nested IF' s, but a close adherence to the established rules is required. Simulating nested IF instructions is sometimes difficult because it is easy for us to lose track of where we are in the instruction. The following discussion should be read carefully and understood completely as an example of how to test instructions that include nested IF'S.

To demonstrate a nested IF instruction, we propose a task that redistributes beepers in a field. This task requires that a robot named karel traverse a field and leave exactly one beeper on each corner. The robot must plant a beeper on each barren corner and remove one beeper from every corner where two beepers are present. All corners in this task are constrained to have zero, one, or two beepers on them. One sample initial and final situation is displayed in Figure 5-3. In these situations, multiple beepers on a corner are represented by a number. We can assume that karel has enough beepers in its beeper-bag to replant the necessary number of corners.

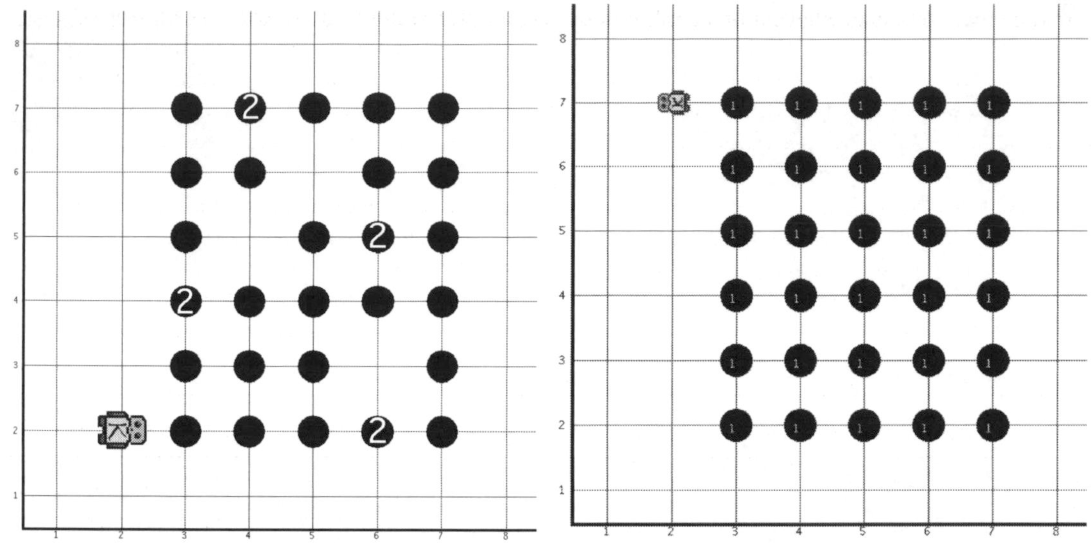

Figure 5.3: A Beeper Replanting Task

The heart of the program that solves this task is a method that enables karel to satisfy the one-beeper requirement for each corner. Here is the method. We can provide an override method for the harvestCorner method of the Harvester class.

```
public class Replanter extends Robot
{
      public void harvestCorner()
      {         if( ! nextToABeeper() )
                {  putBeeper();
                }
                else
                {  pickBeeper();
                   if ( ! nextToABeeper() )
                   {      putBeeper();
                   }
                }
       }
       ...
}
```

The outer IF statement in this definition is an IF/ELSE and the nested IF statement is an ordinary IF. The nested IF instruction is inside the ELSE clause of the outer IF. Next, we simulate karel in the three possible corner situations: an empty corner, a corner with one beeper, and a corner with two beepers.

In the empty corner situation, karel executes the outer IF and determines that the test is true. The robot executes the putBeeper message in the THEN clause placing one beeper on the corner. Karel has now finished executing the outer IF instruction and thus has finished executing harvestCorner.

Next we assume that there is one beeper on karel's corner. Karel first executes the outer IF. The test is false so the robot executes the ELSE clause. This clause consists of two instructions, pickBeeper and the nested IF instruction. Karel picks the beeper and performs the test associated with the nested IF. The test is true so karel executes the THEN clause of this IF instruction and puts a beeper back on the empty corner. Karel is now finished with the nested IF, the ELSE clause, the outer IF, and the entire harvestCorner instruction.

Finally, we assume that karel is on a corner with two beepers. Karel executes the outer IF, finds the test is false, and then executes the ELSE clause. Karel picks up one of the two beepers on the corner. Up to this point karel has duplicated its actions in the one-beeper situation, but now comes the difference in execution. Karel executes the nested IF instruction, finds the test is false, and skips the nested IF'S THEN clause. Once again, karel is now finished with the nested IF, the ELSE clause, the outer IF, and the entire harvestCorner instruction.

We want to emphasize that when nested IF instructions seem too intricate we should try replacing the nested IF with a new message instruction. The definition of the associated method must command karel to perform the same actions as the nested IF and may help us better understand what karel is doing. Because nesting also makes an instruction less readable, a good rule of thumb is to avoid nesting IF instructions more than one level deep. The harvestCorner method, which has one level of nesting, is rewritten below using an auxiliary method. Simpler methods are easier to understand and, therefore, easier to use.

```
public void harvestCorner()
{       if ( ! nextToABeeper()   )
        {       putBeeper();
        }
        else
        {       nextToOneReplantOne();
        }
}
```

We write the nextToOneReplantOne method by copying the ELSE clause from our original definition of harvestCorner.

```
public void nextToOneReplantOne()
{       pickBeeper();
        if ( ! nextToABeeper() )
        {       putBeeper();
        }
}
```

Given the entire program from Section 3.9.1 along with either of these new definitions of the harvestCorner method, do we have a correct solution for the beeper replanting task? We may consider using our old method of verification and test the program with karel in every possible initial situation, but there are more than 200 trillion[8] different fields that this program must be able to replant correctly! Attempting verification by exhaustively testing karel in every possible initial situation would be ludicrous.

---

[8] There are 3 different possibilities for each corner; and there are 30 corners in the field. The total number of different fields is thus 3 multiplied by itself 30 times. For you mathemagicians, the exact number of different fields is 205,891,132,094,649.

Instead, we will try to establish correctness based on the following informal argument: (1) we have verified that harvestCorner works correctly on any corner that is empty or contains one or two beepers, and (2) we can easily verify that our program commands karel to execute this instruction on each corner of the field. Therefore, we conclude that the program correctly replants the entire field.

This argument further enhances the claim that karel's mechanism for instruction definition is a powerful aid to programming. Usually, we can informally conclude that an entire program is correct by verifying that: (1) each new instruction in the program works correctly in all possible situations in which it can be executed, and (2) the program executes each new instruction at the appropriate time. This method allows us to verify a program by splitting it into separate, simpler, verifications, just as stepwise refinement allows us to write a program by splitting it into separate, simpler instructions.

Suppose that a robot is in a situation in which it must determine if there are exactly two beepers on the current corner. We would like to write a predicate to return true if this is so, and false otherwise. We imagine that this is needed in some replanting task, so we will add it to the Replanter class. We can write such a predicate if we pick up beepers one at a time and then ask if there are any more. We must remember to put back any beepers that we pick up, however. Note that if we have picked two beepers up, we still need to ask if there are any more to determine if there are exactly two beepers on the current corner.

```
public boolean exactlyTwoBeepers()
{       if (nextToABeeper())  // one or more beepers
        {       pickBeeper();
                if (nextToABeeper())  // two or more beepers
                {       pickBeeper();
                        if(nextToABeeper()) // more than two
                        {       putBeeper();
                                putBeeper();
                                return false;
                        }
                        else // exactly two beepers
                        {       putBeeper();
                                putBeeper();
                                return true;
                        }
                }
                else // only one beeper
                {       putBeeper();
                        return false;
                }
        }
        else  // no beepers
        {       return false;
        }
}
```

This is about the limit of how far we should nest such statements. Any more than this and they become very difficult to understand. Actually two levels is much better than three. You should always define a new instruction for the inner IF statement and if you name it well, the entire structure will be much easier to understand.

5.6 More Complex Tests

It may not be a trivial matter to have a robot make two or more tests at the same time. Programming languages provide the capability to make multiple tests within an IF or an IF/ELSE instruction. We can do this but we must be clever with our programming as illustrated by the following example.

Let's assume we are still working on the Lost Beeper Mine problem introduced earlier. Recall that the Lost Beeper Mine is a very large pile of beepers. We have another assignment from that problem--a very important landmark along the way is found where all of the following are true:

* karel is facing west,

* karel's right side is blocked,

* karel's left side is blocked,

* karel's front is clear, and

* there is at least one beeper on the corner.

Following these requirements we must plan an instruction that will test all of these conditions simultaneously. If we do what seems logical we might try to write something like this:

```
if (     facingWest()
         AND rightIsBlocked()
         AND leftIsBlocked()
         AND frontIsClear()
         AND nextToABeeper() )
{   . . .
```

This seems very logical, but there is one major problem. If we use a sequence of nested IF instructions to do the job the result will be very ugly.

```
if (facingWest() )
{       if ( ! rightIsClear()  )
        {       if ( ! leftIsClear()  )
                {       if (frontIsClear() )
                        {       if (nextToABeeper() )
                                {
                                        <instruction>
                                }
                        }
                }
        }
}
```

If we trace this, we will find that all of the tests must evaluate to true before karel can execute <instruction>.

Fortunately, Java and the robot programming language have an operator for AND, but it is spelled && with two ampersand characters. So we can actually say:

```
if (    facingWest()
        && rightIsBlocked()
        && leftIsBlocked()
        && frontIsClear()
        && nextToABeeper()
        )
{   . . .
}
```

Another way to build complex tests is to define new predicates. Suppose we would like to write

```
if (nextToABeeper() && leftIsBlocked()) { . . .
```

This can be done if we write a new predicate in the class in which we need such a test. There is no real need for this, given the && operator, but it is instructive to examine it. For example:

```
public boolean nextToABeeper_AND_leftIsBlocked()
{       if(nextToABeeper())
        {       if ( ! leftIsClear())
                {       return true;
                }
                else
                {       return false;
                }
        }
        return false;
}
```

This can be simplified to:

```
public void nextToABeeper_AND_leftIsBlocked()
{       if(nextToABeeper())
        {       return ! leftIsClear();
        }
        return false;
}
```

One way to help determine if a predicate with two or more conditions is correct is to look at the truth table, which gives all possible combinations of the parts of the predicate. The truth table for AND is shown below.

nextToABeeper	leftIsBlocked	AND
T	T	T
T	F	F
F	T	F
F	F	F

The IF instruction in the predicate says that when nextToABeeper is true we should return the negation of leftIsClear, which is the same as leftIsBlocked. Note that the first two lines of the truth table also say this. On these two lines nextToABeeper is true and the leftIsBlocked lines exactly match the AND lines here. Likewise, the predicate says that when nextToABeeper is false we should return false. Again, this matches the truth table exactly, since on the last two lines, where nextToABeeper is false, we return false.

Note that in the nextToABeeper_AND_leftIsBlocked instruction there is no need to check that the left is clear if we have already determined that we are NOT next to a beeper. We can simply return false in this case. We only need to check the second part of the AND when the first part is true. This is known as "short-circuit evaluation" of the predicate, and it is very useful. To use it wisely when you write your own predicates, however, so that a user isn't misled, you must check the leftmost part (nextToABeeper) first. The Java && operator also uses this short circuit evaluation.

Similarly we can say

```
if (nextToABeeper() || leftIsBlocked()) { . . .
```

The Java operator || means OR. The truth table for an OR is as follows. Notice that when nextToABeeper is true the OR is also true, and when nextToABeeper is false the result is the same as leftIsBlocked.

nextToABeeper	leftIsBlocked	OR
T	T	T
T	F	T
F	T	T
F	F	F

Note also that the && operator has a higher precedence than the || operator. This means that in a sequence of terms separated by these operators the && operators are applied first. If you wish it otherwise, you can use parentheses, just as in arithmetic expressions using addition and multiplication. The rules are that you apply the operators in parentheses first, otherwise apply the higher precedence operators before lower, and also work left to right among operators of the same precedence. The || operator also uses short-circuit evaluation. If the left expression (nextToABeeper, here) is true the result is already known to be true.

5.7 When to Use an IF Instruction

Thus far we have spent most of our time and effort in this chapter explaining how the IF and the IF/ELSE instructions work. It is at this point that students are usually told, "Write a program that uses the IF and the IF/ELSE instructions so that a robot can . . . " It is also at this point that we hear the following question being asked by students, "I understand how these work but I don't understand when to use them." It is "understanding when to use them" that is the focus of this section.

Let's review what the IF and the IF/ELSE instructions allow robots to do in a robot program:

* The IF instruction allows a robot to decide whether to execute or skip entirely the block of instructions within the THEN clause.

* The IF/ELSE instruction allows a robot to decide whether to execute the block of instructions in the THEN clause or the ELSE clause.

* Nesting these instructions allows karel to make more complex choices if required.

We can use these three statements to build a decision map. A decision map is a technique that asks questions about the problem we are trying to solve. The answers to the questions determine the branch we follow through the map. Here is the section of the decision map that a programmer would use for choosing between an IF and an IF/ELSE.

To use this part of the decision map we must be at a point during our implementation where a robot needs to choose from among alternatives. We use the map by asking each question as we encounter it and following the path that has the answer. If done correctly, we eventually arrive at an implementation suggestion. If the map does not work, we probably do not need to choose between alternatives or have not correctly thought out our plan. By the way, we say we choose from among one alternative as a shorthand for the situation where the choice is simply to do something or not.

Suppose a robot must face north if there is a beeper on the current corner and face south otherwise. How many tests does the robot have to make? One-either nextToABeeper or !nextToABeeper. This answer directs us down the left path to the next question, how many alternatives does the robot have available? Two-the robot must either face north or face south. This takes us down the path to the IF/ELSE instruction. Our implementation looks like this.

```
if( nextToABeeper() )
{       faceNorth();
}
else
{       faceSouth();
}
```

Note that Java has other instructions, including one called *switch* that can help with the case of more than two tests in some circumstances. We don't discuss switch in this book.

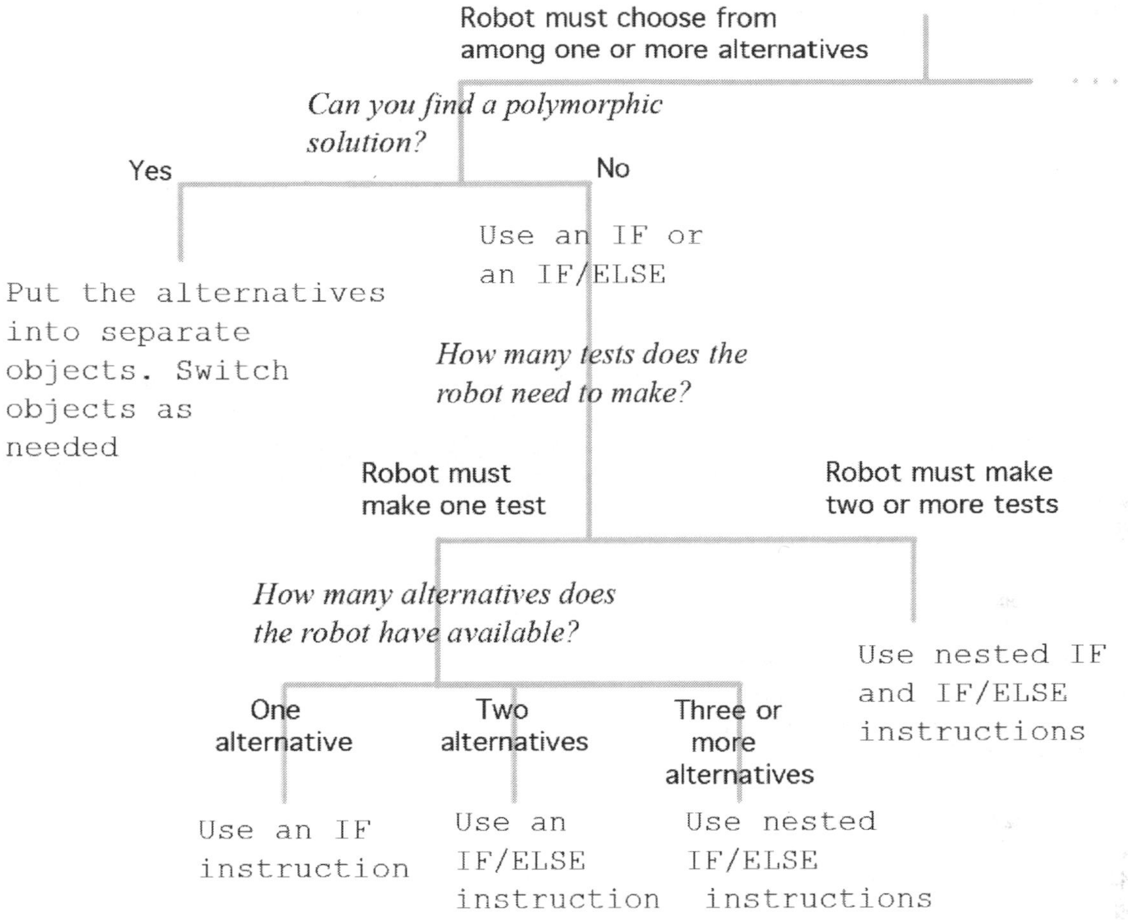

Figure 5-4 Part of the Decision Map

5.8 Transformations for Simplifying IF Instructions

This section discusses four useful transformations that help us simplify programs containing IF instructions. We start by observing that when two program fragments result in a robot's performing exactly the same actions, we call this pair of fragments execution equivalent. For a simple example, `turnLeft(); putBeeper();` is execution equivalent to `putBeeper(); turnLeft();`.

In general, we can create one execution equivalent IF/ELSE instruction from another by replacing <test> with its opposite and interchanging the THEN and the ELSE clauses as illustrated below. We call this transformation *test reversal*. Notice that if we perform test reversal twice on the same instruction, we get back to the instruction with which we started.

```
if(frontIsClear())
{       move();
}
else
{       jumpHurdle();
}
```

```
if( ! frontIsClear() )
{       jumpHurdle();
}
else
{       move();
}
```

Generally speaking we prefer the positive, rather than the negative forms of tests, so we prefer the first of the above forms over the second. This is not an absolute rule, but it is the reason why the built in predicate is called frontIsClear rather than frontIsBlocked. The first seems to be stated more positively.

Test reversal can be used to help novice programmers overcome the following difficulty. Suppose that we start to write an IF instruction and get ourselves into the dilemma illustrated below on the left. The problem is that we want a robot to do nothing special when its front is clear[9] but when its front is blocked we want karel to execute <instruction>. We would like to remove the THEN clause, but doing so would cause a syntax error -- karel does not understand an IF/ELSE instruction without a THEN clause. The solution to our problem is illustrated on the right.

```
if(frontIsClear())
{       doNothing();
}
else
{       <instruction>
}
```

```
if( ! frontIsClear())
{       <instruction>
}
```

To transform the IF on the left into the IF on the right, we use test reversal. First we change <test> to its opposite, then switch the doNothing instruction into the ELSE clause and bring <instruction> into the THEN clause. By the previous discussion of test reversal, execution equivalence is preserved. Finally, the new ELSE clause (which contains the doNothing instruction) can be removed, resulting in the simpler IF instruction on the right.

The second transformation we discuss is *bottom factoring*. Bottom factoring is illustrated below, where we will show that the IF/ELSE instruction on the left is execution equivalent to the program fragment on the right. We have kept the bracketed words in these instructions because their exact replacements do not affect this transformation.

[9] We can define the method doNothing as four left turns. Executing this instruction would leave karel's position unchanged, and this instruction is also immune to error shutoffs. This would be wasteful of the Robot's battery capacity, however. We could also simply not write anything between the braces of the THEN part.

```
if(<test>)
{       <instruction_1>
        <instruction_3>
}
else
{       <instruction_2>
        <instruction_3>
}
```

```
if(<test>)
{       <instruction_1>
}
else
{       <instruction_2>
}
<instruction_3>
```

In the program fragment on the right, we have factored <instruction_3> out of the bottom of each clause in the IF. We justify the correctness of this transformation as follows: If <test> is true, the instruction on the left has the robot execute <instruction_1> directly followed by <instruction_3>. In the program fragment on the right, if <test> is true the robot executes <instruction_1> and then, having finished the IF, it executes <instruction_3>. Thus, when <test> is true, these forms are execution equivalent. A similar argument holds between the left and right fragments whenever <test> is false.

In summary, <instruction_3> is executed in the IF on the left regardless of whether <test> is true or false. So we might as well remove it from each clause and put it directly after the entire IF/ELSE instruction. Moreover, if the bottoms of each clause were larger, but still identical, we could bottom factor all of the common instructions and still preserve execution equivalence. Think of this process as bottom factoring one instruction at a time until all common instructions have been factored. Since execution equivalence is preserved during each factoring step, the resulting program fragment is execution equivalent to the original instruction.

The third transformation we discuss in this section is *top factoring*. Although this transformation may seem as simple and easy to use as bottom factoring, we will see that not all instructions can be top factored successfully. We divide our discussion of this transformation into three parts. First, we examine an instruction that can safely be top factored. Then we show an instruction that cannot be top factored successfully. Finally, we state a general rule that tells us which IF instructions can safely be top factored.

Top factoring can safely be used in the following example to convert the instruction on the left into the simpler program fragment on the right. These two forms can be shown to be execution equivalent by a justification similar to the one used in our discussion of bottom factoring.

```
if(facingNorth())
{       move();
        turnLeft();
}
else
 {      move();
        turnRight();
}
```

```
move();
if(facingNorth())
{       turnLeft();
}
else
{       turnRight();
}
```

In the next example, we have incorrectly used the top factoring transformation. We will discover that the program fragment on the right is not execution equivalent to the instruction on the left.

```
if(nextToABeeper())
{       move();
        turnLeft();
}
else
{       move();
        turnRight();
}
```

```
move();
if(nextToABeeper())
{       turnLeft()
}
else
{       turnRight();
}
```

To show that these forms execute differently, let's assume that a robot named karel is on a corner containing one beeper, and that the corner in front of the robot is barren. If karel executes the instruction on the left, the robot will first find that it is next to a beeper, and then will execute the THEN clause of the IF by moving forward and turning to its left. The program fragment on the right will first move karel forward to the next corner and then will instruct it to test for a beeper. Since this new corner does not contain a beeper, karel will execute the ELSE clause of the IF, which causes the robot to turn to its right. Thus, top factoring in this example does not preserve execution equivalence.

Why can we correctly use top factoring in the first example but not in the second? The first instruction can be top factored safely because the test that determines which way karel is facing is not changed by having it move forward. Therefore, whether karel moves first or not, the evaluation of the test will remain unchanged. But in the second example, the move changes the corner on which karel checks for a beeper, so the robot is not performing the test under the same conditions. The general **rule** is that we may top factor an instruction only when the conditions under which the test is performed do not change between the original and factored versions of the instruction.

The fourth and final transformation is used to remove redundant tests in nested IF instructions. We call this transformation *redundant-test-factoring* and show one application of this rule.

```
if(facingWest())
{       move();
        if(facingWest())
        {       turnLeft();
        }
}
```

```
if(facingWest())
{       move();
        turnLeft();
}
```

In the instruction on the left, there is no need for the nested IF instruction to recheck the condition facingWest. The THEN clause of the outer IF is only executed if karel is facing west, and the move inside the THEN clause does not normally change the direction that karel is facing. Therefore, facingWest is always true when karel executes this nested IF instruction. This argument shows that karel always executes the THEN clause of this nested IF. So, the entire nested IF instruction can be replaced by turnLeft, as has been done in the instruction on the right. Once again, this transformation preserves execution equivalence. Of course, if we have given move a new meaning in the class of which this is a member, then we cannot guarantee that move doesn't change the direction. In this case the two fragments would not be equivalent. A similar transformation applies whenever we look for a redundant test in an ELSE clause. Remember, though, in an ELSE clause <test> is false.

This transformation is also a bit more subtle than bottom factoring, and we must be careful when trying to use it. The potential difficulty is that intervening instructions might change karel's position in an unknown way. For example, if instead of the move message we had used a turnAroundIfNextToABeeper message, we could not have used redundant-test factoring. Here we cannot be sure whether karel would be facing west or east when it had to execute the nested IF.

These four transformations can help us make our programs smaller, simpler, more logical, and--most important--more readable. Readability is a very important property of programs since we spend so much time trying to understand programs and modify them. This may not seem too important to you now, but programs that do something significant are usually built by teams of people who need to communicate effectively through the programs they write.

We said above that we prefer the positive form of a test when possible. There are some other tricks that you can use to make your programs more readable. One is not to use deeply nested structures, defining new predicates as necessary. Another is, when writing an IF-ELSE statement to arrange things so that if one of the clauses (THEN or ELSE) is very short and the other long, then choose a predicate so that the short one comes first as the THEN clause. This lets you read and understand it and move on to the other before you forget what the predicate is.

5.9 Polymorphism Revisited (Advanced Topic)

Since polymorphism is in many ways the most important topic of this book, we would like to say a few more things about it and see how it can be used in conjunction with IF statements to do some wonderful things. In a certain sense IF statements achieve a measure of polymorphism, called ad-hoc polymorphism, since the program must make explicit (or ad-hoc) decisions. In some circumstances we don't have a choice of using IF statements or polymorphism to achieve an end, but when we do, polymorphism gives a more satisfactory result. This is because problems change and when they do, IF statements usually need to be modified. When a program contains a large number of IF statements and only some of them need to be changed for the new problem, it can be a major task keeping the updates consistent. In this section we will solve a few problems that use both IF statements and polymorphism to get a sense of the difference.

The situations in which we cannot use polymorphism in the robot language as in Java involve those things that cannot behave polymorphically. Beepers and walls are not objects, so we can't use polymorphism to deal with them. Robots on the other hand can behave (and always behave) polymorphically so with robot behavior we prefer polymorphism.

Here is a simple problem that we looked at in Chapter 4, but can extend here. Suppose we have a bunch of robots, one on each corner of first street from some avenue to some avenue farther on and we want to ask each of them to put down one beeper. We want to write a program that will work no matter how many robots there are. To make it explicit, suppose there is a robot on first street and n'th avenue and we want a robot with one beeper on each corner between the origin and this robot and then we want to ask them all to put down their beepers. We will use IF statements to set up the situation and then use polymorphism to get the robots to put down their beepers.

To do this we need at least two classes of robots, just as before. We will make a few changes to our BeeperPutter hierarchy of classes that we built in the prevous chapter. We will make these classes a bit more polymorphic as well as illustrating how we can use IF statements to set up later polymorphic actions. Previously, BeeperPutter was an interface, but here we will use an abstract class instead.

```
public abstract class BeeperPutter extends Robot implements Cloneable
{       public abstract void distributeBeepers();

        public abstract void createNeighbor();
}
```

First, every subclass will need a createNeighbor instruction. In Chapter 4 we used the constructor to tell a robot who its neighbor is. Here we will not need to do that since each robot will create its own neighbor. Therefore, we want a createNeighbor method with no parameters. We will also want this method to be polymorphic. Since a NoNeighbor robot has no neighbor it needs to do nothing at all when it performs *createNeighbor*. Therefore we will implement a "no action" version of *createNeighbor* in the NoNeighbor subclass of BeeperPutter. Thhe body of this version of createNeighbor has no instructions.

In the createNeighbor method of NeighborTalker we will have a robot create its own neighbor. We want to be able to do this so that the neighbor is one street to the left of the given robot. Furthermore, if the robot is standing on second avenue then the neighbor it creates (on first avenue) will be a NoNeighbor robot rather than a NeighborTalker robot. If it creates a NeighborTalker, then it will send the createNeighbor message to the newly created neighbor.

We have a problem with this, however. No robot knows the corner on which it is standing, so it can't create this neighbor using *new*. To do so would require knowing the street and avenue on which to place it. We will therefore need to use another way to create this neighbor. Any robot can ask the factory to create a robot exactly like itself. When it does so, the newly created robot will be delivered to the corner on which the robot sits when it makes the request and will be set up in the same state as the existing robot: facing the same direction, with the same number of beepers. To do this we send the robot the *clone* message. A robot can even send this message to itself, of course, as it can with any other message. The clone message takes no parameters, but returns a new robot of the same class as the original. Thus, we see again that methods can return things other than boolean values. For the clone message to be recognized, however, we need to implement the Cloneable interface, as we have done in BeeperPutter. This gives us access to the built-in clone method.

Note that the clone method itself is highly polymorphic. It can be executed in any robot class and it always returns a robot of the same class and in the same state as the original.

Since we want the neighbor on the adjoining corner, we will move to that corner before sending the *clone* message. Then we can return to the original corner and send the newly-created neighbor the *createNeighbor* message. The exception will be when we discover that after the first move we find that front is blocked, meaning that we are about to create a robot on first avenue. In this case we want to create a NoNeighbor robot instead of a clone.

```
public class NeighborTalker extends BeeperPutter
{       ...
        public void createNeighbor()
        // PRE: facing West on first street and front is clear
        {       move();
                if (frontIsClear())
                {       neighbor = (BeeperPutter) clone();
                }
```

```
                else
                {       neighbor = new NoNeighbor(1, 1, North, 1);
                }
                goBack();
                neighbor.createNeighbor();
        } // POST: facing North on original corner.
        ...
}
```

More on Java Cloning can be found in Section 6 of the Appendix.

With these changes our main task block becomes especially simple.

```
public static void main(String [] args)
{       NeighborTalker aRobot = new NeighborTalker(1, 6, West, 1);
        aRobot.createNeighbor();
        aRobot.distributeBeepers();
}
```

When a robot is sent the createNeighbor message it creates the neighbor, but also sends that robot the createNeighbor message, which creates another, etc. This only ends when we reach a noNeighbor robot since its createNeighbor does nothing.

Let's focus for a moment on why we needed IF statements here and why the solution couldn't be entirely polymorphic. In the robot world the walls and beepers are not objects so we cannot build subclasses of them. They are just primitive data. Therefore, they cannot act polymorphically (or act at all, actually). The robots CAN be polymorphic but in this situation the robot needs to interact with a wall to find out if its front is clear. We therefore use the non-polymorphic tool, the IF statement, to set up the situation in which polymorphism can then act. Note that aside from the clone and rememberNeighbor methods the only method of interest here was distributeBeepers which was polymorphic. However, we could also have other polymorphic methods in these classes and, once the situation was set up, all of them would work without additional IF statements. Thus, if our problem changes, we can either add a new class for a new kind of robot that must behave differently from these, or we can add a new polymorphic method to each of these classes. We do not have to visit a large number of if statements and add a new part for each new part of the problem. At most we have to do the rememberNeighbor differently.

Finally, let's consider the Enumeration interface and enumeration objects a bit more. We are now in a position to understand the other method of this interface.

```
public interface Enumeration
{
        public Object nextElement();
        public boolean hasMoreElements();
}
```

The *hasMoreElements* method is a boolean method just like nextToABeeper: a predicate. It tells us if the enumeration has been exhausted yet, either because it was initially empty, or because we have called *nextElement* a sufficient number of times to enumerate all the elements in the collection. We shall see an even more important use of this method in the next chapter, but for now, note that you can protect yourself against a NoSuchElementException by placing the *nextElement* instruction inside an if.

```
Enumeration neighbors = neighbors();
if(neighbors.hasMoreElements())
{
        UrRobot myNeighbor = (UrRobot)neighbors.nextElement();
        ...
}
```

If there are no neighbors at all, this won't do anything.

5.10 Important Ideas From This Chapter

selection
nested instructions
predicate
condition
statement transformation
clone

5.11 Problem Set

The problems in this section require the use of the IF instruction in its two forms. Try using stepwise refinement on these problems, but no matter what instruction you use to obtain a solution, write a clear and understandable program. Keep the nesting level small for those problems requiring nested IF instructions. Use proper punctuation and grammar, especially within the THEN and ELSE clauses of the IF instructions. Carefully simulate each definition and program that you write to ensure that there are no execution or intent errors.

1. Write a new predicate leftIsBlocked that determines if there is a wall exactly one half block away on a robot's left. Be sure that when it terminates, the robot is on the same corner and facing in the same direction.

2. Look at the following instruction. Is there a simpler, execution equivalent instruction? If so, write it down; if not, explain why. Hint: A simplifying transformation for the IF may prove useful. Common sense helps too.

```
if( ! nextToABeeper())
{       move();
}
else
{       move();
}
```

3. Assume that a Prospector robot is on a corner with either one or two beepers. Write a new method that commands the robot to face north if it is started on a corner with one beeper and to face south if it is

started on a corner with two beepers. Besides facing the robot in the required direction, after it has executed this method there must be no beepers left on the corner. Name this method findNextDirection.

4. Write another version of findNextDirection(see the previous problem). In this version the robot must eventually face the same directions, but it also must leave the same number of beepers on the corner as were there originally.

5. Write an instruction that turns a robot off if the robot is completely surrounded by walls, unable to move in any direction. If the robot is not surrounded, it should execute this instruction by leaving itself turned on, and by remaining on the same corner, facing the same direction in which it started. Name this instruction turnOffIfSurrounded. Hint: To write this instruction correctly, you will need to include a turnOff inside it. This combination is perfectly legal, but it is the first time that you will use a turnOff instruction outside the main task block.

6. Program a robot to run a mile long steeplechase. The steeplechase course is similar to the hurdle race, but here the barriers can be one, two, or three blocks high. Figure 5-5 shows one sample initial situation, where the robot's final situation and path are shown on the right. Call the class of this new robot Steeplechaser. It should have Racer as a parent class. Override appropriate instructions of Racer to implement the new behavior.

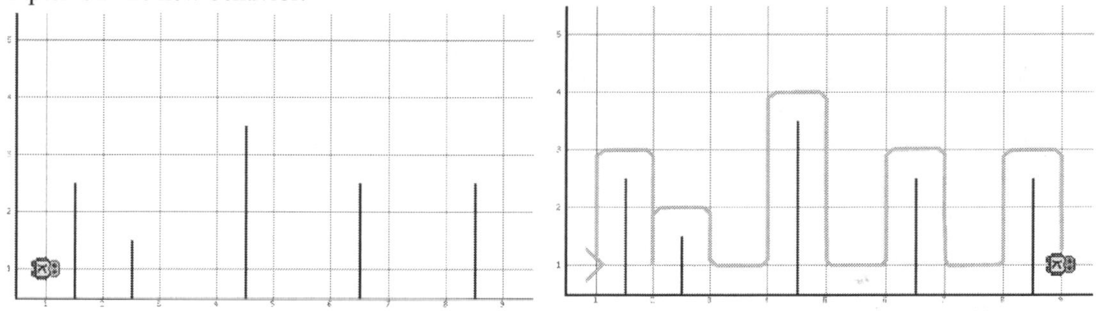

FIGURE 5-5 Steeplechase Race Task

7. Rewrite and check the following new instruction, taking care to interpret all of the robot programming grammar rules correctly. This instruction uses nested IF'S to face a robot toward the east; verify that it is correct by simulation. Hint: When trying to check this instruction, ignore the instruction indentation. One way of doing this is to have someone read you the instruction. While they are reading the instruction, you should keep track of the meaningful components of the instruction. This is exactly what the factory does when it reads instructions to robots at the factory.

```
public void faceEast()
{
        if(! facingEast())
{
                if(facingWest()){
                        turnLeft();
                        turnLeft();}
        else
                { if(facingNorth())
{
                        turnRight();}
                else    {
                        turnLeft();
                        }
                }
        }
}
```

8. The current version of mysteryInstruction is syntactically correct, but very difficult to read. Simplify it by using the IF transformations.

```
public void mysteryInstruction ()
{
        if(facingWest())
        {
                move();
                turnRight();
                if(facingNorth())
                {
                        move();
                }
                turnAround();
        }
        else
        {
                move();
                turnLeft();
                move();
                turnaround();
        }
}
```

9. Write an instruction for the MazeWalker class named followWallRight, assuming that whenever a robot executes this instruction there is a wall directly to the right. Figure 5-6 shows four of the different position changes that the robot must be able to make. This instruction is the cornerstone for a program that directs a robot to escape from a maze (this maze escape problem is Problem 5.9-17).

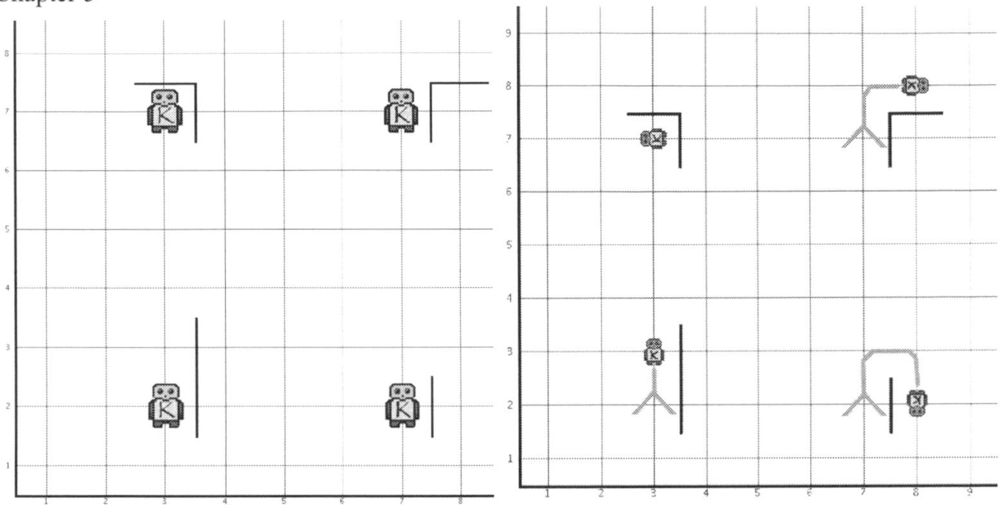

Figure 5-6 The follow-wall-right Specification

10. Program a robot to run a mile-long steeplechase where the steeples are made from beepers instead of wall segments. The robot must jump the steeples in this race by picking the beepers that make up the steeples. Each steeple is made from beepers that are positioned in columns that are one, two or three blocks long. Corners have either zero or one beeper. There are no gaps in any of the steeples. Figure 5-7 shows one sample initial situation.

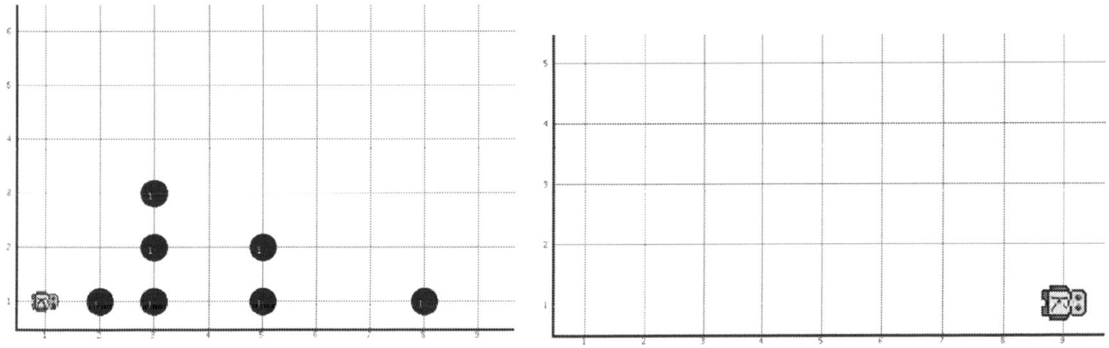

Figure 5-7 Different Steeplechase

11. A robot named karel has been hired to carpet some "small rooms" along a one mile section of its world. A "small room" is a corner that has a wall segment immediately to the west, north, and east. The door is to the south. Karel is to put a single beeper in only the "small rooms" and on no other corners. Figure 5-8 shows one set of initial and final situations. You may assume that karel has exactly eight beepers in its beeper-bag.

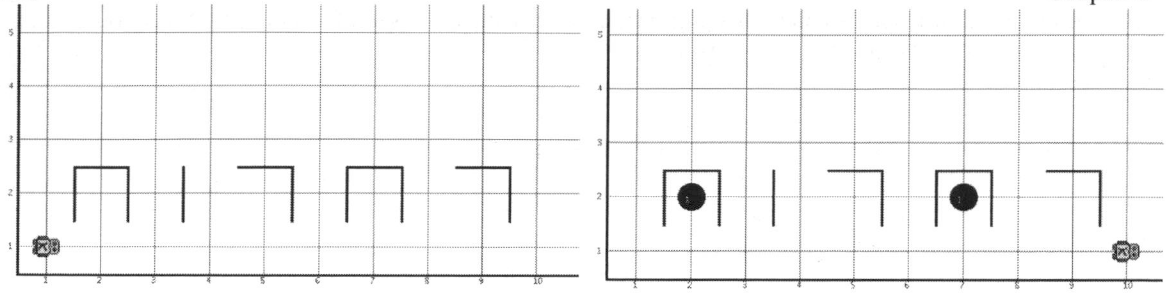

Figure 5-8 Carpeting Some Small Rooms

12. Karel did so well on the job in Problem 5.10-11 that the robot has been hired for a more complex carpeting task. The area to be carpeted is still one mile long. The rooms are now one, two or three blocks long. The room must have continuous walls on its west and east side and at its northern end. If any walls are missing, the area must not be carpeted. Also, karel must not reuse beepers. This means that once a beeper has been put down, it must not be picked up. Figure 5-9 shows one set of initial and final situations. You give karel exactly twenty-four beepers during construction and delivery.

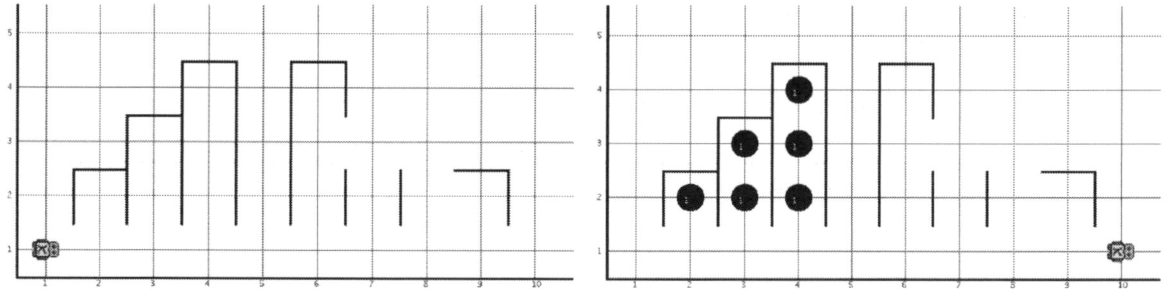

Figure 5-9 More Complex Carpet Laying

13. Write a predicate that will return true if and only if the robot executing it is both next to a beeper AND its left is blocked. Write another predicate that will return true if the robot executing it is either next to a beeper OR its left is blocked. In this latter case if the robot is next to a beeper with its left blocked it should also return true. Recall that nested IF's can be used to implement AND. Similarly, a sequence of IF's can be used to implement OR. What general conclusions can you draw from this exercise?

14. Write a predicate that will return true if and only if the robot executing it is has exactly two beepers in its beeper-bag. Can we write a predicate that will return true if and only if the robot executing it is on a corner with exactly two other robots? Why or why not? Write another predicate that will return true if and only if the robot executing it is on a corner with at most two beepers.

15. We are used to writing tests to be sure that a robot doesn't get into trouble. For example:

```
if(karel.frontIsClear())
{
        karel.move();
}
```

However, there is a situation in some robot programs in which this is not safe. For example, if we override move. Suppose we do override move to do something other than move one block. What can we also do in the same class to make the above safe again?

16. Modify your solution to Problem 4.12-21 so that the spiral walking robot properly shuts off when it reaches a wall.

17. Rewrite the exactlyTwoBeepers predicate to simplify it and make it easier to read and use. Write additional predicates as usual. Try to think of really good names for the parts.

6 Instructions That Repeat

This chapter completes our discussion of the instructions built into the robot programming language vocabulary. The two new instructions we will learn are FOR-LOOP and WHILE. Both instructions can repeatedly execute any instruction that a robot understands, including nested FOR-LOOP and WHILE instructions. These additions greatly enhance the conciseness and power of the robot programming language. In Section 6.7 we will construct a complex robot program by using stepwise refinement and all of the instructions we have learned.

Since we are becoming experienced robot programmers, an abbreviated view of the robot world will be used for some figures. To reduce visual clutter, the street and avenue labels and, occasionally, the southern or western boundary walls will not be shown. As usual, our examples will use a single robot, often named karel. Since most of our examples will involve manipulation of beepers, we suppose that we are building a class named BeeperController.

6.1 The FOR-LOOP Instruction

When we program a robot, having it repeat an instruction a certain number of times is sometimes necessary. We previously handled this problem by writing the instruction as many times as needed. The FOR-LOOP instruction gives us a mechanism which allows karel to repeat another instruction a specified number of times. Here we will introduce a simple form of a powerful Java statement. One can actually do much more with this statement than we will here, however. Before we introduce it, we need to say a few things about a kind of data that is built into Java, but not used much in robot programs. An int variable represents a subset of the integers of mathematics. The range of allowed values is from approximately - 2 billion to + 2 billion. Strictly speaking it is from -2^{31} to $+2^{31}-1$. The values that an int can hold are familiar to you as values such as -85, and 42. A variable of type int can hold one of these values at a time, and the value can be changed in an assignment. For example, we can create and initialize an int with

```
int x = 0;
```

We can then later give it a different value with

```
x = 42;
```

Note that the declaration only occurs once. One way to change a value is to give an int a value one more than its current value. This is simply done with just

```
x++;
```

If x had value 42 before executing this, then it has value 43 afterwards.

By the way, it isn't often necessary to know this, but if you increment the largest positive value, you get the smallest negative one.

In Java and in the Robot programming language, a simple FOR-LOOP has the following structure.

```
for ( int <variable-name> = 0;
      <variable-name> < <positive-number>;
      <variable-name> ++
    )
{
         <instruction-list>
}
```

This instruction introduces the reserved word **for**. The bracketed word <positive-number> tells the robot how many times to execute the instruction list that replaces <instruction-list>. We refer to <instruction-list> as the *body* of the FOR-LOOP instruction. The three instances of <variable-name> are to be replaced with any convenient name. This instruction is called FOR-**LOOP** because one can imagine the instructions of the <instruction-list> arranged in a circle. If we execute them one after the other, we will come to the first one just after the last one. Our first example of a FOR-LOOP instruction is an alternate definition of turnRight. Here we have used i as the <variable-name>. Notice there are three integer values that are >= 0 and < 3, namely [0, 1, 2].

```
public class BeeperController extends Robot
{
        public void turnRight()
        {       for (int i = 0; i < 3; i++)
                {       turnLeft();
                }
        }
...
}
```

The body of the FOR-LOOP will be executed three times, once when i is 0, once when it is 1, and again when it is 2. The three parts of the loop control in parentheses are separated by semicolons. The first is called the initialization. The second is the termination test. The last is executed after each of the repeated executions of the body. So, in effect, the above FOR-LOOP is similar to the following statements.

```
int i = 0;
if( i < 3)
{       turnleft();
        i++; // i is now 1
}
if(i < 3)
{       turnleft();
        i++; // i is now 2
}
if(i < 3)
{       turnLeft();
        i++; // i is now 3
}
```

The FOR-LOOP is actually much more flexible than what we use here, but this simple form is an important idiom and should be learned. It is all that we need for now.

As a second example, we rewrite the harvestOneRow method that was written in Section 3.8.3. This definition originally comprised nine primitive instructions, but by using FOR-LOOP we can define the method more concisely. With this new, more general version of harvestOneRow, we can now easily increase or decrease the number of beepers harvested per row; all we need to change is <positive-number> in the FOR-LOOP instruction.

```
public class Harvester extends Robot
{
        public void  harvestOneRow()
        {       harvestCorner();
                for (int i = 0; i < 4; i++)
                {       move();
                        harvestCorner();
                }
        }
...
}
```

Remember that the robot is originally on a corner with a beeper, so we need to harvest the first corner before we move. The above is equivalent to the following version, however. In this version we must remember to harvest the last corner after the loop completes, since we ended with a move and have only harvested the first four corners in this row.

```
public void harvestOneRow()
{       for (int i = 0; i < 4; i++)
        {       harvestCorner();
                move();
        }
        harvestCorner();
}
```

Finally, we show one FOR-LOOP instruction nested within another. Carefully observe the way that the inner loop both begins and ends within the outer loop. The <variable-name> of the control variable must be different for each loop.

```
public void walkSquareOfLength_6()
{       for (int i = 0; i < 4; i++)
        {       for (int j = 0; i < 6; i++)
                {       move();
                }
                turnLeft();
        }
}
```

If we assume no intervening walls, this instruction moves the robot around the perimeter of a square whose sides are six blocks long. The outer FOR-LOOP instruction loops a total of four times, once for each side of the square. Each time the outer FOR-LOOP's body is executed, the robot executes two instructions. First the robot executes the nested FOR-LOOP, which moves it six blocks. Then it executes the turnLeft, which prepares it to trace the next side. Thus, the robot executes a total of twenty-four moves and four left turns, which are arranged in an order that makes it travel in a square.

6.2 The WHILE Instruction

In this section we explain the WHILE instruction and analyze many of its interesting properties. It is the most powerful instruction that is built into the robot programming language.

6.2.1 Why WHILE is Needed

To motivate the need for a WHILE instruction, we look at what should be a simple programming task. Assume that a robot is initially facing east on some street, and somewhere east of it on that same street is a beeper. The robot's task is to move forward until it is on the same corner as the beeper, and then pick it up. Despite this simple description, the program is impossible to write with our current repertoire of instructions[10]. Two attempts at solving this problem might be written as follows.

```
if ( ! nextToABeeper())
{       move;
}
if ( ! nextToABeeper())
{       move();
}
                .
                .
                .
if ( ! nextToABeeper())
{       move();
}
pickBeeper();
```

```
for(int i = 0; i < ?; i++)
{       move();
}
pickBeeper();
```

We can interpret what is meant by these instructions, but robots understand neither ". . . " nor "?". The difficulty is that we do not know in advance how many move instructions the robot must execute before it arrives at the same corner as the beeper; we do not even have a guaranteed upper limit! The beeper may be on the robot's starting street corner, or it may be a million blocks away. The robot must be able to accomplish this task without knowing in advance the number of corners that it will pass before reaching the beeper. We must program our robot to execute move instructions repeatedly, until it senses that it is next to the beeper. What we need is an instruction that combines the repetition ability of the FOR-LOOP instruction with the testing ability of the IF instruction.

---

[10] Unless we use the technique called recursion that is discussed in Chapter 7.

6.2.2 The Form of the WHILE Instruction

The WHILE instruction commands a robot to repeat another instruction as long as some test remains true. The WHILE instruction is executed somewhat similarly to an IF instruction, except that the WHILE instruction repeatedly executes itself as long as <test> is true. The general form of the WHILE instruction is given below.

```
while ( <test> )
{
        <instruction-list>
}
```

The new reserved word **while** starts this instruction, the parentheses enclose <test>, and braces enclose the <instruction-list> in the usual way. The conditions that can replace <test> are the same ones used in the IF instructions.

A robot executes a WHILE loop by first checking <test> in its current situation. If the <test> is false, the robot is finished with the WHILE instruction, and it continues by executing the instructions following the entire WHILE loop. On the other hand, if the <test> is true, the robot executes <instruction-list> and then re-executes the entire WHILE loop. Here is a sample WHILE instruction that solves the problem that began this discussion.

```
public class BeeperController extends Robot
{
        public void goToBeeper()
        {       while ( ! nextToABeeper())
                {       move();
                }
                pickBeeper();
        }
...
}
```

This method moves a robot forward as long as nextToABeeper is false. When the robot is finally next to a beeper, it finishes executing the WHILE loop. After the loop terminates, the robot picks up the beeper. The following method is another simple example of a WHILE loop, and we will examine its behavior in detail.

```
public void clearCornerOfBeepers()
{       while ( nextToABeeper() )
        {       pickBeeper();
        }
}
```

Suppose we have a robot named karel in class BeeperController and send it the message karel.clearCornerOfBeepers(). This method commands karel to pick up all of the beepers on a corner. Let's simulate karel's execution of this instruction on a corner containing two beepers. Karel first determines whether nextToABeeper is true or false. Finding the test true, it executes the body of the WHILE loop, which is the pickBeeper message. Karel then re-executes the entire WHILE loop. The robot finds <test> is true (one beeper is still left), and executes the body of the WHILE loop. After picking up the second beeper, karel re-executes the entire WHILE instruction. Although we know that no beepers are remaining, karel is unaware of this fact until it rechecks the WHILE loop test. Now karel rechecks the test and discovers that nextToABeeper is false, so the robot is finished executing the WHILE loop. Because the entire definition consists of one WHILE loop, karel is finished executing clearCornerOfBeepers. It appears that no matter how many beepers are initially on the corner, karel will eventually pick them all up when this instruction is executed.

But what happens if karel executes clearCornerOfBeepers on a corner that has no beepers? In this situation, <test> is false the first time that the WHILE instruction is executed, so the loop body is not executed at all. Therefore, karel also handles this situation correctly. The key fact to remember about a WHILE instruction is that until karel discovers that <test> has become false--and it may be false the first time--karel repeatedly checks <test> and executes the loop's body if it is true.

6.2.3 Building a WHILE Loop - the Four Step Process

In the previous chapter on IF's we discussed the problems novice programmers frequently face when introduced to a new programming construct. We are in a similar situation with the WHILE loop. We have seen the form of a WHILE loop, looked at an example, and traced the execution of the example. Before using a WHILE loop in a robot program, it would be helpful to have a framework for thinking about the WHILE loop.

We should consider using a WHILE loop only when a robot must do something an unknown number of times. If we are faced with such a situation, we can build our WHILE loop by following the four step process shown below. To illustrate these steps, we will again consider the problem of having a robot named karel pick all beepers from a corner without knowing the initial number of beepers on the corner.

Step 1: Identify the one test (predicate) that must be true when karel is finished with the loop.

In the above problem, karel must pick all beepers on the corner. If we consider only tests that involve beepers we have four from which to choose: anyBeepersInBeeperBag, nextToABeeper, and their opposites. Which one is the test we want? When karel is finished, there should be no beepers left on the corner, so the test we want to be true is

```
! nextToABeeper().
```

Step 2: Use the opposite form of the test identified in step 1 as the loop <test>.

This implies we should use `nextToABeeper`. Does this make sense? The WHILE instruction continues to execute the loop body as long as the test is true and stops when it is false. As long as karel is next to a beeper it should pick them up. When it is done, there will be no beepers on the corner.

Step 3: Within the WHILE, make progress toward completion of the WHILE. We need to do something within the WHILE to ensure that the test eventually evaluates to false so that the WHILE loop stops. Often it is helpful to do the minimum amount of work that is necessary to advance toward the completion of the task.

Something within the body of the loop must allow the test to eventually evaluate to false or the loop will run forever. This implies that there must be some instruction (or sequence of instructions) within the loop that is related to the test. In this problem, what must be done to bring us closer to the test being false? Since we are testing for nextToABeeper, we must pick one (and only one) beeper somewhere in the loop. We can argue that if karel keeps picking one beeper, it must eventually pick all the beepers leaving none on the corner. Why pick only one beeper during each iteration? Why not two or three? If there is only one beeper on the corner, and we instruct karel to pick up more than one, an error shutoff will occur. Picking just one beeper during each iteration of the loop is the minimum needed to guarantee that all the beepers are eventually picked up.

Step 4: Do whatever is required before or after the WHILE instruction is executed to ensure we solve the given problem.

In this example, we have to do nothing before or after the loop. However, there are times when we may miss one iteration of the loop and have to "clean things up" which can be done either before or after the WHILE. Also, we sometimes need to execute an instruction or two before the WHILE loop to get our robot into the correct position.

If we follow these four steps carefully, we reduce the chance of having intent errors and infinite repetition when we test our program. Infinite execution is the error that occurs when we begin to execute a WHILE instruction, but it never terminates. This is discussed in Section 6.3.2.

6.2.4 A More Interesting Problem

Let's apply the steps presented above to a new problem. A robot named karel is somewhere in the world facing south. One beeper is on each corner between karel's current position and the southern boundary wall. There is no beeper on the corner on which karel is currently standing. Write a new method, clearAllBeepersToTheWall, to pick all of the beepers.

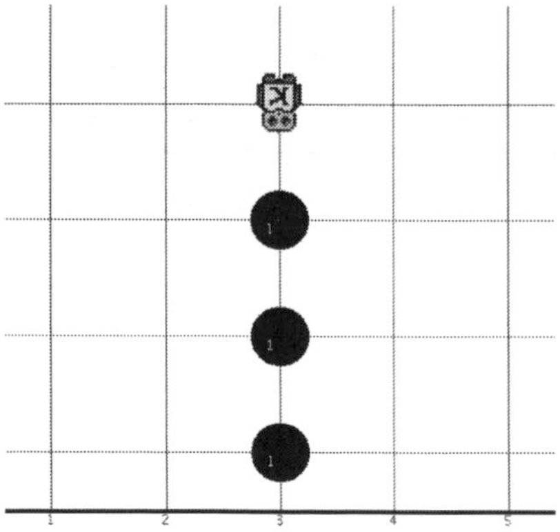

Figure 6-1 Pick All Beepers

As before, let's ask ourselves some questions:

Question: What do we know about karel's initial situation?

Answer: Karel is facing south.

Karel is an unknown distance from the southern boundary wall.

Each corner between karel and the southern boundary wall has one beeper.

Question: Does any of this information provide insight toward a solution?

Answer: Karel can travel forward until it reaches the southern boundary wall. It can pick a beeper from each corner as it travels.

We have the beginnings of a plan. We continue the process below.

Question: What robot instruction can we use to keep karel traveling southward until it reaches the southern boundary wall?

Answer: Since traveling to the southern boundary wall requires an unknown number of move instructions, we can use a WHILE loop.

Question: How do we actually use the WHILE loop?

Answer: We can use the four step process as follows:

Step 1: Identify the one test that must be true when karel is finished with the loop. Karel will be at the southern boundary wall, so the test, frontIsClear(), will be false, so ! frontIsClear() will be true.

Step 2: Use the opposite form of the test identified in step 1 as the loop <test>. FrontIsClear() is the opposite form.

Step 3: Do the minimum needed to ensure that the test eventually evaluates to false so that the WHILE loop stops. Karel must move forward one block within the loop body, but we must be careful here. Karel is not yet standing on a beeper so it must move first before picking the beeper. We can use a single pickBeeper instruction because there is only one beeper on each corner.

Step 4: Do whatever is required before or after the WHILE is executed to ensure we solve the given problem. Since karel is already facing south, we do not have to do anything.

Based on the above discussion we can write the following new method:

```
public void clearAllBeepersToTheWall()
{       while ( frontIsClear())
        {       move();
                pickBeeper();
        }
}
```

Our work is not finished. We must carefully trace the execution before we certify it as correct. Can we test all possible situations that karel could start this task in? No! We cannot test all possible situations but we can test several and do a reasonable job of convincing ourselves that the method is correct. One method of informally reasoning about the instruction follows.

First: Show that the method works correctly when the initial situation results in the test being false. That would mean that the initial situation would look like this:

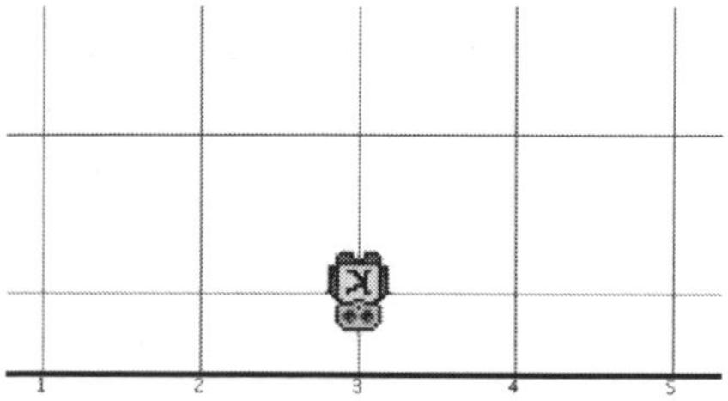

Figure 6-2 The Same Task Without Beepers

Second: We must show that each time the loop body is executed, karel's new situation is a simpler and similar version of the old situation. By simpler we mean that karel now has less work to do before finishing the loop. By similar we mean that karel's situation has not radically changed during its execution of the loop body (in this example a non-similar change could mean that karel is facing a different direction). If our new method is correct, we should see these changes in the following karel world:

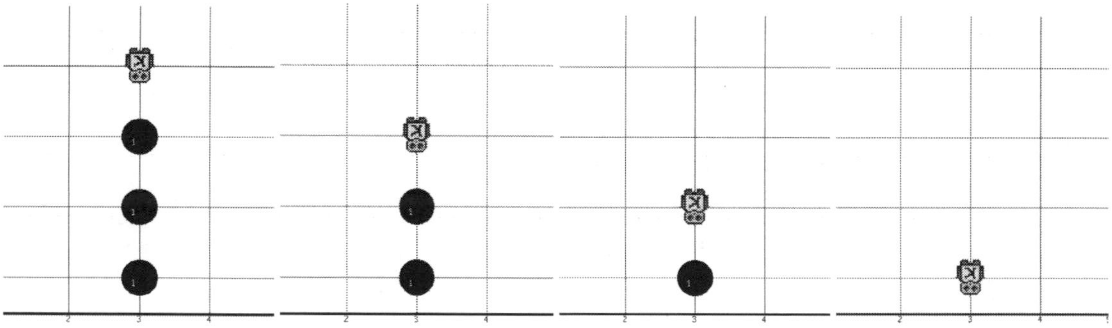

Figure 6-3 Tracing karel's Progress Executing the Loop

After each iteration of the loop, the current corner should have no beepers. Take some time and trace the robot's execution of the loop and verify that it is correct.

6.3 Errors to Avoid with WHILE Loops

The WHILE loop provides a powerful tool for our robot programs. Using it wisely, we can instruct robots to solve some very complex problems. However, the sharper the ax, the deeper it can cut. With the power of the WHILE loop comes the potential for making some powerful mistakes. This section will examine several typical errors that can be made when using the WHILE loop. If we are aware of these errors, we will have a better chance of avoiding them or, at least, an easier time identifying them for correction.

6.3.1 The Fence Post Problem

If we order five fence sections, how many fence posts do we need? The obvious answer is five! But it is wrong. Think about it.

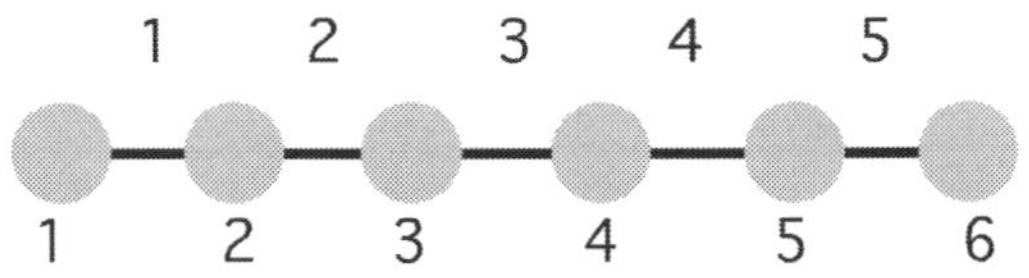

Figure 6-4 The Fence Post Problem

This diagram should help us to understand why the correct answer is six. We can encounter the fence post problem when using the WHILE loop. Let's take the previous problem with a slight twist and put a beeper on karel's starting corner.

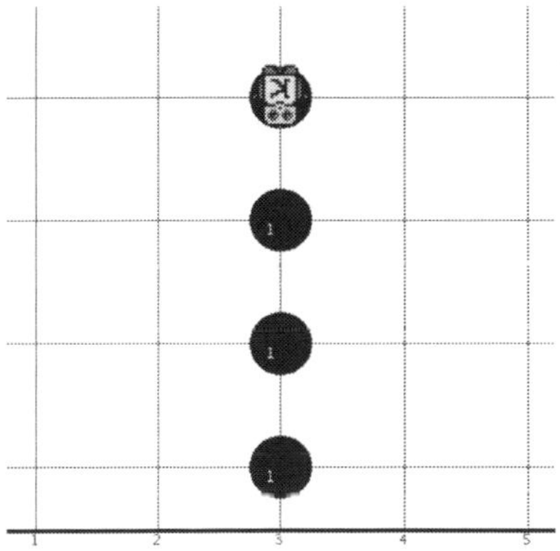

Figure 6-5 Initial Situation

Since this is a slight modification of the clearAllBeepersToTheWall task of the class BeeperController, it would be advantageous to have solutions to both problems available. One good way to do this is to build a new class, say BeeperSweeper, derived from BeeperController, in which to implement this new method, which is just an override of clearAllBeepersToTheWall.

Suppose we decide to solve this problem by reversing the order of the messages in the original loop body and have karel pick the beeper before moving:

```
public class BeeperSweeper extends BeeperController
{
        void  clearAllBeepersToTheWall()
        {       while ( frontIsClear() )
                {       pickBeeper();
                        move();
                }
        }
...
}
```

If we trace the method's execution carefully, we will discover that the loop still finishes--there is no error shutoff--however, the southernmost beeper is not picked.

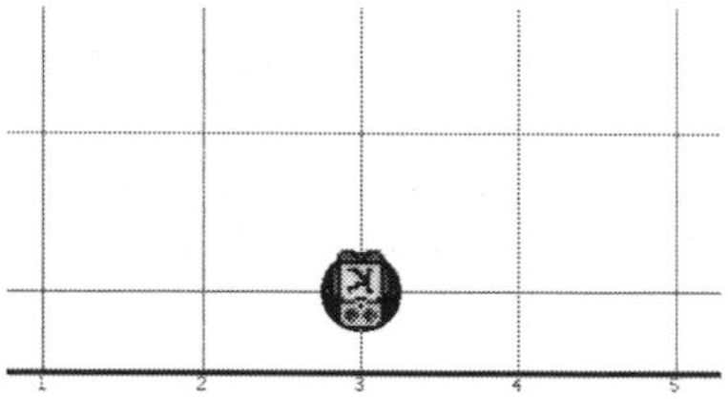

Figure 6-6 Final Situation

In this example the beepers were the fence posts and the moves were the fence sections. The WHILE loop executes the same number of pickBeeper and move messages. Consequently, there will be one beeper left when the loop finishes. This is where step 4 in the four step process comes in. We now have a situation where we must do something before or after the loop to make sure we solve the given problem. There are at least two ways to handle this. Here is one.

```
public void clearAllBeepersToTheWall()
{       while ( frontIsClear() )
        {       pickBeeper();
                move();
        }
        pickBeeper();
}
```

Our solution is simply to pick the final beeper after the WHILE loop stops executing. What is the other way to solve this fence post problem? Ah yes. We could pick up the beeper on the start corner first. This would put us in the initial position of clearAllBeepersToTheWall. This means that we can actually use that instruction to write this one.

```
public void clearAllBeepersToTheWall()
{       pickBeeper();
        super.clearAllBeepersToTheWall();
}
```

6.3.2 Infinite Execution

Having looked at step 4 in the four step process, let's now refocus our attention on step 3: do what is needed to ensure that the test eventually evaluates to false so that the WHILE loop stops. Sometimes we forget to include an instruction (or sequence of instructions) that allows the test to eventually become false. Here is an example:

```
while   ( facingNorth() )
{       pickBeeper();
        move();
}
```

Look at this loop carefully. Is there any instruction within the loop body that will change the robot's direction? Neither pickBeeper nor move does so. The loop will iterate zero times if the robot is initially facing any direction other than north. Unfortunately, if it is facing north we condemn the robot to walk forever (since the world is infinite to the north) or to execute an error shutoff if it arrives at a corner without a beeper[11]. We must be very careful when we plan the body of the WHILE loop to avoid the possibility of infinite repetition.

6.3.3 When the test of a WHILE is Checked

Section 6.2.2 explained how a robot executes a WHILE instruction, yet unless the instruction is read carefully, there may be some ambiguity. In this section we closely examine the execution of a WHILE instruction and explain a common misconception about when a robot checks <test>. Let's examine the following instruction carefully.

```
public void harvestLine()
{       while ( nextToABeeper() )
        {       pickBeeper();
                move();
        }
}
```

This method commands a robot to pick up a line of beepers. The robot finishes executing this method after moving one block beyond the final corner that has a beeper.

Let's simulate this new method in detail for a line of two beepers. Karel starts its task on the same corner as the first beeper. The robot is again named karel. Karel executes the WHILE instruction and finds that the test is true, so it executes the body of the loop. The loop body instructs karel to pick up the beeper and then move to the next corner. Now karel reexecutes the loop; the test is checked, and again karel senses that it is next to a beeper. The robot picks up the second beeper and moves forward. Karel then executes the loop again. Now when the test is checked, the robot finds that its corner is beeperless, so it is finished executing the WHILE loop. The definition of harvestLine contains only one instruction--this WHILE loop--so harvestLine is also finished.

---

[11] Of course, if we have overridden pickBeeper or move, then anything is possible. One of the new versions could change the direction, and then the robot would exit the WHILE.

The point demonstrated here is that karel checks <test> only before it executes the body of the loop. Karel is totally insensitive to <test> while executing instructions that are inside the loop body. A common misconception among novice programmers is that karel checks <test> after each instruction is executed inside the loop body. This is an incorrect interpretation of when karel checks <test>.

Let's see what would happen if karel used the incorrect interpretation to execute the harvestLine method in the two-beeper situation. This interpretation would force karel to finish the WHILE loop as soon as it was not next to a beeper. Karel would start by determining if it were next to a beeper. Finding the test true, karel would execute the loop body. This is fine so far but, after executing the pickBeeper, karel would not be next to a beeper anymore. So, according to this incorrect interpretation, karel would now be finished with the loop and would be limited to picking up only one beeper regardless of the length of the beeper line.

Recall again the fence sections and fence posts. Notice that the body of a while is like a fence section and the test is like a fence post. The number of test evaluations is always one more than the number of executions of the body of the WHILE instruction.

6.4 Nested WHILE Loops

We have already discussed nesting, or the placing of one instruction within a similar instruction. Nesting WHILE loops can be a very useful technique if done properly and in this section we will look at both a good and a bad example of nesting.

6.4.1 A Good Example of Nesting

We will use a modification of a previous problem. A robot named karel is somewhere in the world facing south. Between its current location and the southern boundary wall are beepers. We do not know how many beepers are on each corner (some corners may even have no beepers). Write a new method that will direct karel to pick all the beepers between its current location and the southern boundary wall.

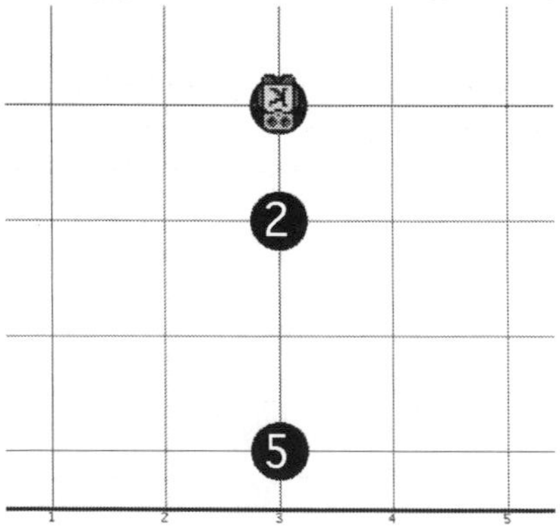

Figure 6-7 A Problem to Move and Pick Beepers

We can use our question/answer format to plan a solution to this problem.

Question: What is the problem?

Answer: We must move karel an unknown distance and have karel pick an unknown number of beepers from each corner it passes.

Question: What does karel have to do?

Answer: Karel must perform two tasks:

- First, karel must walk an unknown distance to the southern wall.

- Second, karel must pick all the beepers on each corner it encounters. There may be from zero to a very large number of beepers on each corner.

Let's concentrate on the first task and save the second task for later.

Question: What instruction can we use to keep karel moving forward to the southern boundary wall?

Answer: Since this requires an unknown number of iterations of the **move** instruction, we can use the WHILE loop.

We can apply the four step process for building WHILE loops and write the following code for karel to test.

```
while   ( frontIsClear() )
{       move();
}
```

If karel executes this instruction correctly, then our plan is on the right track. However, if karel stops before arriving at the boundary wall or executes an error shutoff when it tries to move through the wall, we must reanalyze our plan. This instruction works properly so we now consider the second task--the picking of all beepers on each corner karel encounters as it travels to the boundary wall.

Question: What instruction will allow karel to pick all the beepers that might be on a corner?

Answer: Since this requires an unknown number of iterations of the pickBeeper instruction, we can use the WHILE instruction to do this task also.

We can apply the four step process for building WHILE loops and write the following implementation.

```
while   ( nextToABeeper() )
{       pickBeeper();
}
```

We simulate this and it appears to work. We now have to decide which loop to nest inside which loop. Do we put the loop that moves karel to the southern boundary wall inside the loop that picks beepers or do we put the beeper picking loop inside the loop that moves karel to the wall?

Question: Can we interchange these two actions?

Answer: No, we cannot. Arriving at the wall should stop both karel's moving and picking. Running out of beepers on one corner should NOT stop karel's moving to the wall. As we move to the wall we can clean each corner of beepers if we nest the beeper picking loop inside the loop that moves karel to the wall.

Our new method definition will look like this.

```
public void clearAllBeepersToTheWall()
{       while ( frontIsClear() )
        {       while ( nextToABeeper() )
                {       pickBeeper();
                }
                move();
        }
}
```

To solve the problem of deciding which WHILE loop is to be the outer loop, we can apply the each test. Do we need to pick up all of the beepers for each single step we take to the wall, or do we need to walk all the way to the wall for each single beeper that we pick up? Here, the answer is the former and the outer loop is the stepping (move) loop.

When we nest WHILE loops we must be very sure that the execution of the nested loop (or inner loop) does not interfere with the test condition of the outer loop. In this problem the inner loop is responsible for picking beepers. The outer loop is responsible for moving the robot. These two activities do not affect each other so the nesting seems correct.

We are not done. We must now test this new method. Take some time and trace karel's execution of it using the initial situation shown in Figure 6.7. As much as we would like to believe it is correct, it isn't. We appear to have forgotten the fence post discussion of section 6.3.1. The way we have written the new method, the last corner will not be cleared of beepers; this last corner is our forgotten fence post. To ensure the last corner is cleared of beepers, we must make one more modification.

```
public void clearAllBeepersToTheWall()
{       while ( frontIsClear() )
        {       while ( nextToABeeper() )
                {       pickBeeper();
                }
                move();
        }
        while ( nextToABeeper() )
        {       pickBeeper();
        }
}
```

This third loop is outside the nested loops and it will clear the last corner of beepers.

One note here about overall design of our new method: As a rule we prefer to perform only one task (e.g., moving to a wall) in a new method and move secondary tasks (e.g., picking the beepers) into a different new method. We believe the following represents a better programming style for the previous problem.

```
public void clearBeepersThisCorner()
{       while ( nextToABeeper() )
        {       pickBeeper();
        }
}

public void clearAllBeepersToTheWall()
{       while ( frontIsClear() )
        {       clearBeepersThisCorner();
                move();
        }
        clearBeepersThisCorner();
}
```

This programming style is easier to read and, if we suddenly find that clearing the beepers requires a different strategy, we only have to make a change in one place, clearBeepersThisCorner.

6.4.2 A Bad Example of Nesting

A robot named karel is facing south in the northwest corner of a room that has no doors or windows. Somewhere in the room, next to a wall, is a single beeper. Instruct karel to find the beeper by writing the new method, findBeeper.

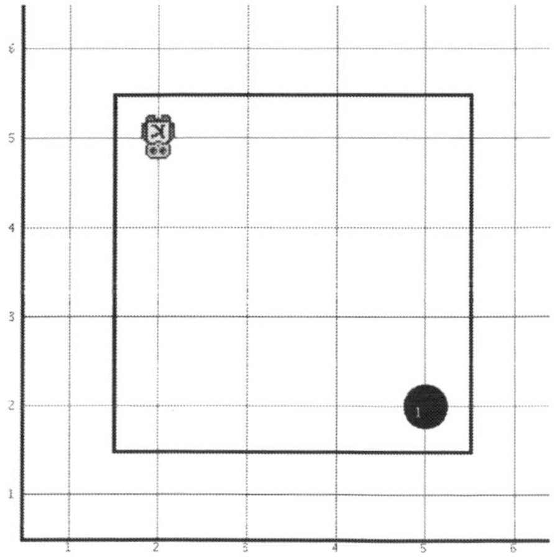

Figure 6-8 Initial Situation #1

We begin with our usual question/answer planning.

Question: What is the problem?

Answer: We must instruct karel to find a beeper that is somewhere in the room next to the wall. We do not know how far away it is, and we do not know how big the room is.

Question: What instruction can we use to move karel to the beeper?

Answer: Since the distance karel must travel is unknown, we can use a WHILE loop.

Using the four step process to build a WHILE loop we develop the following new method.

```
public void findBeeper()
{       while  ( ! nextToABeeper() )
        {       move();
        }
}
```

If we carefully analyze this new method, we find, as shown in Figure 6-9, that karel executes an error shutoff when it arrives at the southern wall.

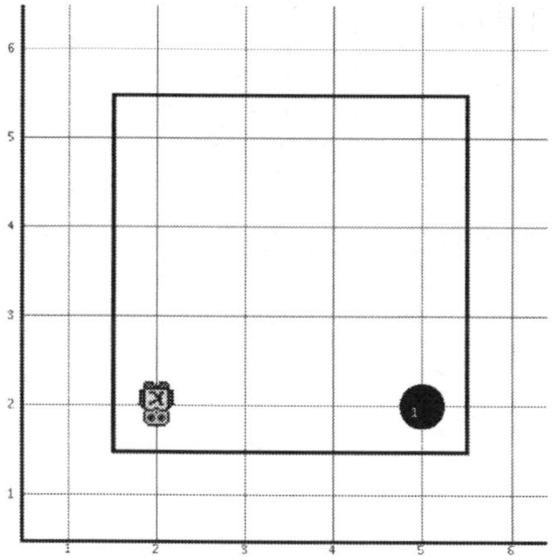

Figure 6-9 Karel Executes an Error Shutoff

Question: What happened?

Answer: We forgot about turning karel at the corners.

Question: How can we fix this problem?

Answer: Let's walk karel forward until it detects a wall.

Question: What instruction can we use to do this?

Answer: Since the distance karel must travel is unknown, we can use a WHILE loop.

Again we use the four step process to build a nested WHILE loop and develop the following new method.

```
public void findBeeper()
{       while ( ! nextToABeeper() )
        {       while ( frontIsClear() )
                {       move();
                }
                turnLeft();
        }
}
```

We must test this to see if it works. Since this problem is somewhat involved, we should use several different initial situations. Will the following situations be sufficient to test our code completely?

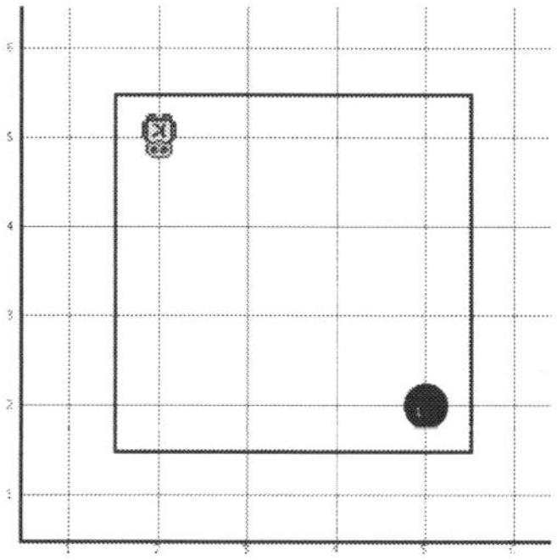

Initial Situation #1

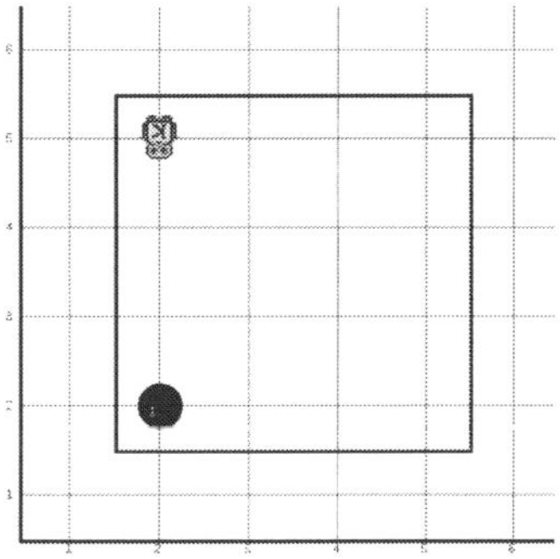

Initial Situation #2

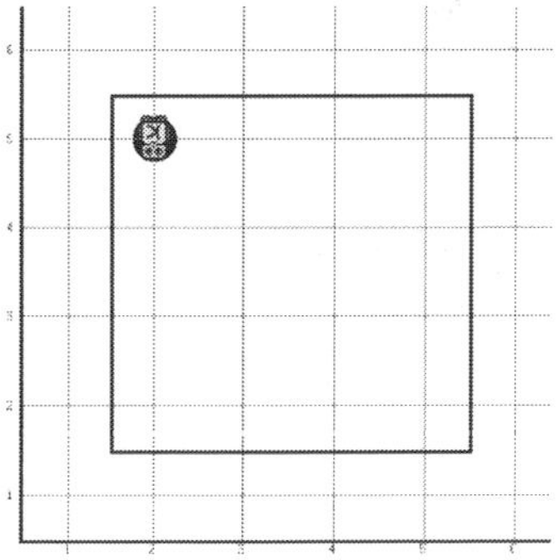

Initial Situation #3

Figure 6-10 Three Different Initial Situations

If we trace our program using these situations, it appears that our method is correct. However, does the original problem statement guarantee that the beeper will always be in a corner? It does not. The original problem statement says that the beeper is somewhere next to a wall. Our three test situations each put the beeper in a corner. We should try an initial situation such as this.

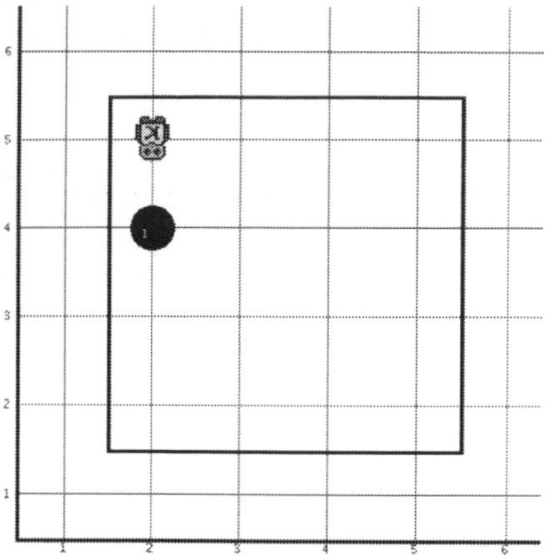

Initial situation #4

Figure 6-11 Another Situation With Which to Test Our method Definition

Let's see what happens here: karel makes the outer test, ! nextToABeeper, and it is true so it begins to execute the outer loop body.

Karel makes the inner test, frontIsClear, which is true so karel moves forward one block coming to rest on the corner with the beeper. What happens now? Karel remains focused on the inner loop. It has not forgotten about the outer loop but its focus is restricted to the inner loop until the inner loop stops execution. Karel is required to make the inner test, frontIsClear, which is true and moves one block forward away from the beeper. This is now karel's situation.

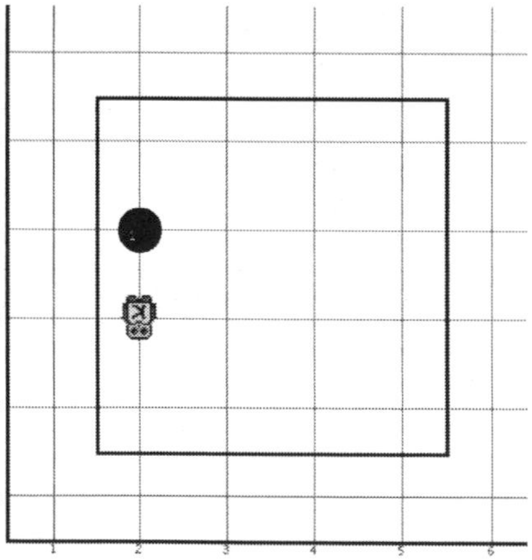

Current Situation

Figure 6-12 Karel Misses the Beeper

Karel remains focused on the inner loop and makes the inner test again. It is true so karel executes the move and is now in this situation:

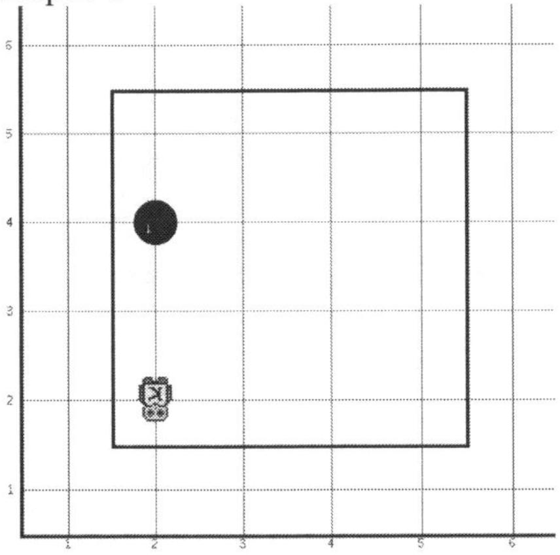

Current Situation

Figure 6-13 Karel Arrives at the Wall

The inner test is false, so karel ceases execution of the inner loop, executes the turnLeft and is done with the first iteration of the outer loop. Now karel makes the outer test, !nextToABeeper, which is true. Karel has no memory of once standing next to a beeper, consequently, karel will continue to walk around this room and keep going and going and going . . . Our method will execute infinitely in this case!

There must be something wrong with our initial reasoning. Let's look at the initial planning segment.

Question: What is the problem?

Answer: We must instruct karel to find a beeper that is somewhere in the room next to a wall. We do not know how far away it is, and we do not know how big the room is.

Question: What instruction can we use to move karel to the beeper?

Answer: Since the distance karel must travel is unknown, we can use a WHILE loop.

We then found that karel performed an error shutoff because we instructed karel to move forward when the front was blocked by a wall. Our next planning segment appears below.

Question: What happened?

Answer: We forgot about turning karel at the corners.

Question: How can we fix this problem?

Answer: Let's walk karel forward until it detects a wall.

Question: What instruction can we use to do this?

Answer: Since the distance karel must travel is unknown, we can use a WHILE loop.

This is where our plan began to go wrong. We decided to walk karel forward until the front was blocked. We reasoned that we could use a WHILE loop to move karel forward and that was the mistake. If the robot moves more than one block forward without allowing the test of the outer WHILE loop to be checked, it will violate step 4 of the four step process--"Do whatever is needed to ensure the loop stops." Karel should only move one block forward within the outer WHILE loop. We should not use an inner WHILE loop to move karel toward the wall! The reason is that karel's execution of the inner WHILE loop can cause the outer WHILE loop to never stop. Both the outer and inner WHILE loops require karel to execute the move instruction so both loops will eventually terminate. Unless both tests, `!nextToABeeper` and `frontIsClear`, are false at the exact same time, the outer loop will never stop. We must discard the inner WHILE loop and find a different way to keep karel from trying to move through the wall.

Question: How can we move karel forward without the WHILE loop?

Answer: Karel should only move forward one block inside the WHILE loop so we must use an IF/ELSE statement to check for a wall. Karel will move when the front is clear and turn left when a wall is present.

Following our new reasoning, we have the following new method.

```
public void findBeeper()
{       while ( ! nextToABeeper() )
        {       if ( frontIsClear() )
                {       move();
                }
                else
                {       turnLeft();
                }
        }
}
```

Nesting WHILE loops is a powerful programming idea, but with this increased power comes the increased need for very careful planning and analysis.

An alternate way to solve this is to start as we did previously with a simple while loop, but suppose the existence of a method moveTowardBeeper.

```
public void findBeeper()
{       while ( ! nextToABeeper() )
        {       moveTowardBeeper();
        }
}
```

What do we have to do to move toward the beeper? If we don't interpret it literally, but rather as "make one step of progress toward the goal of finding the beeper" then we easily arrive at:

```
public void moveTowardBeeper()
{       if ( frontIsClear() )
        {       move();
        }
        else
        {       turnLeft();
        }
}
```

6.5 WHILE and IF Instructions

Novice programmers frequently use WHILE and IF instructions in a conflicting, unnecessary, or redundant manner. Examine the following program fragments to find improperly used tests.

```
if ( facingSouth() )
{       while ( ! facingSouth() )
        {       turnLeft();
        }
}
```

In this fragment there are conflicting tests. When the IF's test is true the WHILE's test must be false. This fragment will do nothing.

Let's try another one.

```
while ( ! frontIsClear())
{       if ( frontIsClear())
        {        move();
        }
        else
        {       turnLeft();
        }
}
```

In this fragment there is an unnecessary test. When the WHILE's test is true, the IF's test must be false so the ELSE is the only part of the loop body that is ever executed.

Here is another.

```
while ( nextToABeeper() )
{       if ( nextToABeeper() )
        {       pickBeeper();
        }
}
```

In this fragment there are redundant tests. The WHILE's test is the same as the IF's test. When the WHILE's test is true so is the IF's.

Problems such as these usually enter our programs when we attempt to fix execution or intent errors. We sometimes get so involved in the details of our program that we forget to take a step back and look at the overall picture. It is often very helpful to take a break and come back to the program with fresh eyes.

6.6 Reasoning about Loops

In section 6.2.3 we discussed the four step process for building a WHILE loop.

Step 1. Identify the one test that must be true when the robot is finished with the loop.

Step 2. Use the opposite form of the test identified in step 1 as the loop <test>.

Step 3. Do what is needed to make progress toward solving the problem at hand and also ensure that the test eventually evaluates to false so that the WHILE loop stops.

Step 4. Do whatever is required before or after the WHILE is executed to ensure we solve the given problem.

We also presented an informal way to reason about the correctness of WHILE loops.

1. Show that the instruction works correctly when the initial situation results in the test being false.

2. Show that each time the loop body is executed, the robot's new situation is a simpler and similar version of the old situation.

We'd like to spend a little more time discussing this last concept of correctness. Remember that a robot will do exactly what it is told and only what it is told. It is up to us to make sure that it is provided with a correct way to solve a given problem. At the same time, we need a way to "prove" (in some sense) that our solution is correct. It will be impossible for us to simulate every possible situation, so we need a way to think through our solution in a formal way to verify that it does what it is supposed to do.

In order to reason about WHILE loops, we will need to understand a key concept called a loop invariant. A loop invariant is an assertion (something that can be proven true or false) which is true after each iteration of the loop. For our purposes, loop invariants will be assertions about the robot's world. In particular, the items that we need to be concerned about after ONE iteration are the following:

* How has the robot's direction changed, if at all?

* How has the robot's relative position in the world changed, if at all (this may involve thinking about wall segments as well)?

* How has the number of beepers in the robot's beeper-bag changed, if at all?

* How has the number and location of other beepers in the world changed, if at all?

Let's look at these items using the example given in section 6.2.4, clearAllBeepersToTheWall. After one iteration of the following loop,

```
while ( frontIsClear() )
{       move();
        pickBeeper();
}
```

what can we say (assert) about the items mentioned above? We can assert the following:

* The robot's direction is unchanged,

* The robot's position has been advanced one corner,

* That corner has one less beeper, and

* The robot's beeper-bag has another beeper.

Which of these statements are "interesting?" By "interesting" we mean which item is important in terms of the problem being solved. Since we're removing beepers from the world as the robot moves forward, we're interested in the second and third assertions. A loop invariant captures the interesting change during one iteration of the loop. Thus, for this problem, the loop invariant is that the robot has advanced one corner and removed one beeper from that corner, but there is still one beeper on each corner in front of it to the wall.

What else have we learned? Let's look at our loop test, frontIsClear. When the loop ends, it will be false, thus the front will be blocked. So we know that when the loop terminates, the robot has removed one beeper from each corner it has passed and the robot's front is now blocked. We have learned that as long as each corner had one beeper on it, our loop must have solved the problem of picking up beepers to the wall.

Let's look at the fencepost problem presented in section 6.3.1. What is the loop invariant for the first attempt at solving that problem? Here's the loop:

```
while  ( frontIsClear() )
{       pickBeeper();
        move();
}
```

What can we assert about this loop?

* The robot's direction is unchanged.

* The robot's position has been advanced forward one corner.

* The previous corner has one less beeper, but every corner to the wall, including the current has a beeper.

* The robot's beeper-bag has one more beeper.

What do we know about the robot and the world when the loop finishes? We know that any previous corners have had one beeper removed from them. Finally, we know that the robot's front is blocked.

What about the robot's current corner? Since the loop invariant only mentions previous corners, we know nothing about the corner on which the robot is standing when the loop terminates--it may have a beeper, it may not. How we choose to remedy this situation is up to us, but at least in reasoning about the loop we have become aware of a potential problem with our loop--the fencepost problem.

Loop invariants can be powerful tools in aiding our understanding of how a loop is operating and what it will cause a robot to do. The key lies in determining how executing the loop changes the state of the world during each iteration and capturing that change as succinctly as possible. Once we've discovered the loop invariant, we can use it and the loop's termination condition to decide if the loop solves the problem. If not, we must look back over the steps for constructing a WHILE loop to see where we might have gone wrong.

Another use of loop invariants is to help us determine what instructions we want to use in the loop body. So far we've used the loop invariant as an after-the-fact device, to verify that a loop we've written solves a specific problem. If we decide what we want the invariant to be before we write the body of the loop, it can help in deciding what the body should be. As an example, consider the following problem: A robot is searching for a beeper that is an unknown distance directly in front of it and there may be some one-block high wall segments in the way.

What do we want to be true when the loop terminates? Since the robot is looking for a beeper, we want it to be next to a beeper. Thus, our test is ! nextToABeeper. What do we want to be invariant? The robot must move one (and only one) block forward during each iteration of the loop to ensure that each corner is examined. Our first pass at a loop might look like this:

```
while ( ! nextToABeeper() )
{       move();
}
```

Unfortunately, this will cause an error shutoff if we happen to run into one of those intervening wall segments before reaching the beeper. How can we maintain our invariant and still avoid the wall segment? A little insight might suggest the following modification:

```
while ( ! nextToABeeper() )
{       if ( frontIsClear() )
        {       move();
        }
        else
        {       avoidWall();
        }
}
```

where avoidWall is defined as:

```
public void avoidWall()
{       turnLeft();
        move();
        turnRight();
        move();
        turnRight();
        move();
        turnLeft();
}
```

In defining avoidWall, we must keep the loop invariant in mind. We want to make progress toward our goal, but as little progress as possible so that we don't accidentally miss something. We should spend some time convincing ourselves that this loop maintains the initial invariant: the robot moves exactly one block forward during each iteration of the loop. Then we can also convince ourselves that this loop does solve the problem.

6.7 A Large Program Written by Stepwise Refinement

In this section we will write a complex program by using stepwise refinement. Suppose that we need to patrol the perimeter of a rectangular field of beepers. Imagine that there has been theft of the beepers and we need a robot guard to walk around the edge of the field. Let us build a class of Guard robots with a method walkPerimeter. The robot will initially be positioned somewhere in the field, but not necessarily on an edge.

To make the problem more definite, let's suppose that the field is at least two beepers wide and two beepers long. The path we want the robot to follow is one that walks along corners that actually contain the beepers marking the outer edge of the field. In the sample initial situation shown in Figure 6.14, the path should include 2nd and 9th Streets and 3rd and 7th Avenues.

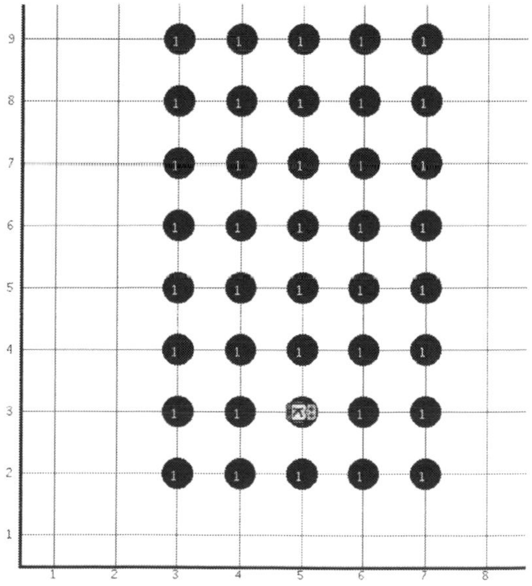

Figure 6.14 Initial Situation

As an initial strategy suppose that we walk our robot, say tony, to the south-east corner and have it walk the perimeter from there. We may need other methods to help us build these, but a first approximation to our class definition is as follows.

```
public class Guard extends Robot
{       public void moveToSouthEastCorner()
        {
                ...
        }

        public void walkPerimeter()
        {
                ...
        }
        . . .
}
```

First, lets attack the `walkPerimeter` method, assuming that we can begin it at the south-east corner. Since it is easier for a robot to turn left (faster anyway) than to turn right, lets program the robot to walk around the field in a counter-clockwise direction, turning left at each corner. Since there are four edges to be walked we can use a for loop instruction. For each execution of the body of the loop we should walk one edge and then turn left at the end of it.

```
public void walkPerimeter() // Robot begins at a corner of the field
{       for(int j = 0; j < 4; j++)
        {       followEdge();
                turnLeft();
        }
}
```

This solution, of course, requires that we add an additional method, `followEdge`, to the Guard class. What does it take to follow an edge? Since the edge is marked by beepers the robot can simply move along it until there is no beeper on the current corner.

```
private void followEdge() //Robot starts on a corner with a beeper
{       while (nextToABeeper())
        {       move();
        }
}
```

If we try to simulate this by hand we find an error. After executing followEdge, tony is left on a corner without any beepers. Since turnLeft doesn't change the corner, we find that after executing followEdge and then turnLeft once, we are not in a legal position to execute followEdge again. What actually happens when we execute followEdge, is that tony walks outside the field and then turns completely around in place. Well, suppose that we have tony back-up as the last step in followEdge, so that it is left on a corner with a beeper. Backing up requires that the robot be able to turn around. Thus we must add the following.

```
private void turnAround()
{       turnLeft();
        turnLeft();
}

private void backUp()
{       turnAround();
        move();
        turnAround();
}
```

Now we can correct followEdge.

```
private void followEdge() //Robot starts on a corner with a beeper
{       while (nextToABeeper())
        {       move();
        }
        backUp();
}
```

Now our simulation seems to be correct, so we turn to moveToSouthEastCorner. To do this we can have the robot face south and then move until it is on the edge of the field, turn left and then walk until it reaches the corner. Facing south is not especially difficult since we have a test for facing south.

```
private void faceSouth()
{       while (! facingSouth())
        {       turnLeft();
        }
}
```

To move to the south edge of the field tony now just needs to walk until there is no beeper on the current corner and then backup. But that is exactly what followEdge does.

```
public void moveToSouthEastCorner()
{       faceSouth();
        followEdge(); // Now at south edge of field
        turnLeft();
        followEdge(); // Now at south-east corner of field
}
```

Well, we have carried out our plan, but when we execute it we find that the robot only walks around three sides of the field, not all four, though it does walk part of the fourth side while it is moving to the south-east corner. What is wrong? Each instruction seems to do what it was designed to do, but they don't fit together very well. The problem is that after executing moveToSouthEastCorner, the robot is left facing east. Then, when we ask it to walkPerimeter it begins by walking immediately outside the field. The first execution of followEdge has taken us outside the field. and then back to the corner, "wasting" one of our four executions of followEdge. We should make the *post-conditions* of one instruction match up better with the *pre-*

conditions of the next. A pre-condition for a method is a predicate that the caller of an instruction is required to establish before executing the method to guarantee its correct behavior. For example, a pre-condition for the pickBeeper method is that the robot be on a corner with a beeper. A post-condition for a method is the predicate that is guaranteed to be true when an method completes, if all of its pre-conditions were true before it was executed. The post-condition of the pickBeeper method is that the robot has at least one beeper in its beeper-bag.

Suppose that we add an additional post-condition to moveToSouthEastCorner and require that it turn at the end of its walk to put the field to the left of the robot. We can establish this by adding a turnLeft to the end of moveToSouthEastCorner.

```
public void moveToSouthEastCorner()
{       faceSouth();
        followEdge(); // Now at south edge of field
        turnLeft();
        followEdge();
        turnLeft(); // Now at south-east corner of field facing North
}
```

Now, when we simulate our robot, it will correctly follow all four edges of the field of Figure 6.14. When we try it in other legal fields, however, we find that we have trouble. For example, we find that tony will execute an error shutoff in trying to patrol the field of Figure 6.15.

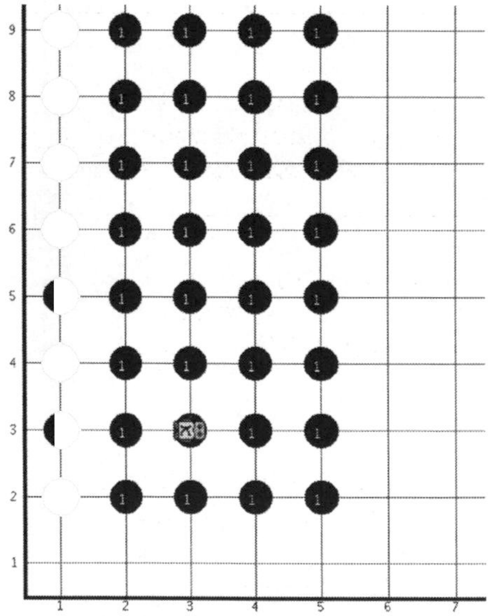

Figure 6.15 Another Initial Position

We call this type of situation a *beyond-the-horizon situation*. Normally, we write a program guided by a few initial situations that seem to cover all interesting aspects of the task. Although we would like to prove that all other situations are not too different from these sample situations, frequently the best we can do is hope. As we explore the problem and learn more about the task, we may discover situations that are beyond our original horizons--situations that are legal, but special trouble-causing cases. Once we suspect a beyond-the-horizon situation, we should immediately simulate a robot's execution in it. If our suspicions are confirmed, and the robot does not perform as we intended, we must modify our program accordingly.

We must reprogram the robot to realize that it is at the edge of a field as soon as it contacts a wall, as well as when it is no longer at a beeper. Since all of our edge sensing is in followEdge, we look there for a solution.

Here is a solution in which we need stop moving when either !nextToABeeper() OR !frontIsClear() become true. Therefore, the opposite of this is our condition for continuing to move. The opposite is:

```
while (nextToABeeper() && frontIsClear()) ...
```

This is, of course, equivalent to the predicate below.

```
public boolean nextToABeeper_and_frontIsClear()
{       if( nextToABeeper() )
        {       return frontIsClear();
        }
        return false;
}
```

It will be instructive, however, to try to use nested constructs as in Chapter 5. Here, however, we have WHILE instructions and not IF instructions. Often the correct solution to this is to nest an IF instruction inside of a WHILE instruction. Suppose we try each of the following to see if they might help us here.

```
while(nextToABeeper())
{       if(frontIsClear())
        {       move();
        }
}
```

```
while(frontIsClear())
{       if(nextToABeeper())
        {       move();
        }
}
```

The second one seems clearly wrong, since once a robot begins executing, execution will continue until it encounters a wall. Since walls aren't necessarily part of the problem, the robot will walk too far afield.

The first also seems to be ok until we simulate it in our beyond-the-horizon situation, in which it will continue to execute forever. The problem is that when we encounter the wall we are still on a corner with a beeper and so we don't exit from the while. We can solve this, however, by picking up the beeper in this situation.

```
while(nextToABeeper())
{       if(frontIsClear())
        {       move();
        }
        else
        {       pickBeeper();
        }
}
```

Now we will exit, but must replace the beeper that we may have picked up. After we exit this while loop, we know that there is no beeper on the current corner, but we don't know if we picked one up or not. We could simply ask the robot to put a beeper if it has any, but this requires that the robot begin with no beepers in its beeper-bag. What else do we know? Well, we know that if we picked up a beeper it was because our front was blocked and we haven't moved or turned so its front must still be blocked in that case. If it is not blocked, it is because we have walked off the edge of the field to an empty corner.

```
public void followEdge() //Robot starts on a corner with a beeper
{       while(nextToABeeper())
        {       if(frontIsClear())
                {       move();
                }
                else
                {       pickBeeper();
                }
        }
        if(frontIsBlocked())
        {       putBeeper();
        }
        else
        {       backUp();
        }
}
```

Well, as it often happens in programming, just when we think we have a solution to a programming problem, the problem changes. When the owner of the field saw our above solution in action, she observed that the robot wasn't going to be especially effective in preventing beeper theft, since, while tony was walking along one edge, someone could steal beepers by entering from the opposite edge. To prevent this, she has changed the specification of the problem to require four robots, starting at the four corners of the field, all walking in unison, to keep better watch. We will look at this problem in Chapter 7 (exercises).

6.8 Enumerations and the While Statement

In the last two chapters we have used Enumerations in simple ways. Finally, we can see the real intent of the Enumeration interface and how it was intended to be used. Suppose you have a robot that has just arrived on a corner and it needs to do somethig with all the robots there, perhaps telling them to lay down their beepers. This is very simple with the combination of the neighbors enumeraton and a while loop.

```
Enumeration neighbors = neighbors();
while(neighbors.hasMoreElements())
{
        UrRobot myNeighbor = (UrRobot)neighbors.nextElement();
        myNeighbor.putBeeper();
}
```

You may, of course, write your own Enumerations. You need to implement the Enumeration interface, of course, but it is also useful to keep in mind the philosophy of an enumeration. First is that the hasMoreElements method returns true or false, but does not modify the collection being enumerated. It makes no state changes in the collection or in the enumeration itself. On the other hand, nextElement, in addition to returning a value if there is one to return, should update its own internal data so that the next time either hasMoreElements or nextElement is called they will do the right thing. Finally, if nextElements is called when there are no more elements, it should "throw" a NoSuchElementException. The discussion of that is beyond the scope of this book. Sending a nextElement message never modifies the collection, however.

6.9 When to Use a Repeating Instruction

As explained at the end of the last chapter, a decision map is a technique that asks questions about the problem we are trying to solve. The answers to the questions determine which path of the map to follow. If we have done a thorough job of planning our implementation, the decision map should suggest an appropriate instruction to use. Take some time and examine some of the discussions presented in this chapter and see how the complete decision map, which is presented below, might have been useful.

Note especially the distinction between the situations in which you use a FOR LOOP and those in which you use a WHILE instruction. The FOR LOOP is based on being able to count the number of iterations. The WHILE is much more flexible, being based on an arbitrary predicate.

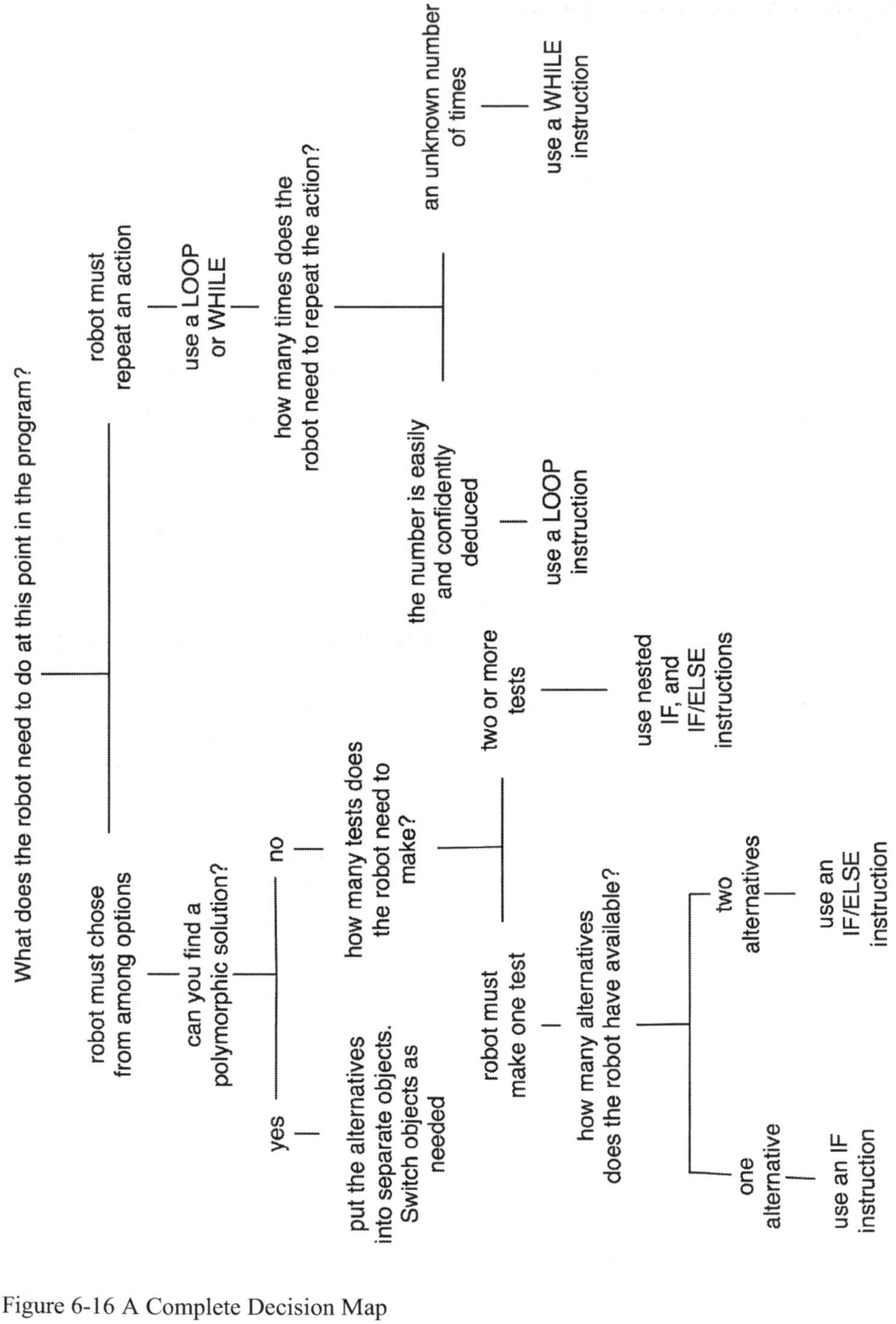

Figure 6-16 A Complete Decision Map

Again, we note for completeness that Java has additional looping statements as well as additional conditional statements.

6.10 Important Ideas From This Chapter

repetition
iteration
fence post problem
infinite execution
loop invariant

6.10 Problem Set

The problems in this section require writing definitions and programs that use FOR-LOOP and WHILE instructions. Try using stepwise refinement and the four step process discussed in Section 6.2.3 when writing these definitions and programs. Test your solutions by simulating them in various initial situations, and try to find beyond-the-horizon situations too. Take care to write programs that avoid error shutoffs and infinite loops.

A common mistake among beginning programmers is trying to have each execution of a while loop's body make too much progress. As a rule of thumb, try to have each execution of a WHILE loop's body make as little progress as possible (while still making some progress toward terminating the loop).

1. Write a new method named emptyBeeperBag. After a robot executes this method, its beeper-bag should be empty.

2. Write a new method called goToOrigin that positions a robot on 1st Street and 1st Avenue facing east, regardless of its initial location or the direction it is initially facing. Assume that there are no wall sections present. Hint: Use the south and west boundary walls as guides.

3. Study both of the following program fragments separately. What does each do? For each, is there a simpler program fragment that is execution equivalent? If so, write it down; if not, explain why not.

```
while( ! nextToABeeper())
{       move();
}
if(nextToABeeper())
{       pickBeeper();
}
else
{       move();
}
```

```
while( ! nextToABeeper())
{       if(nextToABeeper())
        {       pickBeeper();
        }
        else
        {       move();
        }
}
```

Describe the difference between the following two program fragments:

```
while(frontIsClear())
{       move();
}
```

```
if(frontIsClear())
{       move();
}
```

4. There is a menace in Karel's world--an infinite pile of beepers. Yes, it sounds impossible but occasionally one occurs in the world. If Karel accidentally tries to pick up an infinite pile of beepers, it is forever doomed to pick beepers from the pile. karel's current situation places the robot in grave danger from such a pile. The robot is standing outside two rooms: one is to the west and one is to the east. Only one of these rooms has a pile of beepers that karel can pick. The other room has the dreaded infinite pile of beepers. Karel must decide which room is the safe room, enter it and pick all of the beepers. To help the robot decide which room is safe, there is a third pile of beepers on the corner at which karel is currently standing. If this third pile has an even number of beepers, the safe room is the eastern room. If the pile has an odd number of beepers, the safe room is the western room. There is at least one beeper in the third pile. Program karel to pick the beepers in the safe room.

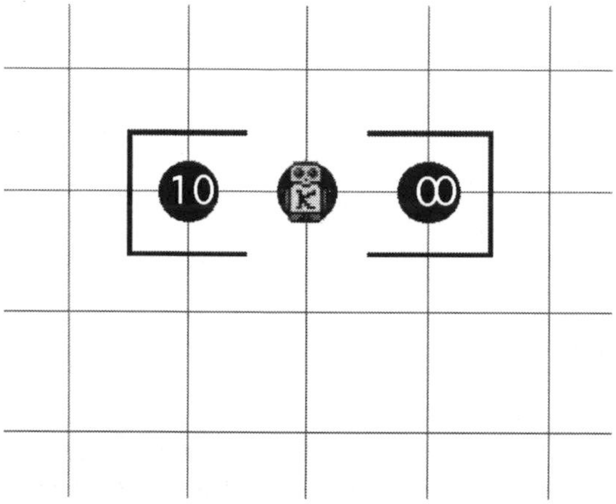

Figure 6-17 A Very Dangerous Task

5. A robot must place beepers in the exact arrangement shown below. Assume that it starts with exactly enough beepers for the task and always starts on the bottom-left corner of the square.

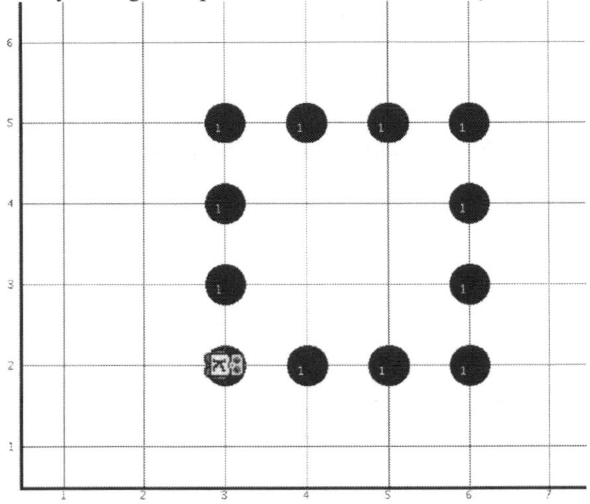

Figure 6-18 A Beeper Arranging Task

6. Instruct a robot to escape from any rectangular room that has an open doorway exactly one block wide. After escaping from the room, the program must command the robot to turn itself off.

7. Program a robot to escape from a rectangular room if it can find a doorway. If there is no doorway, the robot must turn itself off. We may not be able use the program written in Problem 6 for this task, because executing this program in a door-less room could cause the to run around inside the room forever. Hint: There is a slightly messy way to solve this problem without resorting to beepers. You can write the program this way, or you can assume that the robot has one beeper in the beeper-bag, which it can use to remember if it has circumnavigated the room. This program may require a separate turnOff instruction for the completely enclosed situation in addition to a turnOff instruction for the situation with a door.

8. Karel is working once again as a gardener. Karel must outline the wall segment shown in Figure 6-19 with beepers. One and only one beeper is to be planted on each corner that is adjacent to a wall. You may assume that karel always starts in the same relative position and has exactly enough beepers to do the task. A simple variation can be programmed in which karel has infinitely many beepers rather than exactly the right number.

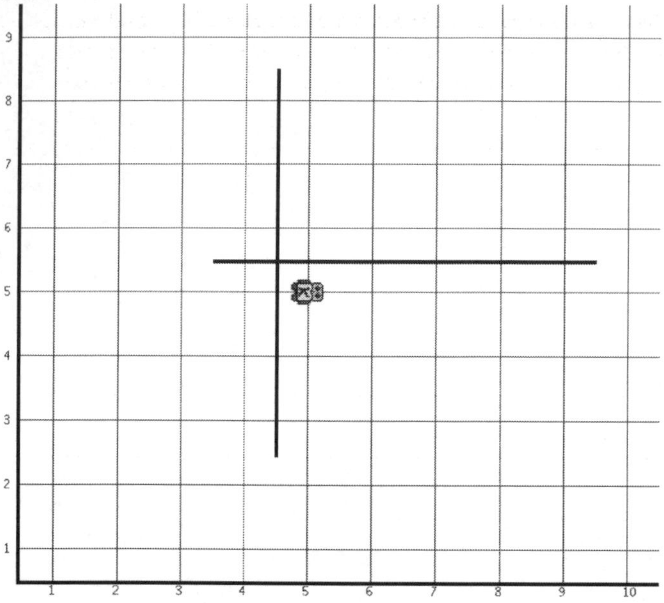

Figure 6-19 Another Gardening Job

9. Karel's beeper crop failed again. The robot is back to carpeting hallways. The hallways always have the same general shape as shown in Figure 6-20 and are always one block wide. To ensure there are no lumps in the carpet, only one beeper can be placed on a corner. Karel has exactly enough beepers to do the job and always starts in the same relative location. Can you write a single program that solves both problems 8 and 9 of this section?

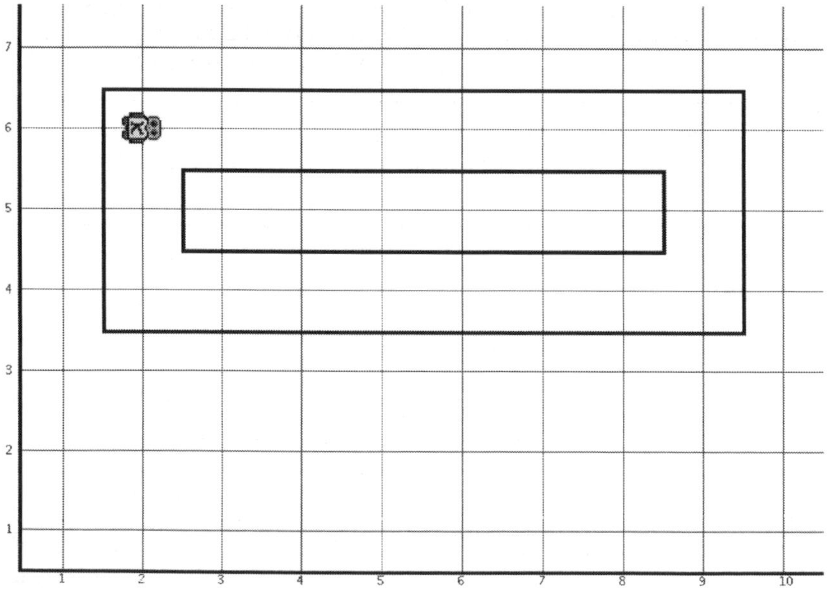

Figure 6-20 Another Carpeting Job

10. Program a robot to run a super steeplechase. In this race the hurdles are arbitrarily high and the course has no fixed finish corner. The finish of each race course is marked by a beeper that the robot must pick up before turning itself off. Figure 6-21 illustrates one possible course. Other courses may be longer and have higher hurdles. Should you modify the class you built in Problem 6 of Chapter 4 or build a new class?

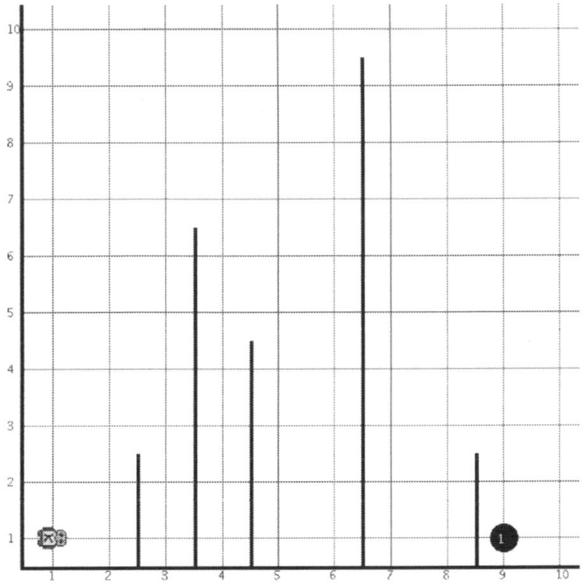

Figure 6-21 A Super Steeplechase

11. Program a robot to run a super-duper steeplechase. In this race the hurdles are arbitrarily high and arbitrarily wide. In each race course the finish is marked by a beeper, which the robot must pick up before turning itself off. Figure 6-22 illustrates one possible race course. The best way to do this exercise, of course, is to build a subclass of the Steeplechaser class you built in Problem 10.

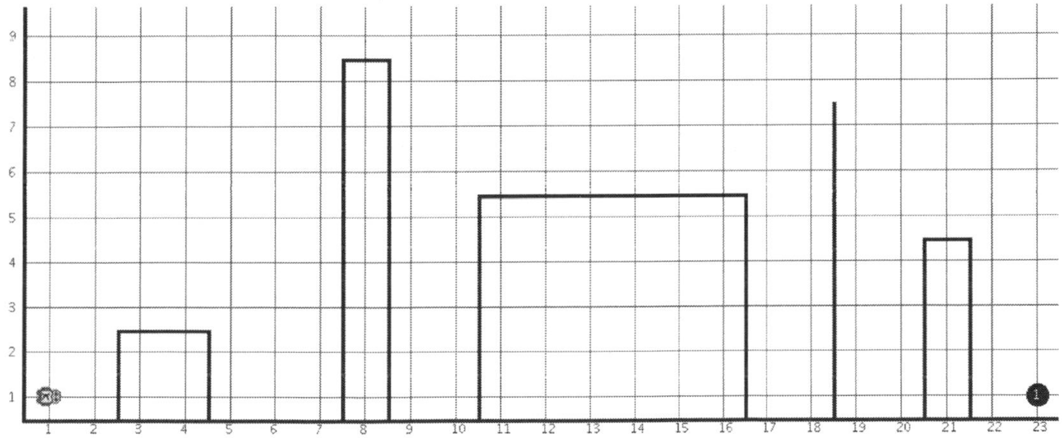

Figure 6-22 A Super-Duper Steeplechase

12. Write an instruction that harvests a rectangular field of any size. The field is guaranteed to be bordered by beeper-less corners. Also, assume that every corner within the field has a beeper on it and that our robot starts facing east on the lower left-hand corner of the field. Should we use a class derived from Harvester?

13. Karel has returned to the diamond shaped beeper field to harvest a new crop. Write a new program for karel that harvests the beepers. The beeper field is always the same size and there is always one beeper on each corner of the field.

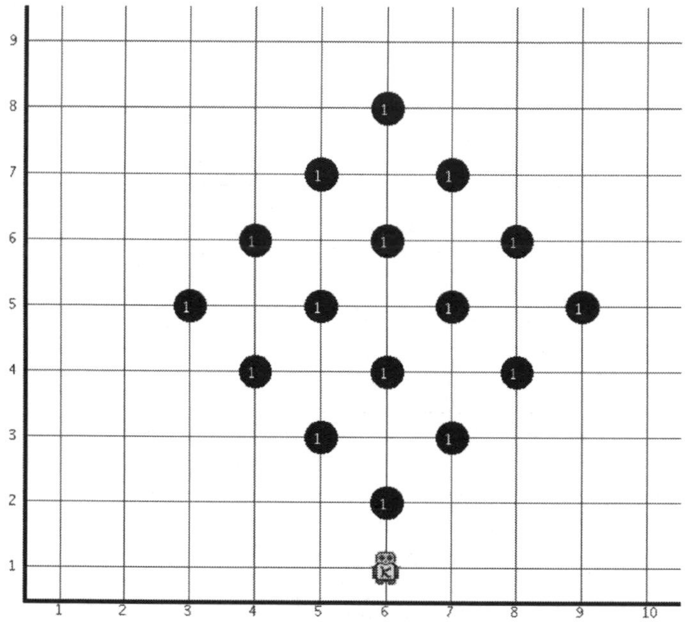

Figure 6-23 Return to the Diamond Shaped Beeper Field

13. A robot named karel is building a fence. The fence will be made of beepers and will surround a rectangular shaped wall segment. The size of the wall segment is unknown. Karel is at the origin facing an unknown direction. The fences (beepers) are stacked somewhere next to the western boundary wall. There are exactly enough beepers in the pile to build the fence. The beeper pile is on the street that is adjacent to the southern edge of the wall segment as shown in the Figure 6-24. The distances to the beeper pile and to the wall segment are unknown. Program karel to build the fence and return to the origin. Assume that there are no beepers in karel's beeper-bag at the start of the program.

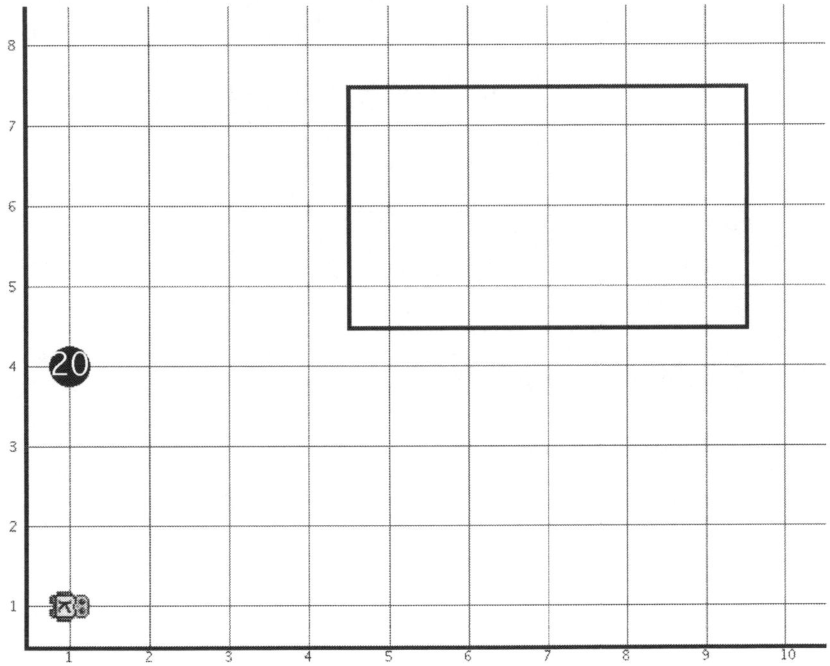

Figure 6-24 Building a Fence

14. A robot named karel likes to take long meandering walks in the woods in the world, and even though it has a built-in compass, the robot sometimes cannot find its way back home. To alleviate this problem, before karel walks in the woods the robot fills its beeper-bag and then it leaves a trail of beepers. Program karel to follow this path back home. There are many questions one can ask about this task. Ignore the possibility that any wall boundaries or wall sections interfere with karel, and assume that the end of the path is marked by two beepers on the same corner. Each beeper will be reachable from the previous beeper by the execution of one move. Also, the path will never cross over itself. See Figure 6-25 for a path that karel must follow. Hint: karel must probe each possible next corner in the path, eventually finding the correct one. It might prove useful to have karel pick up the beepers as it follows the path; Otherwise it may get caught in an infinite loop going backward and forward. How difficult would it be to program karel to follow the same type of path if we allowed for a beeper to be missing occasionally (but not two missing beepers in a row)?

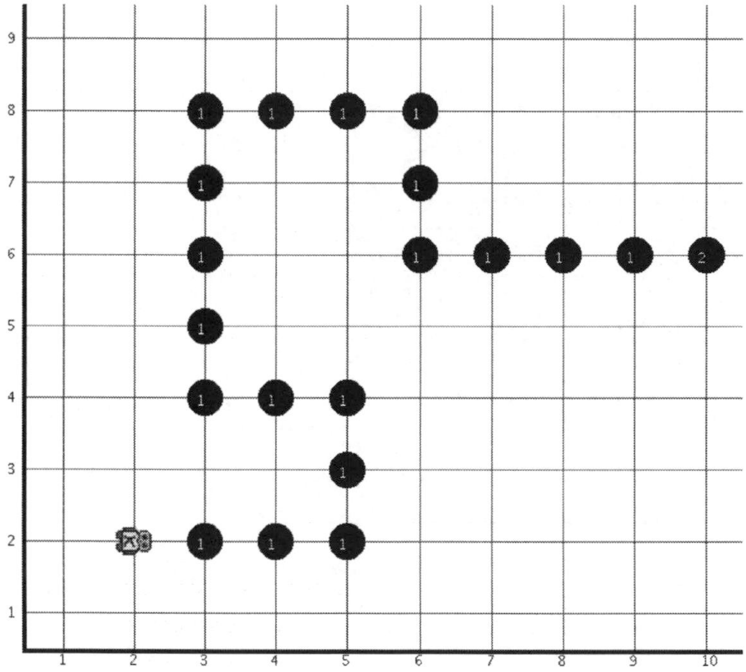

Figure 6-25 A Path of Beepers

15. Assume that a robot is somewhere in a completely enclosed rectangular room that contains one beeper. Program the robot to find the beeper, pick it up, and turn itself off.

16. Program a robot named karel to escape from a maze that contains no islands. The exit of the maze is marked by placing a beeper on the first corner that is outside the maze, next to the right wall. This task can be accomplished by commanding karel to move through the maze, with the invariant that its right side is always next to a wall. See Problem 5.11-9 for hints on the type of movements for which karel must be programmed. Figure 6-26 shows one example of a maze.

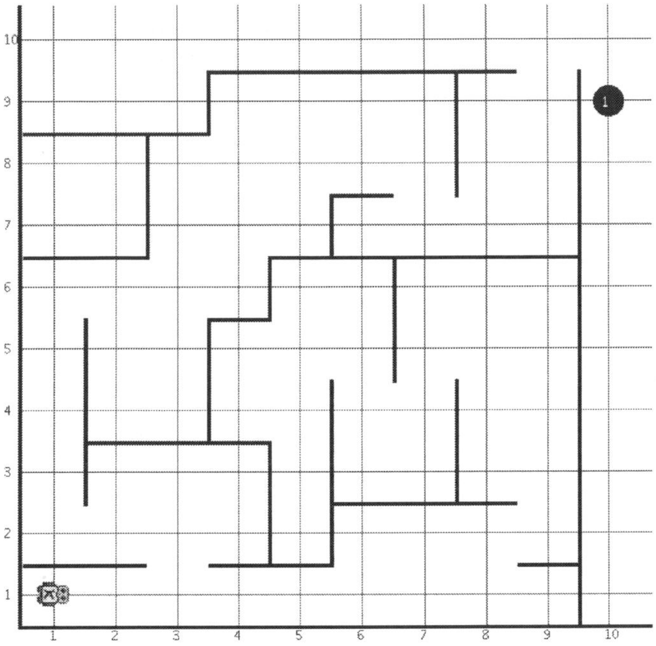

Figure 6-26 A Maze

There is a simpler way to program this task without using the instructions written in Problem 5.11-9. Try to write a shorter version of the maze-escaping program. Hint: Program karel to make the least amount of progress toward its goal at each corner in the maze. Finally, compare the maze escape problem with Problem 6.9 11, the Super Duper Steeplechase. Do you see any similarities? Are there any similarities to the room-escaping problem? What class should we build to solve this problem? What should the parent class be?

17. This problem is inspired by the discussion on the verification of WHILE loops (Section 5.6). Simulate a robot's execution of the following instruction in initial situations where the robot is on a corner with 0, 1, 2, 3, and 7 beepers.

```
void willThisClearCornerOfBeepers ()
{
        for  (int i = 0; i < 10; i++)
        {
                if ( nextToABeeper() )
                {
                        pickBeeper();
                }
        }
}
```

State in exactly which initial situations this instruction works correctly. What happens in the other situations?

18. Program a robot named karel to go on a treasure hunt. The treasure is marked by a corner containing five beepers. Other corners (including the corner on which karel starts) contain clues, with each clue indicating in which direction karel should proceed. The clues are as follows: 1 beeper means karel should go north, 2 means west, 3 means south, and 4 means east. Karel should follow the clues until it reaches the treasure corner where the robot should turn itself off. Figure 6-27 shows one possible treasure hunt.

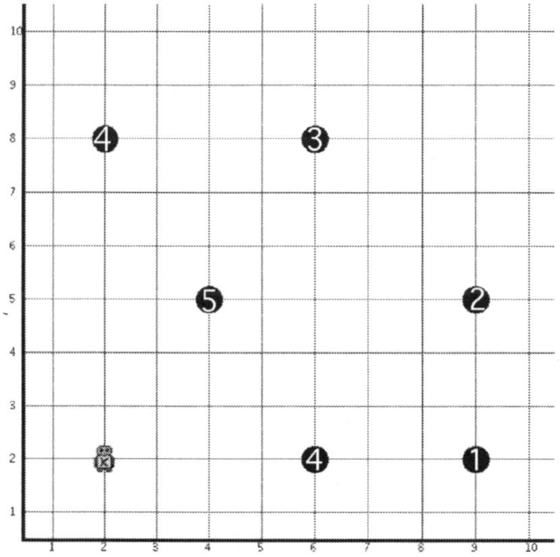

Initial situation

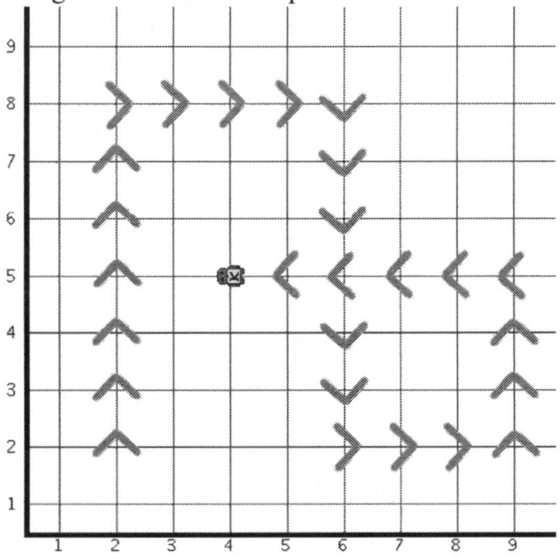

Final situation and karel's path

Figure 6-27 A Treasure Hunt

19. A robot named karel is inside a room that has a number of open windows. There are no windows in the corners of the room. Karel is next to the northern wall facing east. Program karel to close the windows by putting one beeper in front of each window. You may assume that karel has exactly enough beepers to complete the task.

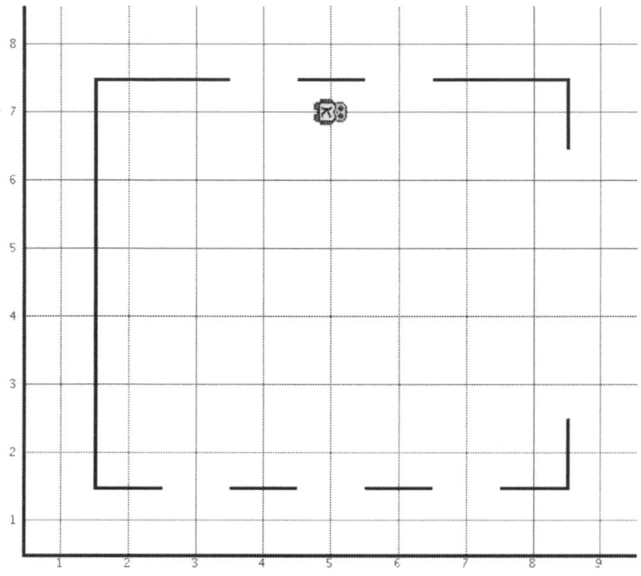

Figure 6-28 Closing the Windows

20. A robot named karel is at the origin facing east. In front of karel, somewhere along 1st Street, is a line of beepers (one beeper is on each corner, with at least one beeper in the line). The length of the line of beepers is unknown but there are no gaps in the line. Karel must pick up and move the beepers north a number of streets equal to the number of beepers in the line. For example, if there are five beepers in the line, the beepers must be moved to 6th Street. The beepers must be moved directly north. If the first beeper is on 4th Avenue, it must be on 4th Avenue when the program is finished.

21. A robot named karel is inside a completely enclosed room with no doors or windows. The robot is in the southeast corner facing south. There is one wall segment inside the room with karel. The wall segment blocks north/south travel and does not touch the walls that form the room. On one side of the wall segment is a beeper (which side is unknown). Program karel to find and move the beeper to the opposite side of the wall segment.

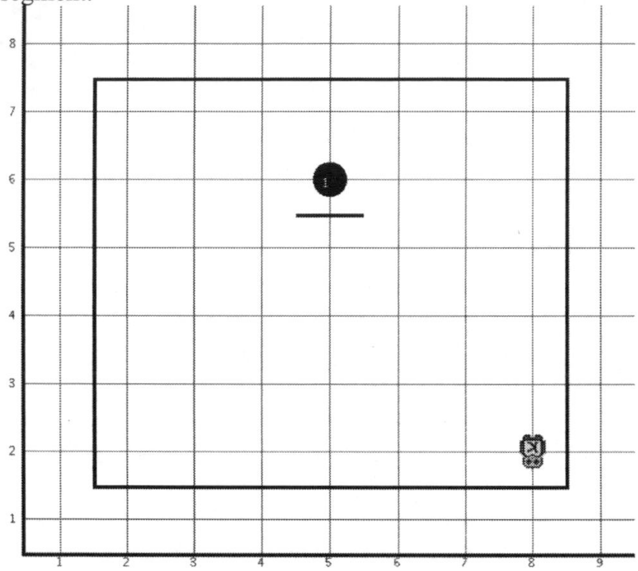

Figure 6-29 Finding and Moving a Beeper

22. Once again karel is working as a carpet layer. Before carpeting a room karel must ensure that the room has continuous walls to the west, north, and east. Only these rooms must be carpeted. The doors to the rooms are always to the south. All rooms are one block wide and there is always a northern wall at the end of each room. Karel's task ends when the robot arrives at a blocking wall segment on 1st Street. Figure 6-30 shows one possible set of initial and final situations.

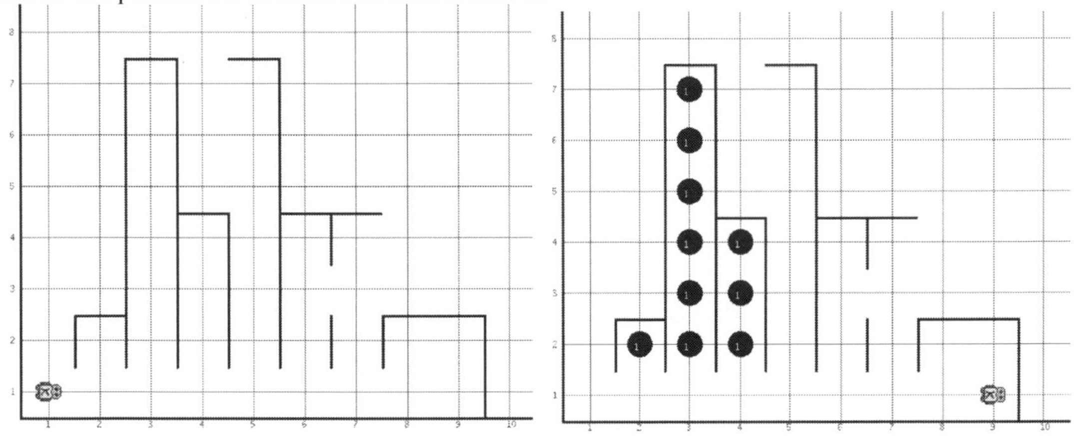

Figure 6-30 A More Complex Carpet Laying Task

23. What will be the effect of executing the following instruction?

```
while (facingNorth())
{
        turnLeft();
}
```

24. Program a robot named karel to arrange vertical piles of beepers into ascending order. Each avenue, starting at the origin, will contain a vertical pile of one or more beepers. The first empty avenue will mark the end of the piles that need to be sorted. Figure 6-31 illustrates one of the many possible initial and final situations. (How difficult would it be to modify your program to arrange the piles of beepers into descending order?)

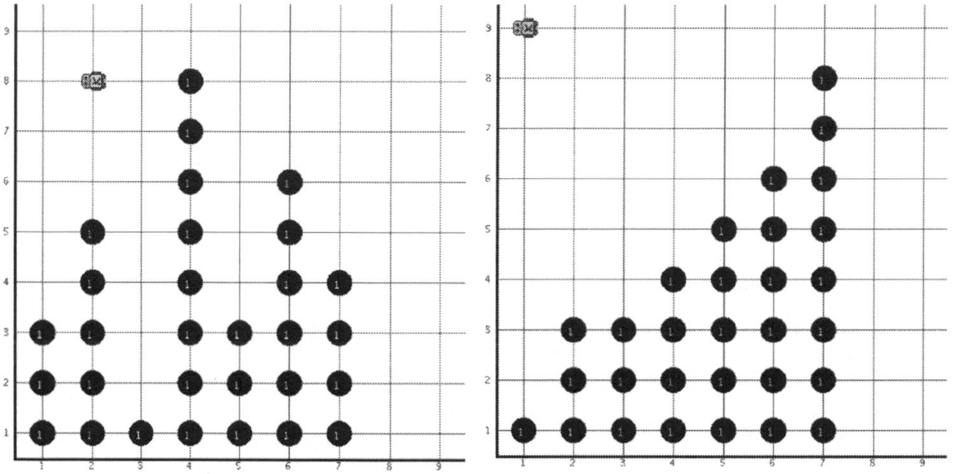

Figure 6-31 A Sorting Task

25. Build a new robot Sweeper class, derived from the Robot class of Chapter 5. The defining property of robots in this class is that they sweep up all beepers on any corner to which they move. Why is this not quite the same thing as saying that they sweep up all beepers on all corners that they occupy?

26. Program the three robots, karel, carol, and karl, to run a relay super steeplechase. karel will start the race at the origin with one beeper in its beeper-bag. Somewhere along 1st street carol will be waiting. When karel gets to carol, karel should pass the beeper to carol and carol should continue the race and karel should stop. When carol gets to karl, karl should likewise continue, with the beeper, and only stop when it comes to a corner with a beeper marking the end of the course. It should put down the beeper it is carrying at this final corner. You may want to put karel and carol in a different class than karl, who can be a Steeplechaser robot. Here you will get a chance to use the predicate nextToARobot.

27. Tony the robot is standing at the origin with some beepers in its beeper bag. Write an instruction that will deposit half of the beepers on the corner. The others should be retained in the beeper-bag. If there are an odd number of beepers then the extra one should be left on the corner.

28. Write a Spy Walk program (See Chapter 4) that continues until the Spy arrives on a corner with no Accomplice robot. This is the treasure corner and it should be marked with three beepers. The Spy should end by picking up these three beepers. Test your program using at least 4 Accomplices and at least three strategies. You may assume there are no other robots in the world besides the single Spy and the Accomplices.

29. After doing (or at least thinking about) Problem 29, go back and answer Problem 4.12-10.

30. Suppose a robot arrives on a corner with a lot of other robots of different classes, some of which have overridden the move method in various ways. What happens if we use the enumeration provided by the neighbors method of this new arrival to send a move message to each of the other robots on this corner?

31. Use the idea of Problem 31 to write a program to build a house using a Contractor and a work crew, where the contractor doesn't even need to know how many robots are in the crew or their types. Be as creative as you like. The contractor will just tell each member of the team where the house is to be built by passing a strategy to each.

32. In Section 6.6, the followEdge instruction has a bug. There is another beyond-the-horizon situation contained in it. Can you identify it? Can you fix it?

33. A robot named karel is at the Origin facing East with an infinite number of beepers in its beeper bag. Somewhere in front of Karel is a wall. Program karel to compute the distance to the wall by placing a number of beepers at the origin equal to the distance between the Origin and the wall.

34. A robot named dersu is in a completely enclosed rectangular room with no beepers in the room. Dersu has an infinite number of beepers in its beeper bag. Program dersu to compute the area of the room by placing a number of beepers in the south-west corner equal to the area of the room.

7 Advanced Techniques for Robots

This chapter presents a number of quite challenging topics. First we will introduce the concept of recursion. Recursion, like loops, allows robots to execute a sequence of statements more than once. We will also look at the formal relationship between recursion and loops. Next, we study two interesting new instructions that give robots the ability to solve some novel beeper-manipulation problems, including numerical computations. Then we will look again at object-oriented programming and see some implications of what we have learned here.

7.1 Introduction to Recursion

Having thoroughly looked at loops in the last chapter, we are now going to examine a different way to get a robot to repeat an action. The technique is called *recursion*. The word means, simply, to recur or repeat. When a programming language allows *recursive definitions* or *recursion*, it means that within a new method we can send the same message (the one with the name of the executing method) to the executing robot. This may seem odd at first, but after a few examples, we hope that it will appear as natural as using a WHILE loop to control a robot's execution. We note that recursion is just another control structure and, while it may appear magical at first, it can be understood as readily as loops. It is another programming tool to add to your collection.

In all of the examples prior to Chapter 6, when we asked a robot to move from one point to another, we knew exactly how far it would move. There are many situations, however, in which this is not true. Suppose, for example, that a robot named kristin is standing at the origin facing east, and suppose that there is a beeper somewhere along 1st Street. We want kristin to go to the beeper and pick it up and return to the origin.

```
kristin.retrieveBeeper ();
```

If we knew that the beeper was on 1st and 23rd, we would be able to write a program without loops to do this. If we knew that it was no more than, say, 15 blocks away, then we could find a solution. (How?) But what if we don't know how far it is. To get started, let's build a new class: BeeperFinder.

```
public class BeeperFinder extends Robot
{
	public void retrieveBeeper ()
	{	findBeeper();
		pickBeeper();
		turnLeft();
		turnLeft();
		returnToWestWall();
	}

	public void findBeeper(){...}
	public void returnToWestWall(){...}
}
```

Well, that will certainly do the job, if we can write the other two new methods. Let's now attack findBeeper. We know that there is a beeper somewhere on 1st Street. We also know that kristin is on 1st Street facing East. It may be that kristin is already on the beeper corner, in which case there is nothing to do. Therefore, we may get started by writing:

```
public void findBeeper()
{       if (! nextToABeeper())
        {
                ...
        }
}
```

This will correctly terminate having done nothing if kristin is already at the beeper corner. Suppose next that the beeper is on some other corner. Then kristin needs to move, of course, and check other corners.

```
public void findBeeper()
{       if (! nextToABeeper())
        {       move();
                ???
        }
}
```

Well, what does kristin need to do after a move? Notice that kristin is on a different corner than the one on which it started and that the original corner was checked and found to lack a beeper. Therefore, we may conclude that the beeper is now (after the move) either at kristin's current location or farther East of it. But this is exactly the same situation (relatively) that kristin was in when it started this task. Therefore, we can conclude that what kristin needs to do now is exactly findBeeper and nothing more.

```
public void findBeeper()
{       if (! nextToABeeper())
        {       move();
                findBeeper();
        }
}
```

Notice that findBeeper has been completely defined, but it has been defined by using findBeeper itself. How can this be done? Well, suppose we needed to empty an ocean with a bucket. To perform emptyTheOcean, we first ask if the ocean is empty. If so, we are done. Otherwise, we just remove one bucket of water from the ocean and then emptyTheOcean.

The important thing in such a definition, called a *recursive* definition, is that we don't define a thing in terms of precisely itself. We define a thing in terms of a simpler or smaller version of itself, and also define the smallest or simplest version separately. Here we define findBeeper as either "nothing", if kristin is already on the beeper corner, or "`move(); findBeeper();`", if kristin is anywhere else. It is also necessary to know before we start executing such an instruction that there is, indeed, a beeper somewhere in kristin's path.

Otherwise, after every move, the reexecution of findBeeper will find that the test is true, generating yet another reexecution of findBeeper without end.

The other method, returnToWestWall is similar, except for the test. Here, however we know that there is a wall to the west. If we can guarantee that the robot is also facing west, then the following method will serve.

```
public void returnToWestWall()
{       if (frontIsClear())
        {       move();
                returnToWestWall() ;
        }
}
```

Programming with recursion is a very powerful and sometimes error-prone activity.

7.2 More on Recursion

Given the problem--a robot must clean all beepers from its current corner--we could easily write a loop that looks like the following.

```
public class Sweeper extends Robot
{
        public void  sweepCorner()
        {       while ( nextToABeeper() )
                {       pickBeeper();
                }
        }
        ...
}
```

This correctly solves the problem and is known as an iterative solution ("iterative" means that a loop of some sort, WHILE or FOR- LOOP, was used). Contrast this solution with a recursive one.

```
public void sweepCorner()
{       if ( nextToABeeper() )
        {       pickBeeper();
                sweepCorner();
        }
}
```

The difference between these two methods is very subtle. The first method, which uses the WHILE loop, is invoked once and the robot's focus never leaves the loop until it is finished, executing zero or more pickBeepers (depending on the initial number on the corner). What happens in the second, recursive, sweepCorner? Let's look at it very carefully.

If the robot is initially on an empty corner when the message is sent, nothing happens (similar to the WHILE loop). If it is on a corner with one beeper when the message is sent, the IF test is true, so the robot executes one pickBeeper instruction (thus emptying the corner). The robot then sends a second sweepCorner message (to itself), remembering where it was in the first execution. When sweepCorner is executed the second time, the IF test is false, so nothing happens and the robot returns to the first invocation.

[initial instantiation of]

```
public void sweepCorner()
{       if ( nextToABeeper() )
        {       pickBeeper();
                sweepCorner(); // <--  This is the second invocation of
        }                              //sweepCorner. The robot will
                                       //return to
}                                      //this point  when that execution
                                       // finishes.
```

[second instantiation of]

```
public void sweepCorner()
{       if ( nextToABeeper() )         // <-- this is now false
        {       pickBeeper();
                sweepCorner();
        }
}
```

Each execution results in a separate instantiation of the instruction sweepCorner. The robot must completely execute each instantiation, always remembering where it was in the previous instance so it can return there when it finishes.

The process for writing recursive robot instructions is very similar to that for writing loops:

Step 1: Consider the stopping condition (also called the base case)--what is the simplest case of the problem that can be solved? In the sweepCorner problem, the simplest, or base, case is when the robot is already on an empty corner.

Step 2: What does the robot have to do in the base case? In this example there's nothing to do.

Step 3: Find a way to solve a small piece of the larger problem if not in the base case. This is called "reducing the problem in the general case." In the sweepCorner problem, the general case is when the robot is on a corner with one or more beepers and the reduction is to pick up a beeper.

Step 4: Make sure the reduction leads to the base case. Again, in the above example of sweepCorner, by picking up one beeper at a time, the robot must eventually clear the corner of beepers, regardless of the original number present.

Let's compare and contrast iteration and recursion:

* An iterative loop must complete each iteration before beginning the next one.

* A recursive method typically begins a new instantiation before completing the current one. When that happens, the current instance is temporarily suspended, pending the completion of the new instance. Of course, this new instantiation might not complete before generating another one. Each successive instantiation must be completed in turn, last to first.

* Since EACH recursive instantiation is supposed to make some (often minimal) progress toward the base case, we should not use loops to control recursive calls. Thus, we will usually see an IF or an IF/ELSE in the body of a recursive new method, but not a WHILE.

Suppose we wanted to use recursion to move a robot named karel to a beeper. How would we do it? Following the steps presented earlier:

* What is the base case? Karel is on the beeper.

* What does the robot have to do in the base case? Nothing.

* What is the general case? The robot is not on the beeper.

* What is the reduction? Move toward the beeper and make the recursive call.

* Does the reduction lead to termination? Yes, assuming the beeper is directly in front of the robot , the distance will get shorter by one block for each recursive call.

The final implementation follows.

```
public void findBeeper()
{       if ( ! nextToABeeper() )
        {       move();
                findBeeper();
        }
}
```

Note that this problem could also have been easily solved with a WHILE loop. Let's look at a problem that is not easily solved with a WHILE loop. Remember the Lost Beeper Mine, the corner with a large number of beepers? Imagine we must write the following method in our search for the mine. A robot named karel must walk east from its current location until it finds a beeper. The Lost Beeper Mine is due north of that intersection a distance equal to the number of moves karel made to get from its current position to the beeper. Write the new method, findMine.

It is not easy to see how to solve this problem with a WHILE loop as we do not have any convenient way of remembering how many intersections have been traversed. Oh, we could probably come up with a very convoluted beeper-tracking scheme, but let's look at a recursive solution that's pretty straightforward. Again, we'll answer our questions:

* What is the base case? Karel is on the beeper.

* What does karel have to do in the base case? turnLeft (this will face karel north).

* What is the general case? Karel is not on the beeper.

* What is the reduction? Move one block forward, make the recursive call and have karel execute a second move after the recursive call. This second move will be executed in all instances but the base case, causing karel to make as many moves north after the base case as it did in getting to the base case.

* Does the reduction lead to termination? Yes, assuming the beeper is directly in front of karel.

Let's look at the complete method:

```
public void  findMine()
{        if ( nextToABeeper() )
         {       turnLeft();
         }
         else
         {       move();
                 findMine();
                 move();
         }
}
```

How many turnLefts are executed? How many moves? How many calls to findMine?

A good way to think about recursion and the recursive call is in terms of the specification of the method itself. In the above case, the specification is that when a robot executes this instruction it will walk a certain number of steps, say k, to a beeper, turn left, and then walk k steps farther. Suppose we start the robot N steps away from the beeper (k = N). When we examine the method above, the ELSE clause has a **move** message first. That means that the robot is now N-1 steps from the beeper. Therefore, by the specification, the recursive (k = N-1) call will walk N-1 steps forward, turn left, and then walk N-1 steps beyond. We therefore need to supply one additional **move** message after the recursion to complete the required N steps.

It will take solving a number of problems and a good deal of staring before recursion becomes as comfortable to use as iteration. A large part of this is because recursion requires some intuition to see the correct reduction, especially in difficult problems. This intuition will come with practice, which is just what the sample problems are designed to provide.

7.3 Tail Recursion and Looping

Suppose we have an method with a WHILE loop and we would like to rewrite it so that it doesn't use a loop, but still carries out the same task. To consider the simplest case, suppose that the outermost control mechanism in a method is a loop. Take, for example, the method

```
public void findBeeper()
{       while ( ! nextToABeeper())
        {       move();
        }
}
```

By the definition of the WHILE given in Section 6.2, this is the same as

```
public void findBeeper()
{       if ( ! nextToABeeper())
        {       move();
                while ( ! nextToABeeper())       <--
                {       move();                  <-- findBeeper
                }                                <--
        }
}
```

However, the nested WHILE instruction in this latter form is exactly the body of findBeeper using the definition of findBeeper given first, so we can rewrite this second form as:

```
public void findBeeper()
{       if ( ! nextToABeeper())
        {       move();
                findBeeper();
        }
}
```

Thus, the first form, a while, is equivalent to the last form, a recursive program. Also notice that we could just as easily transform the second form into the first, since they are execution equivalent.

Notice, finally, that this is a special form of recursion, since after the recursive step (the nested findBeeper) there is nothing more to do in this method. It is, after all, the last instruction within an IF instruction, so when it is done, the IF is done, and therefore the method of which this is the body is done. This form of recursion is called *tail recursion* because the recursive step comes at the very tail of the computation.

It is possible to prove formally that tail recursion is equivalent to WHILE looping. Therefore, we can see that a WHILE loop is just a special form of recursion. So anything that you can do with a loop, you can also do with a recursive program. There are some deep and beautiful theories in computer science (and in mathematics) that have been developed from this observation.

By way of contrast, the findMine method discussed in Section 7.2, was certainly recursive, but it is not tail-recursive, because the final **move** message follows the recursive message. That method is also equivalent to one using only WHILE loops, but, as suggested in Section 7.2, it is very convoluted.

7.4 Going Formal

At the beginning of this chapter we saw that it is possible to get a robot to perform an operation repeatedly without using FOR-LOOP or WHILE instructions. Perhaps you are wondering if there is a relationship between recursive programming and iterative programming. The answer, of course, is yes and we would like to go a bit deeper into the relationship.

In Chapter 6, we learned about the WHILE instruction and how to use it. However, the description we gave of it was somewhat informal, relying on examples and intuition. That is fine at the beginning, but it is also useful to look at a formal definition of a WHILE statement, so that it can be analyzed logically.

Suppose we permit instructions themselves to be named. We don't permit this in the robot language itself, only in talking about the robot language. This is the so-called *meta level*; the level at which we don't use a thing (the programming language), but discuss and analyze it. In any case, suppose that we let the simple WHILE statement form "while (<test>){<instruction-list>}" be known as statement W. Let us also denote the <test> of the WHILE as T and the <instruction-list> as L. Then W can be written as:

W == while (T) { L }

The formal definition of W is

W == if (T){ L; W; }

This says that to perform the while instruction W we must first test T (if (T) . . .) and if T is false, do nothing at all, but if T is true, then we must perform L followed by W, the while instruction itself. By the definition this means that we must test T again and if it is false do nothing else, but if it is true, we must perform L again followed by W again, etc.

The looping should be clear from this description, but if you look at the definition we have written, you see the *recursive* nature of the WHILE. This means that the WHILE statement W is defined in terms of itself, since W appears on the right side of the definition as well as the left. We hope that the W on the right is not exactly the same as the one on the left, but a simpler, smaller version of the W that appears on the left. What that means is that for a while loop to make sense, or be defined, the execution of the instruction list L, must partially solve the problem that the entire WHILE set out to solve, and take us closer to termination of the loop. If that is not the case, and the execution of L leaves the robot in the same state, relative to termination, that it was in at the start, then the loop is guaranteed to run forever. This is because in this case the definition is purely circular and so doesn't define anything.

7.5 Searching

This section introduces two new methods named zigLeftUp and zagDownRight, that move a robot diagonally northwest and southeast respectively. Both of these methods are defined by using only UrRobot's methods such as turnLeft, but we derive immense conceptual power from being able to think in terms of moving diagonally. For reasons that will become clear in the exercises, the class into which we put these methods is Mathematician. It will have the class Robot as the parent class.

The following definitions introduce the stars of this section: zigLeftUp and zagDownRight. These direction pairs are not arbitrary; if a robot moves to the left and upward long enough, it eventually reaches the western boundary wall. The same argument holds for traveling down and toward the right, except that in this case the robot eventually reaches the southern boundary wall.

The other two possible direction pairs lack these useful properties: a robot will never find a boundary wall by traveling up and toward the right, and we cannot be sure which of the two boundary walls it will come upon first when traveling downward and to the left.

The following methods define zigLeftUp and zagDownRight.

```
public class Mathematician extends Robot
{
	public void zigLeftUp ()
	{	// Precondition: facingWest and frontIsClear
		// Postcondition: facingWest
		move();
		turnRight();
		move();
		turnLeft();
	}

	public void zagDownRight()
	{	// Precondition: facingSouth and frontIsClear
		// Postcondition: facingSouth
		move();
		turnLeft();
		move();
		turnRight();
	}
	...
}
```

Assume that we have a Mathematician named karel. Observe that no part of these methods forces karel to move in the intended directions. To execute zigLeftUp correctly, karel must be facing west; to execute zagDownRight correctly, karel must be facing south. These requirements are called the pre-conditions of the methods. Recall that a pre-condition of a method is a condition that must be made true before a robot can correctly execute the method. We have seen many other examples of pre-conditions in this book.

For this example, the directional pre-condition of zigLeftUp is that karel is facing west; likewise, the directional pre-condition of zagDownRight is that karel is facing south. Karel's execution of these methods, when their pre-conditions are satisfied, is shown in Figure 7-1.

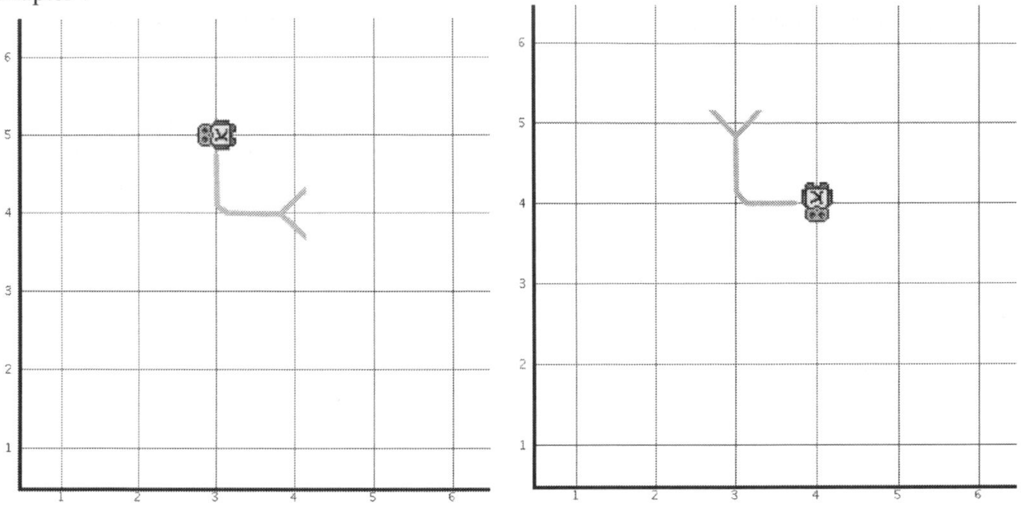

zig-left-up zag-down-right

Figure 7-1: Execution of the Zig-Zag Methods

Here is a statement that is loaded with terminology: the directional pre-conditions of zigLeftUp and zagDownRight are invariant over each instruction's execution. This just means that if karel is facing west and it executes zigLeftUp , the robot is still facing west after the instruction has finished executing. This property allows karel to execute a sequence of zigLeftUp 's without having to reestablish their directional pre-condition. A similar statement holds about karel's facing south and zagDownRight. Also observe that each instruction must be executed only when karel's front is clear. This pre-condition is not invariant over the instructions, because karel may be one block away from a corner where its front is blocked (e.g., karel may execute zigLeftUp while facing west on the corner of 4th Street and 2nd Avenue).

The first major method that we will write solves the problem of finding a beeper that can be located anywhere in the world. Our task is to write a method named findBeeper that positions karel on the same corner as the beeper. We have seen a version of this problem in Chapter 6 where both karel and the beeper are in an enclosed room. This new formulation has less stringent restrictions: the beeper is placed on some arbitrary street corner in karel's world, and there are no wall sections in the world. Of course, the boundary walls are always present.

One simple solution may spring to mind. In this attempt, karel first goes to the origin and faces east. The robot then moves eastward on 1st Street looking for a beeper. If karel finds a beeper on 1st Street, it has accomplished its task; if the beeper is not found on 1st Street, karel moves back to the western wall, switches over to 2nd Street, and continues searching from there. Karel repeats this strategy until it finds the beeper. Unfortunately, a mistaken assumption is implicit in this search instruction: there is no way for karel to know that the beeper is not on 1st Street. No matter how much of 1st Street karel explores, the robot can never be sure that the beeper is not one block farther east.

It looks as if we and karel are caught in an impossible trap, but there is an ingenious solution to our problem. As we might expect, it involves zig-zag moves. We need to program karel to perform a radically different type of search pattern; Figure 7-2 shows such a pattern, and we use it below to define the findBeeper method.

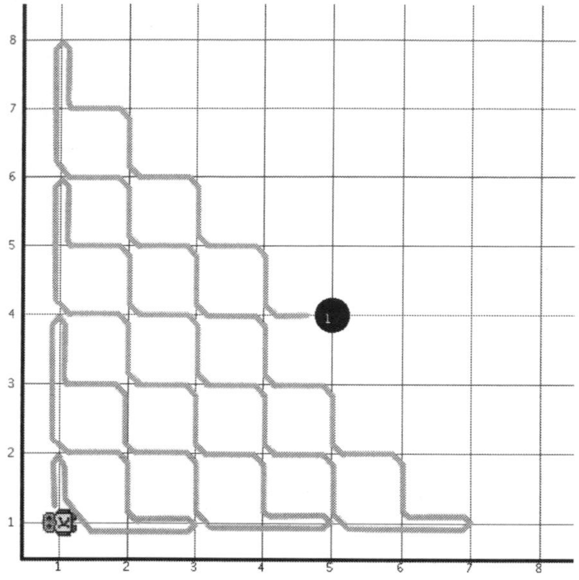

Figure 7-2: A Method for Searching Every Corner

This search method expands the search frontier similar to the way water would expand over karel's world from an overflowing sink at the origin. Roughly, we can view karel as traveling back and forth diagonally on the fringe of this water wave. Convince yourself that this search pattern is guaranteed to find the beeper eventually, regardless of the beeper's location--in our analogy, we need to convince ourselves that the beeper will eventually get wet. We can use stepwise refinement to write the findBeeper method using this search strategy with the zigLeftUp and zagDownRight methods.

```
public void  findBeeper()
{       goToOrigin();
        faceWest();
        while (  ! nextToABeeper() )
        {       if ( facingWest() )
                {       zigMove();
                }
                else
                {       zagMove();
                }
        }
}
```

The findBeeper method starts by moving karel to the origin and then facing west. (We saw how to write the faceWest instruction in Chapter 5.) These messages establish the directional pre-condition for zigLeftUp . The WHILE loop's purpose is to keep karel moving until it finds a beeper, and is correct if the loop eventually terminates. The IF condition, which is nested within the body of the loop, determines which direction karel has been traveling and continues moving the robot along the diagonal in this same direction. We continue the stepwise refinement by writing zigMove and zagMove.

```
public void  zigMove()
{       // Pre-condition: facingWest
        if ( frontIsClear() )
        {       zigLeftUp ();
        }
        else
        {       advanceToNextDiagonal();
        }
}
```

and

```
public void  zagMove()
{       // Pre-condition: facingSouth()
        if ( frontIsClear() )
        {       zagDownRight();
        }
        else
        {       advanceToNextDiagonal();
        }
}
```

The moving methods, zigMove and zagMove operate similarly; therefore we discuss only zigMove. When karel is able to keep zigging, the zigMove method moves it diagonally upward towards the left to the next corner; Otherwise, the robot is blocked by the western boundary wall and must advance northward to the next diagonal. We now write the method that advances karel to the next diagonal.

```
public void  advanceToNextDiagonal()
{       if ( facingWest() )
        {       faceNorth();
        }
        else
        {       faceEast();
        }
        move();
        turnAround();
}
```

The advanceToNextDiagonal method starts by facing karel away from the origin; it turns a different direction depending on whether the robot has been zigging or zagging. In either case, karel then moves one corner farther away from the origin and turns around. If karel has been zigging on the current diagonal, after executing advanceToNextDiagonal, the robot is positioned to continue by zagging on the next diagonal, and vice versa.

Observe that when karel executes a zigLeftUp or a zagDownRight method, it must visit two corners; the first is visited temporarily, and the second is catty-corner from karel's starting corner. When thinking about these methods, we should ignore the intermediate corner and just remember that these instructions move karel diagonally. Also notice that the temporarily visited corner is guaranteed not to have a beeper on it, because it is part of the wave front that karel visited while it was on the previous diagonal sweep.

Trace karel's execution of findBeeper in the sample situation presented in Figure 7-2 to acquaint yourself with its operation. Try to get a feel for how all these instructions fit together to accomplish the task. Pay particularly close attention to the advanceToNextDiagonal method. Test findBeeper in the situation where the beeper is on the origin and in situations where the beeper is next to either boundary wall.

Notice something very important about zigLeftUp and zagDownRight. When their preconditions are met, they have an interesting invariant. Note that the sum of the street number and the avenue number does not change when they execute when the precondition is first true. For example, zigLeftUp decreases its avenue number by one, while increasing its street number. Hence the sum does not change. We will exploit this in the exercises.

7.6 Doing Arithmetic

One of the things that computers do well is manipulating numbers. Robots can be taught to do arithmetic as we shall see. One way to represent numbers in the robot world is to use beepers. We could represent the number 32 by putting 32 beepers on a corner, but we can be more sophisticated. Suppose that we represent the different digits of a multi-digit number separately. Therefore to represent the number 5132 we could, using 2nd street as an example of a place to put the number, put 5 beepers at 2nd Street and 1st Avenue, 1 beeper at 2nd and 2nd, 3 beepers at 2nd and 3rd, and 2 beepers at 2nd and 4th. We could write a whole column of numbers as shown in Figure 7. 3.

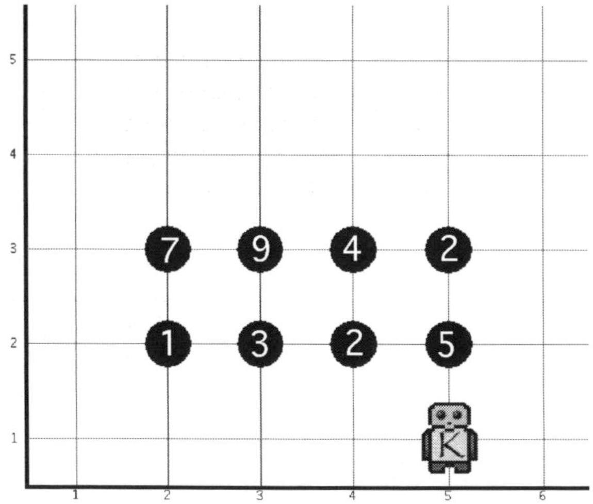

Figure 7.3 A Column of Numbers to be Added.

Let's start with a simpler case, however and just add up a column of single digit numbers. See Figure 7.4 for an example. Suppose we start with an Adder robot on 1st Street with a column of numbers represented by beepers north of it. On each such corner there will be between 1 and 9 beepers. We want to "write" on 1st Street the decimal number representing the sum of the column. Since we must "carry" if the total number of beepers is more than 9 we assume that we are not starting at 1st Avenue.

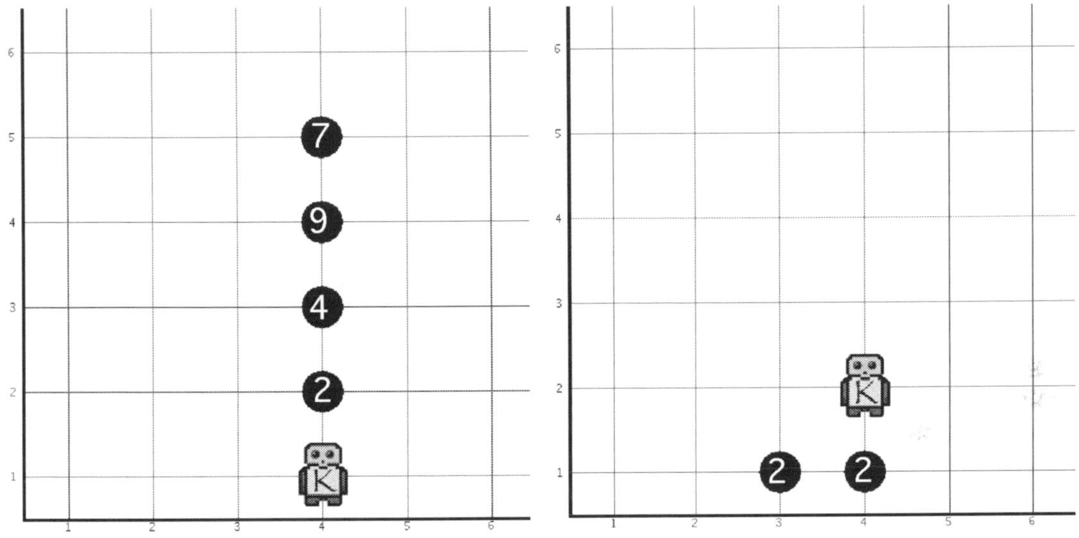

Figure 7.4 Adding Single Digit Numbers Before and After

Our adder robot will utilize two helper robots. The first of these will check to see if a carry is necessary and the second will actually do the carry if it is necessary. Since these robots will need to be created and find the adder robot that created them, we will start with a super (parent) class that provides this finding method. All of our other classes for this problem will be derived as subclasses of this base class; Finder. We won't actually create any Finder robots, however. This class is just a convenient place to place methods that must be common to other classes.

```
public class Finder extends Robot
{
        public void turnAround(){...}
        public void turnRight(){...}

        public void moveToRobot() // Robot directly ahead.
        {       whilc( ! ncxtToARobot() )
                {       move();
                }
        }
        ...
}

public class Carrier extends Finder
{
        public void carryOne(){...} // Carry a "one" to the next column
}
```

```
public class Checker extends Finder
{
        public boolean enoughToCarry(){...}
        // Are there enough to require carrying?
        . . .
}

public class Adder extends Finder
// Always create on 1st Street, facing North.
{
        private Carrier carry = new Carrier(1,1, East, infinity);
        private Checker check = new Checker(1,1, East, 0);

        public void gatherHelpers(){...}
        public void addColumn(){...}
        . . .
}

public void gatherHelpers() // Adder class
{       carry.move();
        carry.moveToRobot ();
        carry.turnLeft();
        check.moveToRobot ();
        check.turnLeft();
}
```

Once the Adder robot has created its helpers, it can execute addColumn. To do this it merely picks up all of the beepers north of it until it finds an empty corner, returns to 1st Street, deposits all of the beepers there and then has the helpers finish the task.

```
public void addColumn() // Facing north on 1st Street.
{       move();
        while(nextToABeeper())
        {       pickBeeper();
                if ( ! nextToABeeper() )
                {       move();
                }
        }
        turnAround();
        while( frontIsClear() )
        {       move();
        }
        turnAround();
        while ( anyBeepersInBeeperBag() )
        {       putBeeper();
        }
        // Compute the quotient and the remainder to separate the digits.
        while(check.enoughToCarry() )
        {       carry.carryOne();
        }
}
```

Carrying is quite simple. Notice that we gave the Carrier an infinite number of beepers in its beeper-bag, so it can't possibly run out.

```
public void carryOne()  // Facing north on 1st Street. -- Carrier class
{       turnLeft();
        move();          // Note:  Error shutoff here if we try to carry
                         // from 1st Street.
        putBeeper();
        turnAround();
        move();
        turnLeft();
}
```

The Checker robot does all of the interesting work. It must determine if there are ten or more beepers on the current corner. If there are it must return true, otherwise false. It can try to pick up ten beepers to check this. However, it has more to do since it is going to be called repeatedly to see how many multiples of ten there really are. Therefore it must find a way to dispose of each group of ten beepers before it attempts to check for the next group of ten. It has another important task also. If it finds less than ten beepers in a group it must leave them on the current corner. This is to account for the first digit of the answer; the one that isn't carried.

```
public boolean enoughToCarry()
        // Facing north on 1st Street. -- Checker class
{       for(int i = 0; i < 10; i++)
        {       if (nextToABeeper() )
                {       pickBeeper();
                }
                else
                {       emptyBag();
                        return false;
                }
        }
        // We have found ten beepers.
        move();
        emptyBag(); // leave them on 2nd Street.
        turnAround();
        move();
        turnAround();
        return true;
}
```

To finish we need only add emptyBag to the Checker class:

```
public void emptyBag()
{       while( anyBeepersInBeeperBag() )
        {       putBeeper();
        }
}
```

Now we are ready to tackle the problem of a multi-column sum. Notice that if we start at the right end of the row of values and just slide the adder and its helpers to the left after adding a column, the three robots will be positioned for the next column. Then, working from right to left, we will compute the correct sum since we carry into a column before that column is added.

We need two additional methods in the Adder class: slideLeft and addAll. Method slideLeft is easy.

```
public void slideLeft()
{       turnLeft();
        move();
        turnRight();
        carry.turnLeft();
        carry.move();
        carry.turnRight();
        check.turnLeft();
        check.move();
        check.turnRight();
}
```

How will addAll know when it is done adding columns? One way is to have the left most number start on Second Avenue so that there is room to carry any value from the left most column. The Adder will then need to check to see if it is on Second Avenue before adding. This requires a new predicate.

```
public boolean onSecondAve()
//precondition facing North and Not on 1st. Ave.
{       turnLeft();
        move();
        if (frontIsClear())
        {       turnAround();
                move();
                turnLeft();
                return false;
        }
        turnAround();
        move();
        turnLeft();
        return true;
}
```

We are now ready to write the addAll method in the Adder class.

```
public void addAll()
{       while( ! onSecondAve() )
        {       addColumn();
                slideLeft();
        }
        addColumn();
}
```

7.7 Polymorphism--Why Write Many Programs When One Will Do?

Polymorphism means literally "many forms." In object-oriented programming it refers to the fact that messages sent to objects (robots) may be interpreted differently, depending on the class of the object (robot) receiving the message. Perhaps the best way to think of this is to remember that a robot is autonomous in its world. We send it messages and it responds. It doesn't come with a remote control unit by which the user directs its actions. Rather, it "hears" the messages sent to it and responds according to its internal dictionary. Recall that each robot consults its own internal dictionary of instructions to select the method that it uses to respond to any message. When we override a method in a new class, the new version of the method, then changes the meaning of the message for robots of the new class but not of the original class.

To illustrate the consequences of this, let's take a somewhat dramatic, though not very useful example. Suppose we have the following two classes

```
public class Putter extends Robot
{
        public void move()
        {       super.move();
                if (anyBeepersInBeeperBag())
                {       putBeeper();
                }
        }
}

public class Getter extends Robot
{
        public void move()
        {       super.move();
                while (nextToABeeper())
                {       pickBeeper();
                }
        }
}
```

Both classes override the move method, and nothing more. Thus, a Putter robot puts beepers on corners that it moves to and Getter robots sweep corners to which they move. Suppose now that we use these two classes in the following task.

```
public static void main(String [] args)
{       Putter  lisa = new Putter(1, 1, East, infinity);
        Getter  tony = new Getter(2, 1, East, 0);

        for (int i = 0; i < 10; i++)
        {       lisa.move();
        }
        for (int j = 0; j< 10; j++)
        {       tony.move();
        }
}
```

If the world contains a beeper on each of the first ten corners of 1st Street and also each of the first ten corners of 2nd Street, then, when the task is done, there will be two beepers on each of the first ten blocks of 1st Street, and none on the corresponding blocks of 2nd Street. There is nothing surprising about this, but note that both lisa and tony responded to the same messages in identical (relative) situations.

The meaning of polymorphism is even deeper than this, however. In fact, the names that we use to refer to robots are not "burned in" to the robots themselves, but only a convenience for the user. A given robot can be referred to by different names, called aliases.

First, we declare that a name will be used as an alias. We won't make it refer to a new robot yet, however.

```
Robot karel = null;   // "karel" will refer to some robot.
```

Secondly, we need to assign a value to the name karel. In other words we need to specify which robot the name "karel" will refer to. We do this with an assignment instruction. This assumes that the name tony already refers to a robot as it would if it were part of the above main task block.

```
karel = tony;
```

This establishes karel as an alternate name (alias) for the robot also known as tony. We could just as easily make the name "karel" refer to the robot lisa. It is very important to note, however, that an alias doesn't refer to any robot until we assign a value to the name.

Then sending a turnLeft message using the name karel will send the message to the same robot that the name tony refers to, since they are the same robot.

```
karel.turnLeft();
```

Suppose now that we consider the slightly revised task that follows. We use the same setup and assume the world is as before. The only difference is that we refer to the robots using the name karel in each case. Note that while we have three names here, we only have two robots.

```
public static void main(String [] args)
{       Robot  karel;
        Putter lisa = new Putter(1, 1, East, 100);
        Getter tony = new Getter(2, 1, East, 0);

        karel = lisa;           // "karel" refers to lisa;
        for (int i = 0; i < 10; i++)
        {       karel.move();   // lisa puts down ten beepers
        }
        karel = tony;           // "karel" refers to tony
        for (int j = 0; j< 10; j++)
        {       karel.move();   // tony sweeps ten blocks
        }
}
```

So note that not only can we have identical messages (move) referring to different actions; even if the message statements as a whole are identical (`karel.move();`) we can have different actions. Notice though, that we are still sending messages to two different robots, and that these robots are from different classes. It is even possible to arrange it so that different things happen on two different executions of the same statement. Consider the following.

```
public static void main(String [] args)
{       Robot  karel;
        Putter lisa = new Putter(1, 1, East, 100);
        Getter tony = new Getter(2, 1, East, 0);

        for (int i = 0; i < 10; i++)
        {       karel = lisa;               // "karel" refers to lisa;
                for (int j = 0; j< 2; j++)
                {       karel.move();   // ??
                        karel = tony;   // "karel" refers to tony

                }
        }
}
```

Note that the move message is sent 20 times, but 10 times it is sent to lisa, and 10 times to tony, alternately. Again, 1st Street gets extra beepers and 2nd Street gets swept.

7.8 Conclusion

Finally, we want to ask the question: When is it appropriate to design a new class, and when should we modify or add to an existing robot class?

The full answer to this question is beyond the scope of this book, because there are many things to be considered in this decision, but we can set some general guidelines here. If, in your judgment, a robot class contains errors or omissions, by all means, modify it. Here omissions mean that there is some method (action or predicate) that is needed to complete the basic functionality of the class or to make robots in the class do what the class was designed to do.

On the other hand, if we have a useful class, and we need additional functionality, especially more specialized functionality than that provided by the class we already have, then building a new class as a subclass of the given one is appropriate. This way, when we need a robot with the original capabilities, we can use the original class, and when we need the new functionality we can use the new one. Sometimes the choice is made because we find that most of the methods of some class are just exactly what we want, but one or two methods would serve better in the new problem if they were modified or extended.

7.9 Important Ideas From This Chapter

recursion
tail recursion
searching
meta
formal definition/proof

7.10 Problem Set

The following problems use the recursion, searching, and arithmetic methods discussed in this chapter. Some of the following problems use combinations of the zigLeftUp and zagDownRight methods, or simple variants of these. Each problem is difficult to solve, but once a plan is discovered (probably through an "aha experience"), the program that implements the solution will not be too difficult to write. You may also assume that there are no wall sections in the world. Finally, you should assume that our robot, karel, starts with no beepers in its beeper-bag, unless you are told otherwise. Do not make any assumptions about karel's starting corner or starting direction, unless they are specified in the problem.

1. Rewrite your program that solves Problem 6.9-21 using a recursive method instead of an iterative one.

2. Karel has graduated to advanced carpet layer. Karel must carpet the completely enclosed room. Only one beeper can be placed on each corner. The room may be any size and any shape. Figure 7-5 shows one possible floor plan. The central area is not to be carpeted by karel. Karel may start from any place within the room and may be facing any direction.

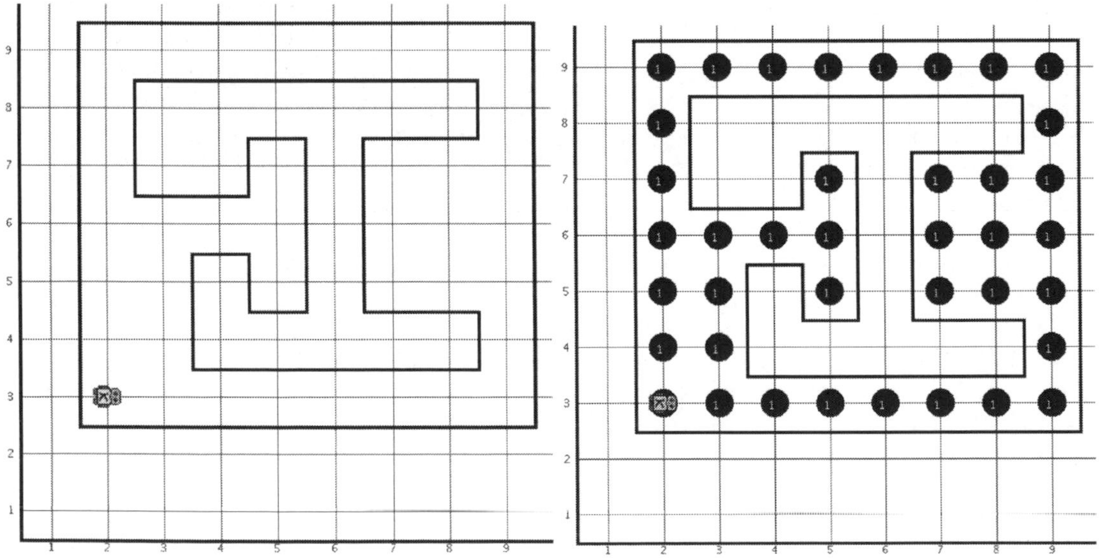

Figure 7-5 A Big Carpeting Job

3. Rewrite both zigLeftUp and zagDownRight so that they automatically satisfy their directional pre-conditions.

4. Assume that there is a beeper on 1st Street and Nth Avenue. Program karel to find it and move to Nth Street and 1st Avenue.

5. Assume that there is a beeper on Sth Street and Ath Avenue, and that karel has two beepers in its beeper-bag. Program karel to put the beepers from its beeper-bag on to 1st Street and Ath Avenue and Sth Street and 1st Avenue. The original beeper must remain at the corner on which it starts.

6. Assume that there is a beeper on 1st Street and Ath Avenue. Program karel to double the avenue number; the robot must move this beeper to 1st Street and 2Ath Avenue. (For example, a beeper on 1st Street and 7th Avenue must be moved to 1st Street and 14th Avenue.) Hint: Use the west boundary wall as in Problem 7.10-4.

7. Assume that karel starts its task with an infinite number of beepers in its beeper-bag. Also assume that there is a beeper on 1st Street and Nth Avenue. Program karel to leave N beepers on the origin.

8. Assume that there is a beeper on Sth Street and 1st Avenue and a beeper on 1st Street and Ath Avenue. Program karel to put one of these beepers on Sth Street and Ath Avenue. Karel must put the other beeper in its beeper-bag. Hint: There are many ways to plan this task. Here are two suggestions: (1) move one beeper south while moving the other beeper north; (2) continue moving one beeper until it is directly over (or to the right of) the stationary beeper. If done correctly, both methods will result in one beeper being placed on the answer corner.

9. Assume that there is a beeper on Ath Street and Bth Avenue. Program a Mathematician robot to find the beeper, pick it up and transport it to 1st Street and (A+B)th Avenue. Hint. When you find the beeper the sum of your street and avenue numbers will be A+B. If you move south one block and also east one block, the sum will still be the same since your Street number will have decreased by one while your Avenue number will have increased by one.

10. Assume that karel has a beeper in its beeper-bag and that there is another beeper on 1st Street and Ath Avenue. Program karel to place one of the beepers on 1st Street and 2 to the Ath power Avenue. This expression is 2 raised to the Ath power or 1 doubled A times. For example, when A is 5, 2 to the Ath power is 32. Hint: This problem uses instructions similar to those used to solve Problem 7.10-6. Karel can use the second beeper to count the number of times it must double the number 1.

11. Repeat Problem 7.10-10, but this time the answer corner is 1st Street and 3 to the Ath power Avenue. Try to reuse as much of the previous program as possible.

12. Program karel to place beepers in an outward spiral until its beeper-bag is empty. Assume that karel will run out of beepers before it is stopped by the boundary walls. One example is shown in Figure 7-6.

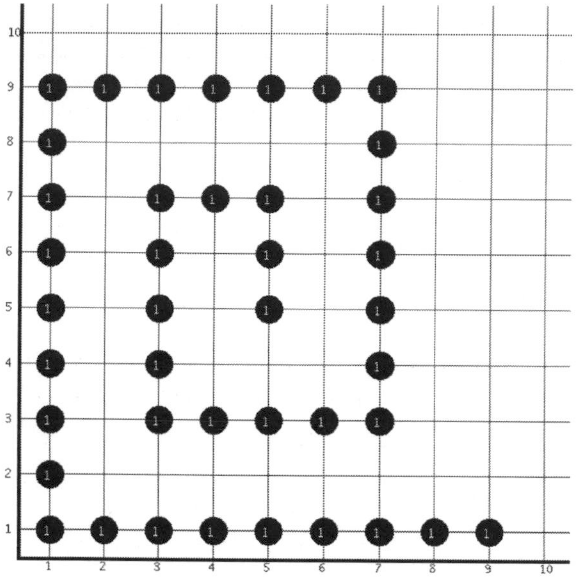

Figure 7-6 A Spiral

13. Assume that karel has two beepers and that there is another beeper on Sth Street and Ath Avenue. Program karel to deposit one of these beepers on the corner of 1st Street and SAth Avenue. (This expression is S multiplied by A.)

14. Assume that karel has three beepers in its beeper-bag and that there is another beeper on Sth Street and Ath Avenue. Program karel to deposit a beeper on the corner of 1st Street and S to the Ath Power Avenue. (This expression is S raised to power of A.)

15. Assume that karel has three beepers in its beeper-bag and that there is another beeper on Sth Street and Ath Avenue. Program karel to put a beeper on the corner of 1st Street and GCD(S,A)th Ave. The GCD of two numbers is their Greatest Common Divisor. For example, the GCD of 6 and 15 is 3. Hint: Use Euclid's subtractive instruction.

16. Assume that karel has N beepers in its beeper-bag. Program the robot to place beepers on 1st Street and all avenues that represent prime numbers between 1st Avenue and (N - SquareRoot of N)th Avenue.

17. Program a robot named karel to pick up a beeper at the west wall and return to the corner on which it starts. There may be other beepers in the path, but it is known that there is a beeper on 1st Avenue directly west of karel's starting position. Hint: Think recursively.

18. Program a robot named karel to pick up a beeper at the origin and return to the corner on which it starts. Hint: Think recursively.

19. Write a recursive program to solve problem 6.10-25. Hint: If all of the piles of beepers were moved one block north, then 1st Street would be clear. The robot could then use two beepers to mark the beginning and ending avenues that it was supposed to sort. An overall plan could be to move the smallest pile between the two markers to the western marker avenue. That marker could then be moved one block East.

20. Write a recursive predicate to determine if the number of beepers in a robots beeper-bag is exactly the same as the number of beepers on the robot's current corner. You may assume that there is no wall immediately to the north of the robot.

21. Karel the Robot meets carol the UrRobot on a corner. How can karel determine if it has exactly the same number of beepers in its beeper-bag that carol has? Each robot should finish with the same number of beepers that it starts with.

22. Karel and carol again meet on a corner. Have them exchange beepers, so that karel ends with the number of beepers carol has initially and conversely. Assume the corner they both occupy has no beepers.

23. The required instruction creates a robot on each of the first ten avenues of 1st Street. They each have zero or more beepers in their beeper-bag. Their task is to sort themselves in order of number of beepers, with the robot with the smallest number on 1st Avenue, etc. Each robot can visit one of its neighbors and between them decide which of their original corners each should occupy. Repetitions of this will sort the robots. When they are sorted have each robot distribute its beepers along the streets of the avenue it occupies, one beeper per corner. The final picture should be similar to the final figure of Figure 5.31. Assume that there are no beepers in the world except the beepers carried by the robots.

24 What happens if we use an Adder robot to add the numbers 3102 and 4027? Devise a solution that covers this beyond-the-horizon situation.

25. Devise a solution to the problem we left unsolved in Chapter 6. Four robots are supposed to patrol a field of beepers, keeping equally spaced around the perimeter. You might try a solution with one leader and three helpers, as we did in the solution to the simpler problem. The leader will belong to a new class that you must design.

26. Do Problem 29 of Chapter 6 again, but have the Spy find the Accomplices recursively.

27. A Contractor wants to build a house with three helpers, a Mason, a Carpenter, and a Roofer, but the helpers are spread around the robot world. Have the Contractor go on a search for its three helpers and pass each a strategy concerning the location of the house when it finds them. It will also need to tell them to get to work. Then have the helpers build the house.

28. Do Problem 28 of Chapter 6 again, but this time tony must remain at the origin throughout.

29. A robot named ilya is in a square room with sides 8 blocks long. Ilya has 8 beepers in its beeperBag. Program ilya to place the 8 beepers so that there is only one on each street, one on each avenue, and one on each diagonal (both left and right diagonals must be considered). This is a classic problem called "Eight Queens." Think of the beepers as queens on a chess board. Queens can move horizontally, vertically, and diagonally. Place 8 queens on a chessboard so that none of them can attack any of the others. HINT: Think recursively.

30. Write a recursive robot program to solve problem 33 of Chapter 6.

31. Write a recursive robot program to solve problem 34 of Chapter 6.

32. Program 8 robots to place themselves on a chessboard (8 by 8 square room) so that when moving according to the chess queen move rules, no robot attacks any other (see problem 1N of this Chapter). Each robot should start on the row on which it will eventually end up. It can leave that row to check if it attacks other robots, but should return to its home row. Hint: use many classes and recursion. You do not need aliases for this exercise. The robots on the first seven streets will need to know the name of the robot on the street immediately to the north. Use local robots for this. Interestingly, all the robots can be named garry.

8 Concurrent Robot Programs

In this Chapter we introduce what has been up to now considered a very advanced topic. Real computer systems today run so fast that they can devote small bits of time to many users in quick succession and it seems as if the entire computer is dedicated to each user. Even more interesting, they can let several "processes" operate with seeming simultaneity for each user. This is called concurrent programming and we will introduce it here, with some of its pitfalls.

8.1 Simple Concurrent Programs

When a program is to run several pieces at the same time, the individual parts are called threads (threads of control). Each thread in a robot program is just like a task: a sequence of robot instructions executed one after the other until the end. We can make a task run in its own thread quite easily. Suppose we again take up the house building task of Chapter 4.

Only one of our Carpenter robots was needed to make two windows. Suppose we write a task function to do just this. This can be a static method of our Main class.

```
public static void carpenterTask()
{       Carpenter linda = new Carpenter(1, 1, North, infinity);
        linda.moveToFirstWindow();
        linda.makeWindow();
        linda.moveToNextWindow();
        linda.makeWindow();
}
```

We next need to create a Runnable class that can be used to control a thread. Such a class implements the Runnable interface and has a run method. Runnable is built into the Java system.

```
class CarpenterRunner implements Runnable
{       public void run()
        {       Main.carpenterTask();
        }
}
```

We could have actually avoided writing the carpenterTask method and just put its statements into this run method.

Finally, from our main task block we need to create a new CarpenterRunner and tell the world to run it in a new thread.

```
public static void main(String [] args)
{       ...
        CarpenterRunner r = new CarpenterRunner();
        World.setupThread(r);
        . . .
}
```

Now this task will run in its own thread along with other threads that we start in the same way. This same thread could be used to control one or more robots. Each thread behaves like an independent main task block, but, of course, all such threads run in the same world. If we make several such threads for our house building task, it will seem like the workers are working all at once.

8.2 Robot Runs In Its Own Thread

One especially nice way to make concurrent robot programs is to let each robot be controlled by its own thread. Each robot then behaves much more like an independent being than has been possible up to now. This is like the helicopter pilot reading a robot's messages to it all at once and then setting it on its way, rather than reading one message at a time and waiting for it to complete.

One simple example is to write a class of robots that can race each other to some goal. For example, suppose we start a Racer robot on 1st street and 1st avenue and another on 2nd street and 1st avenue. Both robots face East. Somewhere in front of each is a beeper. We start them up simultaneously, each in its own thread and see who gets there first.

To arrange this, we are going to do two things differently in the Racer class. We are going to tell the World to run this robot in its own thread and we are going to give the class its own run method. (Note that UrRobot itself implements the Runnable interface, which is what makes this possible.)

```
public class Racer extends Robot
{       public Racer(int Street, int Avenue, Direction direction,
            int beepers)
        {       super(Street, Avenue, direction, beepers);
                World.setupThread(this);
        }
        public void race()
        {       while(! nextToABeeper())
                        move();
                pickBeeper();
                turnOff();
        }
        public void run()
        {       race();
        }
}
```

Then, all we need to do in the main task block is to create our robots. We don't actually even need to name them, but we will here.

```
public static void main(String [] args)
{       Racer first = new Racer(1, 1, East, 0);
        Racer second = new Racer(2, 1, East, 0);
}
```

They will automatically start themselves up, since we told the world to run them in the Racer constructor.

8.3 Cooperation

Robots have a very rudimentary way to communicate with each other. They can meet on a corner and exchange beepers. This can be the basis of sophisticated programs. Here we show part of a simple relay race in which three robots exchange a beeper (the baton) when the first runs up to the second and the second then runs up to the third.

```
public class RelayRacer extends Robot
{       public RelayRacer(int street, int avenue,  Direction direction,
             int beepers)
        {       super(street, avenue, direction, beepers);
                World.setupThread(this);
        }

        public void run()
        {       while(!nextToABeeper())
                {       spin();
                }
                pickBeeper();
                runToRobot();
                putBeeper();
                turnOff();
        }
        private void spin()
        {       turnAround();
                turnAround();
        }
        private void turnAround()
        {       turnLeft();
                turnLeft();
        }
        private void runToRobot()
        {       move();
                while(! nextToARobot())
                {       move();
                }
        }
}
```

If we start one of these on a corner that contains a beeper, facing down a street that contains another of these then the relay will begin properly. You will need to do some additional things to make it end properly, however.

8.4 Race Conditions

When threads run concurrently it is usually impossible to predict the order of operations of the individual instructions in different threads. This sometimes leads to undesirable effects in which two things happen in the wrong order. It is generally difficult to reason about the interleaving of concurrent operations because there are so many possibilities. This needs to be carefully controlled. For example, if two computers are connected to the same printer, and the print driver on each isn't careful, it would be possible for two users to print at about the same time and have the individual characters of the two documents interleaved on the output. The usual method of controlling this kind of thing is to have a queue that holds requests to print. A newly arriving print request is put into the back of the queue and the printer takes requests from the front. Eventually each request works its way to the front and gets printed. But, if the print driver isn't careful and two print requests arrive at about the same time, the print queue can get corrupted.

In this section we are going to illustrate one classic problem with concurrency, called race conditions. Since we are using robots we can do this by actually holding races. The term however, applies whenever the interleaving of operations can cause something to happen at an unexpected time.

Suppose we take our Racer robots of Section 8.2 and make them race to pick up the same beeper. We can start one at 10th street and 1st avenue and the other at 1st street and 10th avenue, racing for a single beeper at the origin. We don't know which will reach the beeper first and pick it up. But the other will slam into the end wall, since it won't see any beeper at all. The first robot to get there will pick it up. Since we aren't going to be sending any messages to these robots, we won't even name them. They will be anonymous.

```
public static void main(String [] args)
{       new Racer(10, 1, South, 0);
        new Racer(1, 10, West, 0);
}
```

Actually, it is possible for both robots to arrive at about the same time and each check to see if there was a beeper there and each find that there was and only then, each try to pick it up. Thus, one of them would do an error shutoff while trying to pick up a beeper that it just checked for and found, rather than when trying to walk through a wall.

Here is another example, contributed by Byron Weber Becker of University of Waterloo.

```
public class Thief extends Robot
{       public Thief(int street, int avenue, Direction direction)
        {       super(street, avenue, direction, 0);
                World.setupThread(this);
        }

        public void run()
        {       pickBeeper();
                move();
                for(int i=0; i<10000; i++)
                 {      turnLeft();
                        turnLeft();
                        if (nextToABeeper())
```

```
                    {  pickBeeper();
                    } else
                    {  putBeeper();
                    }
                    move();
                    turnLeft();
                    turnLeft();
                    move();
                    Thread.yield(); // May not be needed.
                }
                move();
                turnOff();
        }
}
```

Notice that if such a robot successfully picks up a beeper from the first corner, then it should execute to completion with no errors. Assuming a robot can pick up a beeper from its starting corner, it then goes to another corner and either takes a beeper or leaves a beeper depending on whether or not one is already there. It then leaves, comes back and checks again. One robot will execute this just fine. When a second robot is introduced, however, it can "steal" a beeper from the corner between the time the other robot checks and actually picks it up. The other robot then performs an error shutoff.

To see this happen, create two such robots and arrange them so that they will meet on the same corner to place their beepers.

```
World.placeBeepers(2,3,1);
World.placeBeepers(3,4,1);
new Thief(2, 3, East);
new Thief(3, 4, South);
```

This is nearly guaranteed to fail as you can see by trying it.

8.5 Deadlock

Another classic concurrency problem is deadlock. This occurs when different threads hold some resources (say a beeper) that the other threads need and each waits (forever) for the others to release the resource. One classic illustration of this is called Dining Philosophers.

In the traditional story we have a group of philosophers who alternately think and eat. Each has a place at the table and between each pair of places there is a fork. Each philosopher will think for a while and then decide it wants to eat. To do so, however requires picking up both forks by its place, one at a time. If it doesn't get a fork it waits for the philosopher next to it to put down that fork and then it picks up the fork and continues. When it finishes, it puts down its forks, again, one at a time.

The problem arises when each philosopher has picked up its left fork and reaches for the right one. Each will wait for a fork and none will put one down. This is deadlock. Here is a class that illustrates this example. Note, that it won't deadlock every time. Also note that the run method in the class never ends. You will have to stop the program yourself.

```
public class Philosopher extends AugmentedRobot
{       public Philosopher(int street, int avenue,  Direction direction)
        {       super(street, avenue, direction, 0);
                World.setupThread(this);
        }

        public void run()
        {       while(true)
                {       think(die.roll());
                        getForks();
                        eat(die.roll());
                        putForks();
                }
        }

        private void think(int time)
        {       for(int i = 0; i < time; i++)
                {       backUp();
                        move();
                }
        }

        private void eat(int time)
        {       for(int i = 0; i < time; i++)
                {       move();
                        backUp();
                }
        }

        private void getForks()
        {       turnLeft();
                move();
                while(! anyBeepersInBeeperBag())
                {       while(! nextToABeeper()) ; // nothing
                        pickBeeper();
                }
                turnAround();
                move();putBeeper();
                move();
                while(! anyBeepersInBeeperBag())
                {       while(! nextToABeeper()) ; // nothing
                        pickBeeper();
                }
                turnAround();
                move();
                putBeeper();
                turnRight();
                showState("Eat ");
        }
```

```
        private void putForks()
        {       pickBeeper();
                pickBeeper();
                turnLeft();
                move();
                putBeeper();
                turnAround();
                move();
                move();
                putBeeper();
                turnAround();
                move();
                turnRight();
                showState("Think ");
        }
        private Die die = new Die(6);
}
```

The Die class isn't shown here, but it simulates the rolling of a single die (one of a pair of Dice) to achieve randomization. Thus, the philosophers seem to eat and think for random periods of time. To start up the simulation, you need to say something like:

```
public static void main(String [] args)
{       World.placeBeepers(2, 2, 1);
        World.placeBeepers(2, 4, 1);
        World.placeBeepers(4, 2, 1);
        World.placeBeepers(4, 4, 1);
        Philosopher p1 = new Philosopher(2, 3, North);
        Philosopher p2 = new Philosopher(3, 2, East);
        Philosopher p3 = new Philosopher(4, 3, South);
        Philosopher p4 = new Philosopher(3, 4, West);
}
```

If you make the Die one or two sided instead of six sided you greatly increase the chance of deadlock.

Note that the AugmentedRobot just provides some simple methods like turnRight and turnAround that we commonly use.

8.6 Important Ideas From This Chapter

concurrent
race condition
deadlock
thread

8.7 Problem Set

1 Run a super duper steeplechase relay race with three robots that run in concurrent threads. See problem 6.11 and problem 6.27.

2. Have two sets of three robots each race against each other in a super duper steeplechase relay tournament.

3. Do Problem 4.12-17 again, where the two Spy robots run in different threads.

4. Do Problem 11 of Chapter 4.12-19 again, where each of the four robots runs in a separate thread.

5. Repeat Problem 4, except that each robot starts at an arbitrary location and each runs in a separate thread. They rendezvous at the origin to exchange strategies.

6. The deadlock problem for Philosophers can be solved if just one of the Philosophers picks up its right fork before the left one. Use polymorphism to implement such a solution. Not all deadlock problems can be solved this way, but asymmetry might be useful in any such situation.

7. One solution to Philosopher deadlock is to have a philosopher put down its first fork if it can't get the second one. It then returns to thinking for a bit. It then tries again later. However, it is possible for a philosopher to never get to eat with this "solution." Because this philosopher example is so important in the history of concurrent programming, this difficulty has come to be called *starvation:* a thread gets no useful work done. Implement this idea in a subclass of Philosopher.

8. If you enjoy computer science and eventually take a course in computability theory, fondly recall the days you spent programming Karel J Robot and try to solve the following problem: Prove that karel, even without the aid of any beepers is equivalent to a Turing machine. Hint: Use the equivalence between Turing machines and 2-counter automata.

Appendix

1 Java main

For those wanting explanation of some of the Java words required for a main task block and a complete program such as that in Section 2.6 we provide the following somewhat simplified definitions.

A Java *package* is a way to collect different parts of a large program together logically. The Java system (JDK or Java Development Kit) comes with several packages of its own, but you can create your own. The name kareltherobot was created by the authors of the simulator for Karel J Robot as a convenient place in which to collect robot programming code. To use this system include

```
import kareltherobot.*;
```

at the beginning of every file with robot code. It gives you access to the system. See pg. 11 for example. If you prefer not to use the * form of import then you will need at least

```
import kareltherobot.Directions;
import kareltherobot.UrRobot;
import kareltherobot.World;
```

You may need to import a few other things as you go along, such as kareltherobot.Robot.

Every Java program must contain a *main* somewhere. It is a member of some class, perhaps a robot class. Again, see pg. 11 for an example. There is another on pg. 34. Its required form is

```
public static void main(String [] args)
{ ...
}
```

In Java the qualifier *public* means that something is available across packages. It is also possible to restrict visibility of names to a single package or even more.

The particular form of main is required by Java. While the following explanation of its parts is not needed now, and probably not especially understandable, you can return to it later when you know more.

In Java, main is a *static* method. This means the method is part of its class and not part of objects. Robots are objects, which are like things. They are defined by classes, which are like production lines in a factory for the creation of objects of the same kind. In terms of our metaphor for robot programming, a static method is like the instructions read to robots by the helicoptor pilot, not the instructions known by the robots themselves. We will see ordinary (instance) methods in the Chapter 3.

Strings in Java are sequence of characters, like the characters in this sentence. The matched square brackets indicate that an *array* of Strings is required. An array is a certain kind of linear collection of things. The name args is just a name for this array. This name is the only part of the declaration of main that can vary.

The declaration (String [] args) is in parentheses as part of the declaration of main to indicate that when the main method is executed by your computer's operating system, an array of strings can be sent to the program to help with program initialization. Since they are not referenced again in the body of any main (the part between braces {...}) we write they won't be used here. The parentheses, like the rest, are required. There is no space between [and].

Braces { and } are used to collect statements into a "block" in Java and in some other programming languages. Statements in Java end with semicolons.

To execute a Java program you first need to translate it into a machine readable form using the Java compiler. Then you need to use the Java run-time to execute the machine readable version. When you do this you give the run time the name of the class that contains your main method. Any class can contain a main method. It is then sometimes called a "main" class.

2 KarelRunner

Since the above is a bit arcane, we would like to simplify it if we can. The Karel J Robot simulation program provided with the book has a built in class named **KarelRunner** that has a special kind of main built in to it. If you use this technique then KarelRunner will always be your main class and always be the class you name to the Java run time.

Then, when you want to write a robot program, create a class like the following. It should be called GetBeeper.java, since it defines a class called GetBeeper. In Java the name of a public class is in a file with the same name and java for an extension. The name of the file and the name of its public class need to match. The name you give to your class and its file should probably be related to the problem you are trying to solve. Here we are trying to get a beeper. Also, in Java, the convention is that class names begin with a capital letter and method names do not.

```
import kareltherobot.*;

public class GetBeeper implements RobotTask
{
        public void task()
        {
                UrRobot karel = new UrRobot(1, 1, East, 0);
                // Deliver the robot to the origin (1,1),
                // facing East, with no beepers.
                karel.move();
                karel.move();
                karel.move();
                karel.pickBeeper();
                karel.turnOff();
        }
}
```

Your class needs to implement **RobotTask** so that the other class, RobotRunner knows how to interpret this and run the task method here. Note that task here is NOT a static method. RobotTask is an interface. Java interfaces are discussed in Chapter 4.

In the book we often speak of the "main task block." You can interpret this to either mean a static main method as in the program in Section 2.9, in which your class implements the Directions interface, or as a task method in some class that implements RobotTask. Either will serve, though the latter is a bit easier to use.

3 Compiling and Executing Robot Code

Once you have a complete Robot program (or any Java program) you will want to execute it to see its effect. This is a two step process. First you must "build" your program and then "execute" it. If you have a Java environment like Eclipse or JBuilder, you create a "project" in the environment and add your files to it. This will include any code you write as well as the robot simulator code that you can get from the authors. Then it is just a matter of pushing buttons or selecting menu options to build and execute.

However, if you do not have an environment to work with then you need to use the JDK (Java Development Kit) from Sun Microsystems. You can get this from http://java.sun.com. You create your robot programs with a text editor and make sure that the file names end in ".java". The build step is then carried out by the "Java compiler" called javac. Suppose we want to compile the MileWalker.java file of Section 3.3. A command to do this would be something like

```
javac -d . -classpath .;KarelJRobot.jar MileWalker.java
```

This assumes you are working in a Windows environment and have established a working directory with all of your files. On a unix system (including Macintosh OS X) the semicolon would be replaced by a colon. This command is typed into a command window on your computer.

I also assume that you put all of your robot code into the default package by not including any package statement at the beginning of each file you write containing robot program code.

If there are no errors in your program then (for robot programs) the compiler, javac, will create machine readable versions of your program in one or more "class" files. If you include a package statement in the file then these will be in a subdirectory with the package name instead.

Once you have done the above, you can execute your program with the "Java Virtual Machine", java. The command would look like this.

```
java -classpath .;KarelJRobot.jar MileWalker
```

The command is case sensitive. You may be able to abbreviate classpath in the above with cp instead. This latter instruction tells java to look for the file MileWalker.class and execute the main that it finds there. Note that you name the class here that contains the main task block that you want to execute. The name of the class is prefixed by the name of the package, but has no suffix. Here we have no prefix as we assume the file is not in any package.

All of the above is needed and must appear just about as shown. In particular you need the -classpath option followed by what is shown above as well as the -d option followed by a space and a period in the compile instruction. Also replace the single semicolon in each with a colon on a unix machine.

It is possible to have many files to compile. You can do this all at once just by including them all where we have shown MileWalker.java. Just include a list of filenames in the javac instruction separated by spaces.

In the java command, however, you always name just one class, the one that contains the main that you want to execute.

Note that I assumed in the above that the simulator for robot programs is called KarelJRobot.jar, which is true when this is written. Jar stands for "Java archive". It must be included both when you compile and when you execute (or "run") your robot program. For Java programs other than robot programs, you don't need this file.

4 Constructors in Java

In the robot programming language, a delivery specification for a UrRobot looks like this:

```
UrRobot karel = new UrRobot(1, 2, North, 0);
```

These specifications need to be defined in the classes that we write. Java calls them constructors, since they are used to construct objects. The UrRobot class defines a constructor (among others) that requires that we give a positive integer for the street and another for the avenue as well as a Direction in which to face the robot initially, and another integer for the number of beepers in its beeper-bag. These values given in the new construct are called *parameters* or *arguments*. Even the word infinity that is used to indicate infinitely many beepers is just a name for a special integer. In Java, an integer value is given a type named int. A constructor looks similar to a method, with some important differences, both in its form and its meaning.

You need to define a new constuctor (and may define several) in every robot class that you write. For example, in the MileWalker class of Section 3.3, the constructor would look like the following. It belongs within the braces that delimit the class definition.

```
public MileWalker(int street, int avenue, Direction direction,
    int beepers)
{       super(street, avenue, direction, beepers);
}
```

Note that the word void does not appear before the name of the constructor (as it would in the methods we have seen so far) and that the name is identical to that of the class. Constructors are not inherited in the way that methods are, but if a class has only constructors that require parameters (as UrRobot requires four parameters) then you must define a constructor in every sub class, such as MileWalker and it must "invoke" the constructor of the super class with the super(…) construct shown above.

The meaning of this, in reality, is that in order to construct a MileWalker, we must first construct a super class object (UrRobot) and then specialize it if necessary. We could also put additional instructions in the constructor body (after super…) and even add additional parameters if we need them.

In general, in Java, you may not need to write a constructor for a class. You will need to if any of the following situations occur.

(a) The superclass has a constructor that requires arguments, and has none without parameters.
(b) You need to do something when you create the object to make it immediately sensible and usable.

In this case, both (a) and (b) hold. It wouldn't make much sense to create a robot and not deliver it to the world to a specific place, for example. Therefore UrRobot has constructors that require the four parameters above and then sub classes like MileWalker must include a compatible constructor as well.

There is one situation in which you can modify this a bit, actually. Suppose you want to create a class of robots in which it only makes sense to deliver them in one specific configuration. You can then write a constructor without parameters, but in the super construct specify the configuration you need. A somewhat abstract example might be

```
public class OriginSitter extends UrRobot
{       public OrignSitter()
        {       super(1, 1, North, infinity);
        }

        ...
}
```

The delivery specification would be just:

```
OriginSitter karel = new OriginSitter();
```

We still need to write a constructor, but we can be more free in its own parameter structure. The important thing is that we do in fact construct a UrRobot that is then specialized to an OriginSitter. You can provide some (rather than all or none) of the parameters and use your fixed values for the rest. The order in super(…) is important, however. You can even add additional parameters of your own to a constructor. This is shown in Section 4.5.

5 Controllers and Inner Classes

The Controller objects of Problem 4.12-9 require a way to obtain a reference to some robot so that you can put useful instructions into the controlIt method. Here is a program that shows how this can be done using constructors of the Controller subclasses. After we see this version, we will examine a somewhat nicer version.

Our task is to lay down a 4 by 5 field of beepers. We will use Controllers to implement the alternating strategy used to turn at the ends of the rows as we move back and forth. First, we examine two controller classes.

```
public class LeftTurn implements Controller
{
```

```
        public LeftTurn(UrRobot aRobot)
        {
                myRobot = aRobot;
        }
        public void controlIt()
        {
                myRobot.turnLeft();
                myRobot.move();
                myRobot.turnLeft();
        }
        private UrRobot myRobot = null;
}

public class RightTurn implements Controller
{
        public RightTurn(UrRobot aRobot)
        {
                myRobot = aRobot;
        }
        public void controlIt()
        {
                myRobot.turnRight();
                myRobot.move();
                myRobot.turnRight();
        }
        private UrRobot myRobot = null;
}
```

Using these is not difficult. Here is the robot class that uses them. We remember two controllers, one of each kind and we swap them whenever we turn. These controllers are remembered in instance variables intialized with the robot itself.

```
public class ControlLayer extends UrRobot
{
  public ControlLayer(int street, int avenue, Direction direct,
      int beeper)
  {
          super(street, avenue, direct, beepers);
  }
  public void turnRight()
  {
          turnLeft();
          turnLeft();
          turnLeft();
  }
  public void layRow()
  {
          putBeeper();
          move();
          putBeeper();
          move();
```

```
            putBeeper();
            move();
            putBeeper();
            move();
            putBeeper();
    }
    public void turn()
    {
            currentTurn.controlIt();
            Controller temp = currentTurn;
            currentTurn = otherTurn;
            otherTurn = temp;
    }
    private Controller currentTurn = new LeftTurn(this);
    private Controller otherTurn = new RightTurn(this);
}
```

Finally, the task for this robot is quite simply stated.

```
public static void main(String [] args)
{       ControlLayer george = new ControlLayer(2, 4, East,
                infinity);
        george.layRow();
        george.turn();
        george.layRow();
        george.turn();
        george.layRow();
        george.turn();
        george.layRow();
        george.turnOff();
}
```

The key here was letting each Controller know which robot it would be "talking" to. Actually, there is an error in the above. Did you catch it? The RightTurn controller sends turnRight to an UrRobot. This is a pesky bug, requiring either spelling out the turnRight as three turnLeft instructions or a cast. If we cast (to ControlLayer, which does implement turnRight), then the RightTurn controller becomes available only to that class (and sub classes).

There is another way to fix this, however. If we define the two controller classes inside of the ControlLayer class they will become part of each each such robot created and hence a simple turnLeft() within the controlIt method will refer to that robot. More important, turnRight will be available as well. So here is the same program done with **inner classes** for the two controllers. Note that the complete class definition of LeftTurn and of RightTurn is within the definition of ControlLayer.

```
public class ControlLayer extends UrRobot  {
    public ControlLayer(int street, int avenue,
        Direction direct, int beepers)
    {
            super(street, avenue, direct, beepers);
    }
```

```
	public void turnRight()
	{
		turnLeft();
		turnLeft();
		turnLeft();
	}
	public void layRow()
	{
		putBeeper();
		move();
		putBeeper();
		move();
		putBeeper();
		move();
		putBeeper();
		move();
		putBeeper();
	}
	public void turn()
	{
		currentTurn.controlIt();
		Controller temp = currentTurn;
		currentTurn = otherTurn;
		otherTurn = temp;
	}
	private class LeftTurn implements Controller
	{
	    public void controlIt()
		{
			turnLeft();
			move();
			turnLeft();
		}
	}
	private class RightTurn implements Controller
	{
		public void controlIt()
		{
			turnRight();
			move();
			turnRight();
		}
	}
	private Controller currentTurn = new LeftTurn();
	private Controller otherTurn = new RightTurn();
    }
```

The differences between this version and the one previous are subtle. Notice the following. The instructions within the two controlIt methods don't need to refer explicitly to any robot, since they implicitly refer to "this" robot. We are, after all writing instructions for a particular robot. Next, we don't need constructors for the Controller classes, since all we needed them for was to make an association with a robot, and that is automatic here. Thus, we don't have parameters when we create the two controllers. Making the inner classes private means that other classes do not have access to them. They are private to this class. This is another form of information hiding, just as inner classes themselves are another form of encapsulation. When a class is needed only by a second class, the first can often be inner to the second one. This is an important technique.

By the way, the task for this robot class is just the same as that for the first.

Note that observers can also be built as inner classes and it is often advantageous to do so.

Problem Set

1. Why is the inner class solution more secure than passing a strategy to the robot when it is created? Why is it less flexible?

2. Give the inner class solution, above, two additional inner class Controllers. These will be called from layRow instead of what we have done. Do this in such a way that alternating rows have different characteristics. For example, odd rows have one beeper in each column, and even numbered rows have two..

6 Java Cloning

Cloning in Java is a bit more complicated than we have suggested in the main text (Section 5.9). Java defines an interface called Cloneable that a class must implement in order for its objects to be cloned. We have done this behind the scenes in our UrRobot class, so that all robot classes are Cloneable.

The clone method of Java doesn't formally return robots, actually. In its declaration it returns things of type Object. Object is the supertype of all Java classes, including robot classes, and when you override the clone method you cannot change this return type. Therefore the declaration of clone in class Object is really (something like)

```
Object clone() {...}
```

When we write such a method in a new class (we have done so in UrRobot) overriding this, we need to keep the same declaration, but we can, of course return any object that is from any subclass of Object according to the usual rules of polymorphism. However, the Java processing system (the compiler) still only knows the return type of this function as Object so it will complain if a NeighborTalker tries to create its neighbor with just

```
neighbor = clone();
```

This is because neighbor is of class BeeperPutter, not Object, but clone returns an Object. We can assign a more specific robot to a robot reference, but not a more general one. Therefore, we need to assure the compiler that we know (even though it does not) that the actual returned value is really a BeeperPutter (in fact it is a NeighborTalker, which is even more specific, but all we need here is BeeperPutter). So we need to say instead:

```
neighbor = (BeeperPutter)clone();
```

Putting the name of a robot class (or any class) before an expression tells the compiler that we believe that the expression has the indicated type. It is called a "cast". In this case we assure the compiler that the result of clone is a BeeperPutter or some subclass of it by casting the result of calling clone to BeeperPutter.

So createNeighbor looks like the following.

```
public void createNeighbor() // PRE: facing West and front is clear
{       move();
        if (frontIsClear())
        {       neighbor = (BeeperPutter)clone();
        }
        else
        {       neighbor = new NoNeighbor(1, 1, North, 1);
        }
        goBack();
        neighbor. createNeighbor();
  } // POST: facing North on original corner.
```

When we cast as we have done here, the compiler inserts a check to be sure we are correct in our reasoning. If we are wrong, the running program will result in an intent error (a ClassCastException in Java) and we will be informed of it if it occurs.

Notice that a cast doesn't change the type of anything. It just assures the compiler that a value has a more specific type based on the logic of the program than can be deduced from reading the text of the program itself. Its correctness depends on how the program executes.

Index of Terms

absolute location 2
abstract class 68
alias 202
ancestor class 39
and operator && 120
anyBeepersInBeeperBag 105
argument 220
assignment instruction 82, 202
assignment operator = 82
avenue 1
base case 187
beeper 3
beyond the horizon situation 165
block 1
body (of loop) 137
boolean 90, 105
bottom factoring 124
boundary wall 1
bug 19
case-sensitive 14
cast 89
class 9, 31
client 74
clone (method) 128, 225
collection 89
comment 13
concurrent 209
constructor 35, 81, 220
corner 1
deadlock 213
debugging 19, 58
decision map 122, 167
declaration 14
decorator 94
definition mechanism 31
delegation 74, 83
delivery specification 12
dictionary 30, 39
else clause 114
enumeration 90, 129
error shutoff 7, 9
execute 7, 12
execution equivalent 123
execution error 17, 53
expression 105
extends 31
facingEast 105
facingNorth 105
facingSouth 105
facingWest 105
false 105
fence post problem 145
field 71
final situation 4, 11
focus of execution 38
FOR LOOP instruction 137
formal definition 191
four step process (loops) 141
frontIsClear 105
general case (recursion) 187
helper method 76
IF ELSE instruction 113
IF instruction 103
implements 76
import 90
index
infinite loop 142, 147
infinity 20
inherit 32
initial situation 4
inner class 221
instance variable 71
instruction 7
int 35, 136
intent error 18. 53
interface 75, 76
intersection 1
invariant 83, 87
lexical error 16
loop invariant 158
main (static method) 10
main task block 12

message 7, 12
meta level 192
method 10, 30, 32, 90
move 7
names 10
negation operator 107
neighbors 90
nested IF 115
new (command) 10, 14
nextToABeeper 105
nextToARobot 105
null 202
object 4
Object (class) 90, 225
object-oriented design 73
observable 95
observer 95
or operator || 121
origin 2
override 40
package 217
parameter 81
parent class 39
pickBeeper 9
polymorphism 65, 79, 127. 202
postcondition 47
precondition 47
predicate 105
private 50, 71
problem solving 42
program 3
programming language 3
public 10, 50
putBeeper 9
race condition 212
recursion 184
redundant-test factoring 127
reference (variable) 10, 79
relative location 2
reserved word 14
return 90, 105
Robot (class) 105
robot task 2, 5
run (method) 211
server 74
short circuit 121
simulating execution 12
situation 4
special symbol 14
static 217
stepwise refinement 42
strategy 83
street 1
sub class 32
super (reference) 35, 40
super class 32, 85, 220
syntactic error 17, 21
syntax error 17
tail recursion 190
task (method) 218
test reversal 123
THEN clause 104
this (reference) 20, 33
thread 209
top factoring 125
tracing execution 12
true 105
turnLeft 8
turnOff 9
UrRobot (class) 9
verify 50
visibility 50
void 10
wall section 2
while 140
WHILE instruction 139

Index of Classes Defined in the Book

Accomplice 92
Adder 198
BeeperController 140
BeeperFinder 184
BeeperLayer 68
BeeperPutter 79, 128
BeeperSweeper 145
BigStepper 41
BlockWalker 87
Carpenter 77
CarpenterRunner 209
Carrier 197
Checker 198
CheckerRobot 107
Choreographer 71
Cloneable 128
Contractor 78
ControlLayer 222
Controller 100
Direction 35
Directions 11
Enumeration 90, 129
FieldHarvester 52
Finder 197
GetBeeper 218
Getter 201
Guard 161
Harvester 44, 138
KarelRunner 218
LeftTurn 221
LeftTurnDecorator 94
Mason 76
Mathematician 192
MileMover 40
MileWalker 31
NeighborTalker 80, 128
NoNeighbor 80
NullListener 96
NullStrategy 84
ObservablePicker 97
OriginSitter 221
Philosopher 214
Putter 201
Racer 114, 210
RelayRacer 211
Replanter 116
RightTurn 222
Robot 105
RobotListener 96
RobotTask 218
Roofer 77
Runnable 209
SparseHarvester 109
Spy 92
StairSweeper 37
Strategy 84
StrategyLayer 84
Sweeper 182, 186
Tester 11
Thief 212
ThreeRowLayer 69
ThreeStep 93
TwoBeeperStrategy 85
TwoRowLayer 69
UrRobot 9
WalkListener 96
Worker 75
World 210

Index of Methods Defined in the Book

action 96
addAll 200
addColumn 198
advanceToNextDiagonal 195
anyBeepersInBeeperBag 105
avoidWall 161
backUp 163
captureTheBeeper 113
carpenterTask 208
carryOne 199
clearAllBeepersToTheWall 143
clearBeepersThisCorner 151
clearCornerOfBeepers 140
climbStair 37
clone 128
controlIt 221
createNeighbor 128, 226
distributeBeepers 80
doIt 84
eat 214
emptyBag 199
enoughToCarry 199
exactlyTwoBeepers 118
faceEast 132
faceNorth 111
faceNorthIfFacingSouth 109
faceSouth 163
faceWest 194
facingEast 105
facingNorth 105
facingSouth 105
facingWest 105
findBeeper 152, 190
findMine 188
followEdge 162
followStrategy 92
frontIsBlocked 107
frontIsClear 105
gatherHelpers 198
getForks 214
getNextClue 92
getToWork 75
glideDown 115
goToBeeper 140
goToNextRow 47
harvest 72
harvestARow 72
harvestCorner 49, 116
harvestField 52
harvestLine 147
harvestOneRow 44, 108, 138
harvestTwoRows 46
hasMoreElements 90
jumpHurdle 114
jumpUp 115
layBeepers 68
layRow 222
longMove 41
main 10, 217
move 7
moveMile 30
moveToRobot 197
moveToSouthEastCorner 162
moveTowardBeeper 156
mysteryInstruction 132
neighbors 90
nextElement 90
nextToABeeper 105
nextToABeeper_and_fron... 165
nextToARobot 105
nextToOneReplantOne 117
not_nextToABeeper 107
onSecondAve 200
pickBeeper 9
placeBeepers 213
positionForNextHarvest 46
putBeeper 9
putForks 214

raceStride 114
register 97
requestStrategy 92
retrieveBeeper 184
returnToWestWall 184, 186
rightIsClear 107
run 209
runToRobot 211
setStrategy 86
setupThread 210
slideLeft 200
spin 211
swapStrategies 87
sweepCorner 186
task 218
think 214
turn 223
turnAround 163
turnLeft 8
turnOff 9
turnRight 37
walkASide 87
walkPerimeter 162
walkSquareOfLentth_6 138
willThisClearCornerOf… 177
zagDownRight 192
zagMove 195
zigLeftUp 192
zigMove 195

66403357R00133

Made in the USA
Columbia, SC
17 July 2019